FIVE RING
FEVER

PERSIST

Laura L

FIVE RING
FEVER

winning is contagious

LAURIE LAWRENCE

Special thanks to all the great athletes from around the world who gave me their time and inspired *Five Ring Fever*. Thanks also to Arch Fraley, friend and photographer of the Australian Olympic Swimming Team, Townsville, 1956, who kindly provided the photographs of that historic visit, and to all the other photograph libraries and individuals who provided photographs for the book.

First published in Australia in 2000

© Laurie Lawrence

Lawrence, Laurie, 1941–
Five ring fever: winning is contagious.

ISBN 0 646 38282 9

1. Olympics – Anecdotes. 2. Olympics – History – Anecdotes.
3. Athletes – Australia – Anecdotes. 4. Athletes – Australia –
History – Anecdotes. I. Title

796.48092

Cover photographs: Herb Elliott, Duncan Armstrong and Jon Sieben
— Allsport; Dawn Fraser — Ern McQuillan

Design concept: Blue Cork
Typesetting and finished art: Brevier Design
Printed in Australia by McPhersons Print Group

C o n t e n t s

YORK®
Air Conditioning and Heating

Supercraft

3M *NEXCARE*™

2GB
8 7 3

 James Hardie

Just because it's not being done doesn't mean it can't be done

After learning from first-hand experience that the publisher, who takes the financial risk, also takes the financial rewards, I was determined to find a way to be able to pay for the publishing of *Five Ring Fever* myself. I have an enormous belief in this project, and wanted to be a part of it from go to whoa. I wanted to give the book every chance to reach as wide an audience as possible. And if I could find some way to finance my 'masterpiece', I might be able to reap some rewards for four years of commitment to my computer while travelling in airplanes around the world.

However, many friends in and aligned with the industry warned me that my self-publishing idea was fraught with danger, as the majority of books published in Australia only sell a few thousand copies. Some books simply don't work at all. They believed that if I printed too many books I could be left, a few months after the book's release, with a garage full of books as well as a hefty bank loan to be paid off.

To be perfectly honest, this situation did not appeal to me at all.

Then one day I was flicking through the pages of a sporting magazine and it hit me — if people paid to advertise in magazines why wouldn't they pay to advertise in a book, so long as the advertising opportunity offered to them was made attractive enough. Just because it's not being done doesn't mean it can't be done.

The idea germinated, and sponsors were soon being sought to lessen my financial risk.

I thank these companies who have had faith in this book. Their logos appear opposite. I must point out that they are sponsoring merely a chapter or two in the book — not the champions written about in these pages. Many of these great athletes are, of course, aligned to their own sponsors.

Citius, Altius, Fortius.

This book is dedicated to every person who dares dream but, more importantly, pursues the Olympic dream of faster ... higher ... stronger.

Those of us who are lucky enough to have a good teacher somewhere in our life owe much to the appetite they give us to learn and improve. They are able to touch our essence and inspire us to fully develop our attitudes and aptitudes.

My coach, Percy Cerutty, was a great teacher. He believed sport, like yoga, prayer or charity, can help us grow into better human beings if we commit and persevere without compromise.

There is much in Laurie Lawrence that reminds me of Percy. His sights have always been set at the highest of world achievement. He is exceptionally inquisitive and observant, constantly looking to learn and to create new ways of doing things.

He is passionate and enthusiastic to a point where he can lift not only a single athlete, but also large audiences to 'have a go'.

Laurie is a person of high energy. Tell me about it! I shared a room with him in the Atlanta Olympic village and sleep was not on the agenda. His whole life is about learning and sharing, which makes some of us around him feel quite lazy and a little wasted.

All his powers of observation, his knowledge of athletic inspiration and his association with some of our great Australian sporting heroes, have ensured that this book is different.

It is easy to read and brings insights to any who wish to learn. In addition, it is full of motivational hints for any aspiring athlete. In fact, anyone who reads read this book will extract from it not only sporting philosophies but also principles that will help them to live a richer, fuller life.

Introduction
by Laurie Lawrence

I consider myself to be among the most fortunate people in the world. I have a supportive wife, three beautiful daughters, I work on my health and fitness. I've been to four Olympic Games and will assist our team in Sydney 2000. I've trained under American master coach Don Gambril. I've observed the late great Sherm Chavoor, coach of Mark Spitz, Mike Burton and Debbie Meyer, in action. I've followed supercoach George Haines around the pool deck like a hungry puppy, waiting for him to drop a tasty morsel of swimming information. I've sniffed chlorine at the stuffy indoor pool at Pymble, in Sydney's northern suburbs, which Australian coaching legend 'pitbull' Forbes Carlile once called his headquarters. I've paddled my feet in the cool waters of the Tobruk pool in Townsville as the Australian team prepared for the Melbourne Olympics. I've continually sought and devoured information and knowledge from swimming experts round the world.

This has been my practical apprenticeship in the sport I love. A sport that has enabled me to coach not only Olympic and world champions, but also people who, while not well-known public sporting figures, have been able to take from the sport of swimming valuable lessons that have made them successful in the sport of life.

My successes have enabled me to rub shoulders with many of the world's great coaches and athletes. I believe these great coaches have many things in common — they are all deep thinkers ... dreamers ... people with active, fertile imaginations. They have all searched for innovations in training technique, dietary supplements, stroke mechanics, stretching, strength training, skill acquisition, ways to improve starts and turns; in fact, any skill, drill or conditioning technique that will develop not only teamwork, but also the quality stroke mechanics, the mental toughness and resilience in their charges that are necessary for success. They, with their athletes, are committed to a relentless march towards common sporting goals.

These people are lateral thinkers, forever seeking new ways to assist their athletes in order to supply them with that little extra something in the gladiatorial world of international sport. Just as great athletes have that indefinable 'it', so, too, do the world's best coaches.

Great coaches are people who lie awake at night dreaming, worrying, conjuring like a magician ways to improve their charges. They are much more than just sports-loving fruit eaters who wear shorts, T-shirts, Nike joggers, and smile while talking in clichés for the TV cameras and as they continually bark instructions to their charges. These are the people I call 'the visionaries'.

They spend a lot of quality time with their athletes, becoming both their friend and mentor. The great coaches have a strong vision for their soul mates but, more importantly, they are able to pass on this vision. It becomes the common passion of the coach and pupil. The story of 'Rowdy' Gaines in Chapter 10 of *Five Ring Fever* exemplifies this. The great coach pursues this goal like a bloodhound — urging, driving, cajoling, reminding his or her athlete 'why' as they strive to get higher, longer, faster, stronger, whether it be as part of a team or as an individual in pursuit of sporting excellence.

Winning teams are not captained by pessimists. The leader must be enthusiastic, positive, have a clear vision of the goal and be able to have their team believe that its common dream is not only possible but also inevitable. Australian women's hockey team coach Ric Charlesworth certainly does this.

To quote George Bernard Shaw ...

You see things and you say, "Why?" But I dream things that never were; and I say, "Why not?"

A postcard of the 'now famous' Tobruk swimming pool in Townsville, printed not long after the pool had hosted the Australian swimming team's preparations for the 1956 Melbourne Olympics.

As for myself, after some initial coaching successes placing swimmers on Australian teams, 'Superfish' Steve Holland became my first, and swimming's youngest-ever male world record holder and world champion, in 1973. However, I reluctantly retired from international swimming coaching in 1975, to spend more time with my wife and newly born daughter, Jane. I also needed to attend to family financial commitments; at that stage in Australia swimming, you could not earn a decent living from coaching alone. As a newly wedded husband and father, I discovered a few harsh realities about my passion for swimming and its relationship to life and supporting a family. Unfortunately, in those days, the time spent coaching a world record holder and a world champion, and many other elite young swimmers, did not pay the family's grocery bill.

By teaching babies how to swim and doing stroke correction I remained closely involved with the sport that had become an integral part of my life since my Dad, 'Stumpy' Lawrence, had taken on the position as Tobruk swimming pool manager for the Townsville City Council in the early 1950s. I had initially been taken to the pool especially for my health, to strengthen weak and sickly lungs. My little story, the first in this book, involving Dawn Fraser and Jon Henricks, recalls those early days around Tobruk pool.

Chlorine was, and remains, well and truly in my blood!

I was in heaven when the Australian Olympic team chose our pool as the training venue for their assault on the 1956 Olympic Games in Melbourne. Dawn Fraser, Murray Rose, Lorraine Crapp, Jon Henricks, David Theile, John Devitt, all household names and living legends, became by necessity friends of a snotty-nosed kid ... the son of the Tobruk pool manager.

Even though I had to stop coaching Stephen Holland the year before the Montreal Olympics, I still had the passion and a strong desire to coach an Olympic champion. I returned to coaching in 1980, when I was financially secure and knew my family would not be disadvantaged by me pursuing my 'hobby'. I returned with one goal in mind — to coach an Olympic champion — having read somewhere that ...

For the resolute and determined there is time and opportunity.

My vision of having someone stand on the victory dais at the Olympics was real and strong, and I continually sold this dream to my young charges, many of whom embraced the concept with enthusiasm, concentration, and commitment. It culminated when Jon Sieben, at 17 years of age, defeated the six foot seven 'albatross', Michael Gross, to be crowned the Olympic champion for the 200 metres butterfly in Los Angeles in 1984 and, further, when Duncan Armstrong won gold, beating the great Matt Biondi in the 200 metres freestyle in Seoul in 1988. Dreams are important and the story on Duncan Armstrong reinforces the action and commitment required to make them come true.

This book of short stories chronicles some of the champion coaches and athletes I've been fortunate to meet. I hope these tales will inspire some young athlete or coach to aspire towards the ultimate, or to at least go to places they never thought possible.

My aim is to show that dreams are an important first step in achieving success. However, without accompanying action, they are merely a fantasy. High achievements always come from people with high

With Dawn, a true legend of Australian and world swimming.

expectations. If you reach for the stars you may not get there, but with commitment and persistence you will get very close.

If you want the elusive edge in life or sport there are no shortcuts. You must dream, plan, work hard and sacrifice as you march daily towards your goal. Even then, there are no guarantees that you will be totally successful. There will be many disappointments. Failure is a constant companion on the journey of anyone striving for excellence. These disappointments can only be softened and rationalised if you have truly given your all in the pursuit of excellence.

If you really want to win you must 'pay the price'. If you don't 'pay the price' you don't deserve to win. The heroes of *Five Ring Fever* have shown us that ...

The will to win is the will to prepare to win!

Enjoy the preparation!

As with my previous book, *Lawrence of Australia*, much of the dialogue in *Five Ring Fever* is a product of both memory and imagination. At times, I have used poetic licence, and although the dialogue may not be word-for-word accurate, the meaning remains true. The story content throughout is based on real competitive experiences, and is certainly not intended to embarrass any athlete. Rather, the intention is to highlight the pressures and agonies suffered and overcome in these athletes' quest for sporting excellence.

15

*The journey of a thousand miles
starts with the first step.*

**Australian women's hockey team
collection**

1 — *The Beginning*
Townsville, 1956

I first contracted Olympic fever when the Australian swimming team used the Tobruk Pool in Townsville as a training base for the 1956 Olympic Games in Melbourne. My father, 'Stumpy' Lawrence, managed the pool, and I was a starry-eyed kid soaking up every precious second of the Olympic training camp. I remember following the great Australian swimming coach Forbes Carlile around, enthralled by his experiments with hypnosis on the swimmers. Carlile would induce the swimmers into a state of relaxation and then suggest to them that their training would become easier and easier. I watched as he hooked them up to wires and machines, made them exercise, recorded their heart rates, and examined their T-waves to test their levels of stress.

I wondered why he had them push themselves to the limit, then hooked them up to gas masks and made them suck in pure oxygen. I was fascinated, yet unaware that I was watching one of those rare individuals who are ahead of their time — a dreamer who believed in cutting his own path, not content to be a mundane follower. Little did I realise the huge influence this crew-cutted eccentric would wield on my coaching career. Later, as a young coach, I continually visited his swim centres to investigate why his team was so successful.

Vivid memories of fit and tanned swimming characters, stretching and doing light weight training around the pool before they entered and swam lap after gruelling lap in preparation for the contest of a lifetime, are burned into my subconscious.

I remember positioning myself between Dawn Fraser and Jon Henricks on the old gal-pipe railings that surrounded the 50-metre pool and watching entranced as a huge crane lifted the old football 'Curleybells' over the silver-frosted wire fence onto the lawn at the Tobruk Pool. A

> **Winners see what they want to happen,
> losers see what they fear might happen.**

huge crowd had been predicted for the Olympic swimming team's final time trials, and the City Council had ordered extra seating be delivered in preparation for the big night.

'Watch the fence, young man!' yelled my dad to the crane operator, as the temporary seating arrangements were lifted over the fence and onto his precious lawn.

'Put it down easy! Careful! Careful! You almost hit that palm tree! That's my favourite tree! It's taken 10 years to grow that tree! Easy, son! Go easy!'

'Stumpy's going off,' Henricks observed to Dawn.

'You go easy, too, Jon! Don't upset him till after I've had my massage. I want to break a world record tonight,' said Dawn casually.

I stared up, so proud and so privileged to be sitting between two of Australia's best Olympic hopefuls. My mind wandered ...

Wait till I tell the kids at school tomorrow ... oh no, this is too much fun. I really don't want to go to school tomorrow ... maybe I can tell Mum I've got a sore chest ... that's it, I'll start coughing and try to wag it again ... she fell for it today ... nah, she won't believe me again ... I could try though ... it's so cool being around these champions ... gee, Harry Gallagher is a good coach ... he reckons Dawn and Jon will win gold medals in Melbourne ... how cool is that ... wish I could go to the Olympics ... I will one day.

'Yeah, Stumpy gives the best massages,' said Henricks, interrupting my musing.

'Wish we could take him to Melbourne with us,' said Dawn.

'What! A masseur on an Olympic team? You're joking! That'll never happen!' replied Jon.

'Look out for that tree!' yelled my father again, visibly agitated. He moved closer to direct the hapless crane driver. The light-framed, scruffy, bearded youth with the roll-your-own cigarette dangling from the corner of his mouth had never struck the likes of Stumpy Lawrence before and probably never would again.

'And son, put that cigarette out. We've got champion athletes here,' he added with conviction.

The young man took one hand off the controls to get rid of the offending article.

'Watch the tree!' screamed Dad again, waving his hands furiously. 'Keep two hands on the wheel son ... two hands on the wheel.'

Soon the job was done, with no damage to the precious lawn or tree. The crane driver, however, was just a little worn out from his protracted ordeal.

'Thanks, son. Well done. I'll be here tomorrow to direct you when you come back to remove these seats,' said Dad, looking the young man right in the eye.

'I can hardly wait!' replied the relieved grease-smeared crane driver, with just a hint of sarcasm dripping from his voice. Immediately, he drove 50 metres to the nearest Moreton Bay fig tree. There, he pulled up in its shade, rolled another cigarette, lit it, drew the smoke deep into his lungs and silently cursed the little bantam rooster who had just hassled him.

Finally, the pool was ready.

Dad showered, shaved, rubbed Californian Poppy hair oil through his ageing locks and sleeked them back. He was ready.

This carnival promised to be a beauty. The local radio station, 4TO, had been pushing it on air all week. Dawn had openly predicted she would break the world record and encouraged locals to come to cheer her on and farewell the other swimmers. I couldn't believe her confidence and collared her while she was getting a massage from my father an hour and a half before the official start time.

'Dawnie, are you really going to break a world record tonight?'

'Probably two,' was her matter-of-fact reply.

'But how can you be so sure?' I quizzed, keen to find out more about Dawn's world record attempt.

'I've done the hard work in training.'

'Yeah, but a world record?'

'Look, I've done everything my coach has asked me to do in training. I'm well.'

'Yeah, but a world record?' I kept up with the questions.

'I've got the best masseur in the world,' she replied, as she mischievously pinched Dad on that area of the body known affectionately as 'gluteus maximus'. He kept rubbing. I kept asking.

'But Dawn, a world record? I've never seen a world record before.'

'Well get ready, boy, you are going to see some tonight.'

'Do you really think so?'

'Laurie!' interrupted my father, and I could detect a slight impatience in his voice. I'd heard that tone before, and I knew I was getting close to a backhander.

'Yes, Dad,' I answered meekly, keen to keep the peace.

'Leave Dawn alone, son! She doesn't want to listen to your incessant ramblings. She's got a race to concentrate on.'

'Leave him alone, Stump. It's okay,' she defended.

'But how do you know?' I started again, buoyed by the knowledge that I now had a staunch ally.

'I've been swimming fast times in training, almost world records. Harry thinks I can. If my coach has faith in me, I know I can do it.'

'Stumpy!' Forbes called and poked his spiky-haired head round the corner. Ursula, his wife, was six paces behind, carrying the gear.

'Yes, Forbes!'

'Forbes, Dawn said she's going to break the world record,' I interrupted.

'Quiet, son!' hissed my father through clenched teeth. Then, smiling,

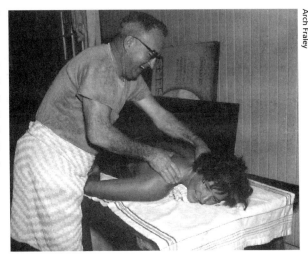

My Dad, 'Stumpy' Lawrence, with Dawn in the Tobruk Pool's 'ambulance room', which was turned into the massage area while the Aussie swim team was in Townsville in '56.

he turned back to Forbes, who had squeezed right inside the cramped little area known as the 'ambulance room' which, for now, was doubling as the massage room.

'Yes, Forbes.'

'Stump, do you think you can put on that hot box sauna you use for your footballers for me tonight?'

'No problems.'

'What do you want that for, Forbes?' I asked. It would be one of the many questions I put to the master over the years in my endless quest for swimming knowledge. Dad kept rubbing, but I could see he was getting mad and I knew I would cop it tomorrow when the carnival was over.

'I believe if you raise the temperature of the human muscle before exercise it will result in an increased performance level in the competitive situation. I'm hoping to collect some further scientific data on this phenomenon tonight,' replied Forbes, happy that someone, even if it was a precocious kid, wanted to listen to his theories.

'It won't help if you don't have good old-fashioned Aussie guts and you're not fit, Forbes,' interrupted Dawn.

*The great coach,
Harry 'The Fox'
Gallagher, with two
of his protégés,
Dawn Fraser and
Jon Henricks,
at the shallow
end at Tobruk.*

Arch Fraley

'True, Dawn,' answered Forbes, unperturbed, 'but let me show you some interesting statistics. Ursula, can I have the notes from the briefcase you have in that new knapsack on your back?'

As Forbes rifled through the knapsack he commented to Dawn, 'I bought this knapsack to make it easier for Ursula to carry all our luggage.'

'Not now, Forbes, I'm getting ready for a world record!' snapped Dawn.

'Really? Well if you were to raise the temperature of your body ...'

'Not now, Forbes,' Dawn's voice had an impatient edge. Forbes didn't notice. Ursula dragged him away still muttering; Dad kept rubbing.

The crowd started arriving. Townsville turned out in full force to see the final time trials and the swimmers didn't disappoint. They gave the locals possibly the greatest exhibition of freestyle swimming ever seen in this country. Dawn swam the 110 yards freestyle in 1:03.3, breaking two world records in the one race, the 110 yards and the 100 metres.

I watched in the dark from the little balcony on top of the pool entrance, immersed in the dreams of youth. World record after world record toppled, and I secretly wished I could go to the Olympics to watch my heroes compete for Australia. They would be held in front of a home crowd in Melbourne for the first time. Why couldn't Dad take us? Wish he was rich. I vowed then that one day I would go to an Olympic Games.

I had no idea of the impact the great Dawn Fraser would have on my career as I followed her unbelievable sporting exploits. It's funny how the dreams of youth can lead to incredible adventures.

To me, she is Australia's greatest Olympian. Her achievements in terms of longevity and class are testament to her athletic ability. Let me list them:

- Olympic gold medals in the same event (100 metres freestyle) at three consecutive Olympics.
- Most medals by an Australian at the Olympics (eight).
- Most gold medals by an Australian at the Olympics (four, tied with Betty Cuthbert and Murray Rose).
- Thirty-nine world records.
- Twenty-seven individual world records.
- First woman to break the minute for the 100 metres freestyle.
- Undefeated in the 100 metres freestyle from 1956 until she was prematurely 'retired' after the Tokyo Olympics in 1964.
- Held the 100 metres freestyle world record for an unprecedented 16 years (including seven years after being banned by the Australian Swimming Union. In fact, her world record at the time was more than a second faster than American Jan Henne's winning performance at the Mexico Olympics in 1968).

Could Dawn have won a fourth consecutive gold had she been given the chance? Sadly, we will never know.

These historic performances do not happen by chance. Winners are very special people, special in that they are prepared not only to dream but, more importantly, to act upon these dreams. They do things that others won't do. Winners are prepared to sacrifice, to pay the price whatever the cost. They set goals and take action to achieve them. Without action, dreams and goals are merely fantasies ... figments of

More memories from '56 ... the immortal Murray Rose, David Dickson, Jon Henricks and a young John Konrads on the night of the final time trials. Konrads, just 14, wouldn't swim competitively in Melbourne — he was there for the experience. But four years later in Rome, he'd win the 1500 metres gold medal.

the imagination which cause undisciplined, unambitious people to meander through life like flightless birds.

Dawn's third 100 metres gold exemplified her superior mental strength and fighting qualities. She was under immense pressure from her fellow Australians, who expected nothing less than gold from their hero. In addition to this she was under close scrutiny from the international media, as no athlete had ever been able to win three successive Olympic gold medals for swimming; indeed, she was being keenly watched by the whole world.

Then disaster. Three months before the Tokyo Games Dawn was driving the car in which her mother was killed. Dawn herself was seriously injured. She damaged the vertebrae in her neck and had to wear a neck brace for support.

One journalist wrote: 'This accident will spell the end of Dawn's glittering career.'

How wrong people can be when they disregard that special inner strength found in humanity and often brought out by champions. Although Dawn was emotionally destroyed by the death of her mother, she dug deep and found this indefinable quality that enables champions to get up when it seems they can't. She somehow disregarded the neck pain and, by sheer willpower, was able to resurrect her interrupted career.

Visions of Dawn racing the American teenager Sharon Stouder, who was half Dawn's age, in Tokyo are strong in my mind's eye. I can see both girls power into the turn, her young rival executing a perfect tumble turn. Dawn, in complete disdain, does the old touch turn before she surges past the 15-year-old to the roar of the huge, mainly Japanese crowd.

Nowadays, Dawn is an integral part of the Aussie Olympic team as an official. Her job is to move around among both the young athletes and the more experienced campaigners, supporting them and being a sounding board, if necessary, for any problems they might have. She is a troubleshooter and, because of her vast experience in the Olympic arena at the real coalface of international competition, where weaknesses are recognised and exploited, she is accorded the highest respect from not only competing athletes and officials but from all Australians.

Few know that this living legend, this former swimming champion, was out on the cross-country course in the stifling heat in Barcelona in 1992 supporting our equestrian team.

The cross-country day is unbelievable. It is a day where man and beast undergo incredible punishment. When Gil Rolton, Matt Ryan and Andrew Hoy galloped their exhausted horses into the 10-minute box for a well-earned rest, Dawn was there with coach Wayne Roycroft icing down the tired animals to get their body temperature down. Only then could horse and rider attack the final gruelling sprint over more hurdles to the finish. Is it any wonder that at the team briefing in Atlanta four years later, Wayne Roycroft was lavish in his praise of this great Australian and Olympic legend, and asked specifically for her to visit them again?

It is fatal to enter a war without the will to win it.

Australian women's hockey team collection

2 — *First Olympics*
Bittersweet

My first Olympic Games as a coach in Los Angeles was not only a personal triumph and amazing experience for me but it was also a resounding Australian success story. It saw 370 athletes and administrators from all over our great nation playing their part, representing their country proudly, all pulling their weight, one team, one direction.

When a team is totally unified and all members pull together unconditionally towards one common goal, it is gratifying to achieve the successes that must inevitably come. Four gold medals were the centrepiece of Australia's Olympic achievements there in Los Angeles, the city of angels. The most memorable for me, of course, was my first gold medal achievement as a coach.

Australia, as a sporting nation, was still clawing back from the horrendous results in Montreal in 1976, when we failed to win even one gold medal, so the medals in Los Angeles held special memories for me.

I'll never forget Dean Lukin's mighty lift in the super-heavyweight weightlifting arena. It was a gem. The 305-pound millionaire tuna fisherman from Port Lincoln in South Australia spent six months of the year at sea on the family fishing trawler. There he trained on board in all weathers, hauling in heavy nets, laden with fish, to help build his phenomenal strength. Once ashore, he began lifting such huge weights in training that his neighbours claimed the walls of their house were cracking from the vibrations.

Dean stayed in Port Lincoln to train in an old tin shed. The big man was roundly criticised for his unusual training methods, the press saying he was not doing the right thing by himself or Australia. But

Go Deano!! Here was a man with the courage and self-belief to go from unknown tuna fisherman to Olympic hero.

Allsport

Dean knew what he was doing ... he was preparing for Olympic Gold.

Champions prepare in different ways. They do, however, have a couple of things in common. One, they are chasing their dream and, two, they are totally committed to excellence and, as a result, they give themselves a great chance of victory by paying meticulous attention to detail in their preparation.

Will you ever forget the big man's exultation? Can you ever forget the look of concentration and determination as Dean slowly sauntered to the bar for his final lift? This lift was to see him attempt a massive 240 kilos in the clean and jerk for the gold. This was a weight he'd never attempted before; in fact, it was five kilos heavier than his lifetime best lift.

Mario Martinez, the American man mountain, had earlier outsnatched Dean by 12 and a half kilos, presenting the Australian with the challenge of a lifetime. However, champions respond to super challenges.

Dean approached the bar with a self-assurance that comes only to athletes who know that they have prepared well. Having paid the price, they are able to exude this aura of quiet confidence, a belief in themselves and their abilities. It is almost an inner arrogance that comes from knowing you have worked hard to gain that elusive edge. Dean hauled the bar high above his head, struggling valiantly to control the swaying bar. Meanwhile, millions of American fans who were cheering for their local hero, silently willed the huge weight to crash unceremoniously onto the lifting apron ...

The bar is up ... it's swaying ... Dean struggles ... finally he exerts control ... he holds the bar still ... controls it ... waits the mandatory three seconds ... the judges give him three green lights for a legal lift. Only then does the big man perform his two-fisted victory leap that would have done justice to any Toyota television commercial. Dean Lukin, the shy South Australian tuna fisherman, lands the biggest catch of his life in Los Angeles ... an Olympic gold medal.

Likewise, who could forget Charlie's Angels, the Australian pursuit cycling team? I can still hear the squeals of delight uttered by Michael Grenda, Kevin Nichols, Michael Turtur and Dean Woods as they crossed the finish line for gold in the 4000 metres team pursuit at the velodrome. They had just crushed the mighty United States team who, on their specially designed aerodynamic bikes, felt the gold was a mere formality for them, especially on home soil. Stories abounded about the US team's use of blood doping techniques for success, so the Aussie underdogs knew they were in for a battle and had to produce a lifetime best for victory. Victory was made a little easier when the Americans lost one rider early in the race and were no match for the tough, superbly fit Aussies.

Charlie Walsh coached his first Olympic gold that day and began a tradition of cycling turbulence and excellence that is still flourishing today. Charlie, a perfectionist, is loved by some for his hard-nosed, no-nonsense approach, built on the premise that ...

Left to right: Turtur, Grenda, Nichols and Woods ... champions!

The only place success comes before work is in the dictionary.

However, he is despised by others because they can't break into the elite AIS cycling team. Charlie's team travels the world for up to nine months of the year, training and using not only the resources available from the Institute of Sport but also living at altitude to build their strength and stamina. Then they are able to race with one goal in mind ... international cycling dominance.

Charlie has made many personal sacrifices in the never-ending quest for perfection. He is passionate and committed about the sport and, like other great coaches of the world, experiments, records, listens, and drives his riders to the brink of exhaustion in the quest for athletic perfection. As I write, Charlie is experimenting with a product that contains colostrum, a mammary secretion that supposedly wards off infection and promotes recovery. Charlie took it himself, but Lucy Tyler-Sharman, a team member, refused to use it.

Do you remember the great Glynis Nunn, winner of the first Olympic heptathlon, the event that crowns the best all-round Olympic athlete?

> *You can't build a strong
> team on weak individuals.*
>
> Ross Perot

For 1984, the five-event pentathlon was replaced by the seven-event heptathlon.

Glynis competed in that heptathlon while secretly nursing an elbow injury that caused her great pain in the throwing events. In order to deaden the pain before throwing she used a 'tens unit machine' to put electrical stimulus into the injured elbow. However, an oversight on her part in administering the treatment too early saw the electrical stimulus wear off and she had to throw the javelin while still in great pain. But champions do what they have to do!

There was no oversight, however, when it came to administering her favourite competition breakfast of pavlova and fresh fruit. Wendy Ey, the track and field manager, made sure the magic egg whites were whisked and ready before competition. Gael Martin, Glynis' roommate, was so impressed with Glynis' gold medal performance she devoured the leftovers and went on to win bronze in the shot put.

Two days before the start of the competition Glynis dreamed of 'flowers' and '13.1'. The flowers duly arrived from Tom McVeigh, the Australian Sports Minister, who was her local politician. The 13.1 arrived too, when she ran a PB into a headwind in the hurdles. The competition remained fierce over the two days. The lead seesawed, finally coming down to the last discipline in the Olympic heptathlon, the 800 metres run. In order to win the gold Glynis had to beat the great Jackie Joyner, whom she was trailing on points, by more than three seconds. Glynis' epic struggle was recorded on television. I can still hear Bruce McAvaney's booming voice as Glynis entered the straight with gold in sight ...

'Nunn's got a great chance of the gold. Joyner is tying right up! Everts leads, 15 metres to Nunn! Joyner's gone I think! Nunn's gonna win the gold if she can hang on. Everts is clear! Nunn's got the gold, I reckon. We'll wait for the official result.'

We should never forget what Glynis Nunn achieved in LA in 1984, and how bravely and dramatically she did it.

There wasn't a dry eye in Australia as Glynis wept unashamedly on the victory dais, clutching her fluffy koala mascot to her breast. She had improved her personal best point score by 108 points. The winning points score: Glynis 6390, Jackie Joyner 6385. A mere five points separated gold and silver. Glynis, by refusing to give in to injury and temporary discomfort, had joined an elite band of Australians whose names are etched in Olympic history.

Finally, of course, there was my own athlete, the fresh-faced 17-year-old Jon Sieben, who broke the world record and, against all odds, conquered the swimming superstar of LA — the mighty German albatross Michael Gross — in one of the biggest upsets of the Games. Jono's victory in the 200 metres butterfly confirmed for me that ...

Perspiration is the lather of success.

The extra hours of hard training that Jono had performed willingly in order to get that elusive 'edge', to be totally prepared, had been worthwhile. For he now carries the mantle of being one of those revered few who can boast Olympic Gold.

Yes, the athletic performances in Los Angeles were magnificent and memorable. Australia finished 15th out of 161 nations. For a small country, this was a reason to celebrate. Australia's performance exceeded the expectations of even the most experienced optimistic officials and pure joy was evident on the faces of officials and athletes alike as they donned team uniforms and headed to the Olympic stadium to celebrate during the Closing Ceremony.

I didn't go to the Closing Ceremony!

I went back to the tiny flat that I'd shared with other Australian coaches and swimmers and sat head in hands, emotionally drained. This flat had been our home for three weeks. I reflected on the wins and losses ...

It had been an emotional rollercoaster, as for 16 days I celebrated with the winners and bled with the others. The losses hit hard! Funny how different performances please you ... Glenn Buchanan's bronze medal in the 100 metres butterfly was pure joy, his personal best performance. That bronze was sweet. I had taught Glenn his first

> *We struggle daily with situations that demand decisions between what we want to do and what we have to do.*
>
> John Maxwell

strokes and guided his career to Olympic bronze ... to me that bronze was pure gold. On the other hand the bronze from Justin Lemberg was sour, pure agony. I buried my head in my hands again as I thought about Lemberg's bronze in the 400 metres freestyle.

'It's not fair,' I muttered to myself. 'It's just not fair.' And I brushed a small tear from the corner of my eye. Overall, it had been a tremendous Olympics from my swimmers — one world record, one gold, one silver and four bronze medals. Still, I was not satisfied. I sat alone in the flat, spitting the dummy bigtime while the majority of the Australian camp were celebrating at the closing ceremony.

'Why couldn't Lemberg's bronze have been gold? Lemberg's bronze should have been gold ... Why?' Justin had lived my coaching philosophy ... 'Success knows no shortcut. Be prepared when the time comes to race.'

He deserved better ... Lemberg had paid the price ... he never missed training ... not once in two years! He was continually searching for the 'edge', looking for little things to give him the advantage ... those turns ... he only missed the gold by 56 100ths ... eight 100ths per turn ... if only ... if only they'd been better ... but they should have been better ... he used to go to the school pool next to his home at Mount Gravatt, Brisbane, every day on his own to practise extra turns ... an hour a day extra on turns ... they should have been better.

Then it hit me. I'd sent that kid to practise turns on his own. On his own! No one to watch, no one to supervise, no one to give feedback. How did he know what he was doing? What sort of coach would do that?

Maybe if I'd gone ... if I'd been there each day to check his turns, they could have been eight 100ths faster? My tardiness may have cost him

the gold medal ... I expect my athletes to be totally disciplined, dedicated, professional ... yet here I acted like a real amateur. I vowed I would never let that happen again. We all make mistakes. But only the fool doesn't learn.

I tried to analyse not only my personal achievements but also the achievements of the more successful nations. A series of questions flashed through my mind, questions that would have to be given serious thought if Australia was to continue its upward spiral in international competition.

Sure, because of the boycott, the Russians and East Germans hadn't been in LA but they'd be in Seoul. How could East Germany, with the same population as Australia, have won so much more gold than us in recent Games?

- What were their coaches doing?
- Were their coaches superior to ours?
- Were they concentrating more on technique?
- Were their athletes stronger?

Jon Sieben with the superb German 'albatross', Michael Gross, on Jono's greatest day.

Justin Lemberg, Justin's coach (me!) and another Australian Olympic squad member, 1500 metres finalist Wayne Shillington, in LA in 1984.

- If so, how did they get them stronger?
- Were the East Germans tougher racers than the Australians? No way, after working with our young kids I really didn't believe this.
- Was their financial support system superior? Was it true East Germany spent $20.64 per head of population on sport compared to our miserly $1.80 per head?
- What do we need to do to get a bigger proportion of medals at the next Olympics?
- How can we turn our weaknesses into strengths?
- How can we turn our strengths into weapons?
- How can I, as a coach, best contribute to the future success of our young athletes? And, more importantly, how can I become a better coach?
- Did they value their athletes more than we did?
- Was their talent identification program so much better controlled, stronger, more far-reaching, more sophisticated than ours?

- Were their special live-in sport schools where talented athletes were housed and trained from an early age the answer to athletic success?

If we want to be competitive against these successful nations, the coaches must analyse what they are doing and ask and answer the questions. Again I asked myself: How can we match the East Germans, Russians, Americans and other major nations in the sporting arena?

Since then, sadly, it has been proven, with the breakdown of the Iron Curtain, that East Germany's sportsmen and sportswomen were on a state-controlled drug program to build strength and endurance. So many of their great performances were drug enhanced. How bitterly disappointing for these nations that many of their champions are now regarded as having given 'ho-hum' performances. There will always be that big question mark hanging over their champions' heads.

When Professor Franke presented undisputed evidence from the Stasi files in a paper at an American swim coaches' conference, detailing evidence of how steroids were systematically fed to many of the young East German swimming stars, as a state-controlled program' I thought of how hard my own swimmer, 15-year-old Jodie Clatworthy, had trained for her fourth place at the Seoul Olympics. As he reeled off name after name I realised that Jodie had been denied her moment of glory by the scourge of drugs!

Coaches and administrators must fight this scourge so that our young people who dream and work so hard are not denied reward for their labours. I would like to publicly praise Forbes Carlile, who is leading the Australian attack on drug cheats. My fax machine continually runs hot with updates on drug cheats from this great man.

The admiration and esteem I held for the great GDR marathon man, Waldemar Cierpinski, victorious in Montreal and Moscow, is now tarnished by the thought that he may have somehow been chemically assisted. Kornelia Ender's string of 10 world records in the 100 metres freestyle, beginning on July 13, 1973, in Berlin, is dulled by the thought that they were drug-assisted. The awe that I held for the tall, slim East German goddess Kristin Otto and her six-gold-medal haul in Seoul, now simply evokes a ho-hum, so-what response. What a tragedy!

*Anyone can wish for something —
and most people do. But only a few
know that a definite plan, combined
with a burning desire, is the only
way to get there.*

3 — Jodie and The Kid
'Seoul, the goal'

The tall, gangly 14 year old with a crew cut, stick-out ears, a nose that could have been sculptured by Michelangelo, and a protruding Adam's apple walked very slowly into the Commonwealth Games pool at Chandler in Brisbane. He seemed a little lost, deep in thought. He had his towel slung casually across his shoulder and his goggles dangling from his little finger, desperately trying to give the appearance of being 'Mr Cool' to the noisy teenagers gathered around the 25-metre pool.

He was really feeling apprehensive, a little nervous. This was his first appearance at the Queensland target squad assembly. This skinny kid from the bush, if you call Rockhampton 'the bush', after gaining places at his first appearance in the age national championships, had sufficiently impressed the Queensland swimming selectors to have them add him to the Queensland target swimming squad. He watched carefully out of the corner of one eye as the gathered hopefuls carefully went through a ritual of pre-training stretching. They'd been to the assembly on a number of occasions and they knew the routine. They were relaxed and familiar.

I walked among the teenagers correcting and encouraging them as they stretched. Seeing the youngster nervously glancing from one to another, trying to follow the stretching as unobtrusively as possible, I questioned him brusquely, revelling a little in his discomfort.

'Armstrong, are you familiar with these stretching exercises?'

'We don't do a lot of stretching in Rocky,' was his measured reply.

'Just follow Jodie Clatworthy,' I ordered back, 'she's familiar with the stretches required for the major muscle groups and the ones you should do. Jodie! Can you help Duncan with these stretches please?'

Jodie Clatworthy, who made the finals of both medley races in Seoul in 1988 (fourth in the 200IM, sixth in the 400). She deserved to be an Olympic medallist, and would have been but for the scourge of performance-enhancing drugs.

'Sure!' she walked confidently to him, looked him in the eye, held out her hand and said, 'Hi! I'm Jodie and I'm going to the Seoul Olympic Games.'

There was something in her confident manner, the way she spoke, and the steely determination that shone from her clear sparkling eyes that made him believe her. She was one special little girl. Already she had set herself lofty goals and her positive mannerisms gave him no reason to doubt her. He could see in her a real strength and could sense that her goals were not just idle daydreams of a young girl bitten with Olympic fever. They were realistic — tangible and attainable. This made him feel good.

'Oh, I'm Duncan,' he replied. Although she was only a slip of a girl, maybe about 11, he could feel the strength in her handshake.

'What do you swim, Duncan?' she asked, with genuine interest.

'I swim freestyle and butterfly,' he replied, but he was feeling a little more at ease now that this girl with the vice-like handshake had befriended him.

This was the start of a friendship that would blossom over a number of years and be built on mutual respect as they sweated in the gym, ran the dreaded stairs, or swam lap after lonely lap fighting and clawing their way towards a common objective ...

'Seoul, the Goal.'

Duncan would go on to be Olympic champion, while Jodie, who gained the admiration of all who came in contact with her for her tenacity, discipline and determination, would come fourth in the gruelling medleys — beaten only by girls who, as I've said, we now know had a serious question mark over their adherence to FINA's drug policy. In fact, some are listed in the Stasi files as being recipients of male hormones.

Soon the teenagers' chatter ceased and they were in the water. They were confident, free and relaxed.

'I want to do a kick set with my group this afternoon!' I yelled. 'Get your kick boards!'

Now the skylarking teenagers were down to serious business. They were in action. There was no talking, just the incessant sound of water splashing as — arms stretched over the kick boards, eyes fixed on the end of the pool — they moved quickly, almost effortlessly, lap after lap through the water. I watched like an eagle, beady eyes shifting left and right, stalking the deck, barking orders, waiting for a mistake. They worked hard. They were almost finished. But the effort required to keep up with the group was starting to tell on Armstrong. His face was red from exertion, like an exhausted turkey that had been chased for hours by some persistent four-year-old determined to get a tail feather. You could see by the pained expression that Duncan was starting to struggle.

Again, I enjoyed his discomfort, secure in the knowledge that it was building character. Still he persisted. His training in Rockhampton had not prepared him for the intensity of this type of workout. I pushed the team harder. Still he persisted. This kid has something, I thought. Maybe it was his pride that kept him going when he was obviously in distress. Then it happened! One of the groups stopped for a split second and their feet momentarily touched the ground. This was what I was waiting for. I saw and I pounced.

'Stop!' I called. 'All over here!'

They obeyed.

'I don't believe it. I just saw someone's feet touch the ground,' I called incredulously. They stood in silence, heads bowed, as I went on.

'This is supposed to be the cream of Queensland swimming,' I said, shaking my finger angrily at the entire team. They stood like naughty little grade-one students being chastised by their teacher, who was stern, straight-faced, but smiling inside.

'I don't care whether it was weakness or a lack of concentration, if you crack like that in training you surely will crack in your races. Your opponents will just rip your jugular out if you show any sign of weakness.'

I looked Armstrong directly in the eye.

'No weaknesses! Start again!' I spat.

Duncan's shoulders slumped. He turned away. His eyes met Jodie's. She smiled. He put his head underwater so she could not see the great tears that threatened to fill his goggles. He held his breath and shook his head underwater. What an animal this Laurie Lawrence is! This was the coach his father wanted him to train with. He must be joking. The kick set was repeated properly. Armstrong struggled but refused to be beaten. He finished the set. Soon the training was over and the chlorine-dipped, wet-headed group filed out.

The 'Kid' from Rocky ... Duncan Armstrong.

As they wandered along the bush path to the carpark, tired but happy, Duncan found himself walking next to his new-found friend.

'That was fun!' Jodie said.

'You call that fun!' he retorted. 'I can hardly walk. I've done more kicking in one session than I've done in a month at home.'

'Yeah, but it was fun!' she insisted.

'It was the hardest thing I've ever done in training,' he said.

'You lucky thing! You must feel great to do a personal best training session!' she continued with enthusiasm.

'Lawrence is over the top. He's mad!' he replied.

'No he's not!' she defended vigorously. 'He's hard, but fair. He challenges you in training to do your best. He tries to make you tough.'

'Make you tough! He nearly killed me!'

'If you continue to do what you've always done you will always get what you've always got. He's a good coach if you want to go to the Olympics, and I do,' she answered simply.

He marvelled at the wisdom expounded by one so young. They walked on in silence. He thought about her words. He was exhausted, but he felt strangely satisfied, proud that he'd finished the training. Sure, there was a bit of salty water in his goggles but the coach had not cracked him, he had not given in, and he vowed he never would. Two months later, the Armstrong family left Rockhampton and Duncan joined the Lawrence team in search of his Olympic dream. Many years later, early in 1988, at the Australian Olympic trials he and Jodie became Seoul soul mates when they both qualified for the Olympic team.

It was in Seoul on Monday, September 19, 1988, that Duncan finally got his chance for Olympic glory. The heats had been a personal triumph for him as he qualified fourth fastest and thus found himself in lane six — ominously, the same lane in which his team mate, 21-year-old Jon Sieben, had won the Olympic gold medal four years earlier. Duncan had worked on the same training principles as Jono Sieben …

When the time comes to race, be ready. Be totally prepared. Leave no stone unturned in the preparation process for only then can you face life with no regrets.

As his coach, I remembered how Duncan had not missed a single training session for two years in his Olympic build-up. He had been totally committed. Duncan, too, could reflect on those cold, lonely, winter nights, when, three times a week after a gruelling swimming training session and a quick bite to eat, he would put on his father's well-worn garden gloves, take his battered old skateboard with the wheels placed sideways and head to the bottom of the street in the company of his father for a little extra strength training. There, the dedicated young man would lie across the skateboard and, using his hands in a swimming action, would haul himself up the incline.

His father, Laurie Armstrong, had been rock solid in support of his son over the years, always encouraging his talents and even transferring

> *Never resist a temporary inconvenience*
> *if it results in a permanent improvement.*

to Brisbane with his job in the bank to give his son the best training opportunity. He would walk slowly beside his son's straining horizontal body in silence as Duncan slowly inched his way up and along the concrete footpath. Once Duncan reached the top they would walk down again, shoulder to shoulder, in a silent communion — one sweating from exertion, the other rugged from the cold but there nevertheless. One chasing the Olympic dream with a clear knowledge of his goal and a burning desire to achieve it; the other giving welcomed support as his son went the extra mile in pursuit of personal excellence.

Duncan could also reflect on those other nights, after his team mates had left the pool and alone with me, the coach, he buckled on the weight belt and jumped into the diving well at Chandler, extended his hands above his head and kicked for an extra half hour to strengthen his legs. He could feel the lactic acid burning in his legs as he fought to keep his head above water.

I have always found this a very good exercise for my charges ... if they don't kick they drown. Human survival is a wonderful motivation. It was during these quiet times together as he worked and I smiled, that I'd remind him of how the pain of a hard workout stops immediately the training session stops but the pain of defeat, if you haven't given your best, lasts a lifetime.

Now in Seoul, I sat quietly on the end of a table, while Duncan relaxed, slowly sipped his dilute sodium bicarbonate drink, and enjoyed a massage in preparation for his clash with three world record holders, American Matt Biondi, German superstar Michael Gross and Polish sensation Artur Wojdat. I felt it was appropriate to revisit the nights that Duncan had, by choice, done the extra work.

'Mate, aren't you glad now you did the extras ... the stairs ... the weights ... the wheels ... the weight belt ... how do you feel?'

'I feel confident, I know I'm going to do my best,' he answered.

Two of the world record holders Duncan faced in the 200 metres final in Seoul. Right: Matt Biondi, 100 metres world record holder. Below: Michael Gross, 200 metres champion.

'I'll bet you these blokes you're racing haven't prepared as well as you ... any money they haven't done the wheels ... any money they haven't done the weight belt'.

'I know I've got nothing to lose. I'm a bit nervous, though.'

'That's good ... that's natural ... a bit of adrenaline pumpin'. But you can approach the final with a confidence and a relaxation that comes only with the knowledge that you have prepared well.'

'Laurie, I know I can go faster tonight. The heats were so very smooth and easy. I'll go better.'

'Of course you will, this is the first time you've been fully tapered in two years. This race is what you've trained for. Did you ring your Dad?' I asked.

'Yeah!'

'What did he say?'

'Break a world record.'

'You're kidding?'

'No, he always says that. He's said it since I was a little kid swimming in Rockhampton,' he told me.

'I've been thinking seriously about tactics for tonight ... I really believe you're the fittest swimmer in the field,' I said. I was trying to give positive vibes for reassurance, but I knew that if the work had been consistent and honest over the training period then the positive feelings and vibes would be there anyway.

'I know I am! Don't worry Laurie, I'll be right,' he said with strong conviction. 'I've prepared well, I'm not frightened of anybody.'

'I think you're in the best lane,' I continued.

'I like lane six,' he said simply.

'Lucky lane six! That's the lane Jono won in Los Angeles!' I enthused, trying to relax him.

'That could be a good omen,' he said. I knew by the quiet confidence in his voice he was already relaxed.

> *Racing at the Olympic level means taking up the personal challenge to be tougher mentally than everybody else, to train longer, to work harder. It is forcing the mind's will on the body when the body cannot give any more. The personal challenge means that when two athletes find themselves evenly matched in the race, the one who can stand pain more wins.*
>
> Canadian women's rowing team

'Do you know I broke into the audiovisual room early today to watch yesterday's heats?' I ventured.

'You're kidding!'

'No! I wanted to watch the way Biondi and company swam their heats.'

'Learn anything?' Duncan laughed with a little twinkle in his eye. He was totally relaxed. This was a good sign.

'Well yes, son, I did! I really think you can win this even though I think the 400 metres is your best event and the event you've trained for ...' Duncan sat up to get his triceps massaged and listened intently as I went on. 'Biondi is going to be out fast. He has great natural speed. You can't let him get too far away or you'll never catch him. You just have to stay in touch if you want to win. Remember, you are fitter than him. If possible you have to use this fitness to your advantage.'

'I'd like to beat him. I'll give it my best shot!'

'You have to be out fast and easy. He has a powerful six-beat kick with a beautiful long stroke ... but his kick creates a mini wave ... I reckon if you get close enough to the wave it will help you stay in touch.'

'Get on the lane rope and suck him up!' Duncan laughed.

'You got it! I reckon if you can stay in touch you're fit enough to run him down in the last 50 metres,' I said.

The masseuse tapped Duncan on the shoulder and said, 'You're ready, son. Good luck!'

I walked with Duncan to the marshalling area, gripped his hand firmly and looked him in the eye.

'Get out there and celebrate your talent. You're fit and ready. Suck him up!' I said, mimicking Duncan's earlier remark.

He looked at me, nodded, smiled, put headphones in his ears, and turned into the marshalling area with a spring and confidence in his step that comes from someone who knows they have prepared well.

I walked into the grandstand with Dick Telford, AIS physiologist, to await the race. This is how I remember it ...

The combatants are called to the deck. Artur Wojdat, the Polish 400 metres world record holder, wearing a white baseball cap, steps forward in lane three and raises his arms high. The defending champion Michael Gross, wearing a green, white and blue track top, is the 200 metres world record holder and the fastest qualifier. He steps forward swinging the long arms that resemble the wing span of a great bird that gave birth to that nickname of 'the Albatross'. Matt Biondi, the 100 metres world record holder, sits. He looks confident in his navy blue USA T-shirt. He is clean-shaven for the final and is in lane five. Duncan, the fourth-fastest qualifier, ranked only 46th in the world before the heats, has qualified with a two-second personal best. He ignores them all. He goes to the diving pool and wets his goggles. He is ready to race.

I'm in the stands, more nervous than the 20-year-old. I'm wearing the multicoloured Aussie team shirt and my Akubra, and I've got the evening's program twisted into a baton to be used as a whip in the home straight should Duncan be close enough for victory. I remember calling to people in the stands, 'Don't forget Duncan Armstrong. Don't forget Duncan Armstrong.'

At the starter's gun Duncan dives in and positions himself on the lane rope next to Matt Biondi. It is a perfect start for him — he's positioned himself perfectly to take advantage of Biondi's bulk, huge kick and resultant drag.

Stuff the silver, we came for the gold!

At the 100-metre mark Anders Holmertz, the Swede, leads, Biondi tumbles second with Armstrong just three quarters of a body length behind but still in touch and hanging on desperately. The announcer calls ...

'Fifty-two, point two, one ... one second ahead of world record pace.'

In the crucial third lap Armstrong moves to within half a body length of Biondi. I sense a chance of victory and start belting Bill Sweetenham, head coach, on the back with my program. As Armstrong tumbles with one lap to go, he moves off the lane rope back to the middle of the lane. He is in a perfect position for the crucial last lap. He must drive his tortured body to the finish line disregarding pain. I know his legs are capable. Those lonely sessions with the weight belt in the diving pool at Chandler are about to strike paydirt. I start screaming, 'Go after him, son! Go after him!'

He doesn't hear me. But I feel pretty good about it anyway and he obliges.

Duncan is in his own private world of total concentration. One mistake and victory will slip from his grasp. Now he thinks of all the extra things he has done in preparing for this race; the skateboard that has made his arms strong like a woodcutter's, the weight belt which has toned his legs to a new level of fitness. He is supremely confident and in control.

'Don't crack! Don't crack!' he calls to himself. I lose control and as Duncan inches closer to the lead I up the belting tempo on Bill Sweetenham's back.

'Cut it out, Laurie!' he screams.

'Shut up, Bill!' I scream back and continue belting.

Duncan inches closer. I sense victory.

When Duncan is 10 metres from the end of the pool I start screaming, 'Don't breathe! Don't breathe!' We have finished every repeat at training for the last four years in this fashion. Would he remember? Five metres out he obliges, obeys, and sprints to the wall not breathing, just as he has done thousands of times in training.

Victory is assured.

I'm a great believer in practising the skills in training that you want in your races so that they may become a mere formality on race day. Duncan is now on automatic pilot. I spin to the electronic scoreboard … it flashes '1' beside the Australian, D. Armstrong, but it also flashes the world record. At last he's obeyed his father!

I'm happy!

Duncan sits on the lane rope and holds his hands high above his head in a victory salute, savouring the moment. All the arduous training sessions, the hours spent honing his rhythmical six-beat technique, the cold nights on the skateboard, the pain of the weight belt, the pain of the race are now forgotten as he enjoys the exhilaration of a victory well earned. At that moment the media and well-wishers surround me.

Dick Telford, who had played his part, slaps me and screams, 'You beauty, Laurie! You beauty!'

Overcome by emotion I throw my arms up and stop belting Bill Sweetenham. He is happy.

Almost simultaneously, Steve Quartermain, a journalist from Channel 10, arrives with cameras and microphone.

'Can you talk, Laurie, can you talk?' he calls above the uproar.

I shake my head, slap the program on my leg and mutter incoherently, 'I can't talk. I can't talk.'

Then, while Duncan enjoys the fruits of his labour below in the brightly lit pool, I start my own private celebration in the stands. Captured on television, my heart is laid bare to the nation ... to the world.

'Lucky lane six! Lucky lane six!' I start screaming and parading as my mind flashes back to Jon Sieben's unexpected Olympic victory four years earlier. But no one knows what I'm thinking. They think I'm a little troppo. I kiss a woman who I'd been joking with before the race. She speaks no English but understands emotion. I continue

Matt Biondi (left), Duncan and Anders Holmertz after the medal presentation.

> *The real winners in life are people who look
> at every situation with an expectation that
> they can make it work and make it better.*
>
> Barbara Pletcher

ranting, waving, jumping, hugging, and kissing. No one is safe. They wish I hadn't been eating Kim Chee.

Steve finally grabs me for the TV. 'How do you feel, Laurie? How do you feel?'

I spin, give him the best left hook, and put him in a headlock that world heavyweight wrestling champion Hulk Hogan would be proud of ...

'We just beat three world record holders, three world record holders! How do you think I feel?'

I continue bouncing down the stairs. Steve rubs his jaw, smiling and stunned. He's not happy with the whack on the jaw but at least he has a television coup.

I see my assistant coach, Ian Findlay, who has been an integral part of this magnificent victory. Ian has, outside training hours on weekends, ridden mountain bikes up hills or gone on long runs with Duncan 'for fun'. Now he is in Seoul as coach of the Malaysian team. I race over. We hug and do a victory jig together. I almost break his back. Lara Hooiveld, a young woman I taught to swim and who is also a member of the Australian Olympic team, is there too. We hug. We are all soul mates in Seoul, bound together by a dream ... a dream that has seen us through good times and bad ... a dream that has kept us persisting when many would have said, 'this is not possible' ... a dream that has fired determination and dedication, commitment and courage. Now we can all rejoice in Duncan's victory.

Steve Quartermain continues to pursue me, like a good journalist, milking every bit of emotion for TV. As I continue on my merry way he gets that famous grab which will remain part of Australian sporting folklore.

I might have been drenched from diving in after Duncan, but ... what the heck ... C'mon Dawn, give us a hug!

'What do you think we came here for silver? Stuff the silver, we came for the gold!'

Nothing can stop me. I push past a security guard and race down to the warm-up pool seeking the new Olympic champion, wanting to congratulate Duncan personally, as it is impossible for him to hear me above the roar of the crowd. He is not there. I wait in vain. He has been taken to a special room to await the victory ceremony. I run back up the stairs, bounding two steps at a time, wanting human contact with the young man with whom I'd spent so much time chasing this elusive dream.

Finally, the victory ceremony. Duncan leads out Anders Holmertz and Matt Biondi. I'm so proud. He bends to receive the gold medal and I push past the TV cameras above the dais and call jokingly to him:

'Duncan! Duncan! I know you! I'm a friend of yours, eh?'

He turns, sees me, smiles and raises two fingers in a sharp upward motion normally used on aggressive drivers who cut you off in traffic. The national anthem plays. He is so proud. I clutch my Akubra and the tears well up. It has been a long hard road. Duncan is now the Olympic Champion.

After the ceremony I go to the warm-up pool to wait for him. It seems an eternity. When at last he arrives. I take off without thinking, diving fully clothed, shoes and stopwatch, into the pool. Contact. Nothing is said. Nothing needs to be said, because we both know that the preparation was perfect, encompassing hard work, sacrifice, discipline and consistency. I hope his fairytale will inspire others to go on and chase their dreams with all the fibre in their being so that win, lose or draw, they can look at themselves in the mirror and honestly say:

I gave it my best shot.

When I arrived home my wife was at the airport with my three daughters to greet me. She gave me a welcome kiss and whispered, 'You made a fool of yourself on national TV. Why did you dive in the pool, you silly cow? I bet you've ruined your good shoes.'

My three girls swarm all over me. 'Daddy! Daddy! What did you bring us, Daddy?'

Gee it's good to be home. Welcome to the real world!

Last season, when we were world champions going for two in a row, everybody was playing us tough. Against the champs, everybody's game goes up a notch. Opponents often play their best game of the season against us ... but knowing is an advantage for us and we'll go a game at a time.

Defending champs are expected to come into the season mentally soft. We've been here before, though. We have been through all the traps and mental potholes of returning champs. Some of the glory of last year's triumph lingers, you get caught up in the relief of having won it all, and then next season is on you immediately.

Kareem Abdul-Jabbar

4 — Bring on the Games
Show no mercy

Act I

The year is 1996. Olympic year, the year long awaited by serious athletes all over the world. The time when the dreams, the striving, the training, the heartache, and the hard work can be realised. This is the year commitment meets opportunity — opportunity hidden deep inside the indomitable human spirit waiting for that special occasion to be released and realised. This is the year when past victories or past defeats count for nothing; they are merely stepping stones along the path to success. The year when past failures and disappointments become strengths, hardened anvils, the fertiliser of success, as athletes the world over unite in Atlanta USA for 16 days of highly publicised cut-throat competition. Their dream is to climb the victory dais to glory and become members of that very special club when they are crowned Olympic Champion.

In order to achieve these dizzy heights, to fulfil the impossible dream, to drink at the 'Olympic Fountain', to experience the Olympic intoxication that lasts a lifetime, there has to be a physical and psychological union, a marriage of body and mind. For without both, even the most talented athlete in the world is doomed to failure. Potential counts for nothing without the great sacrifices. Today there are thousands of young athletes walking around this country with the potential to be world or Olympic champions but, sadly, without an intelligent plan and, more importantly, a commitment to that plan. They are doomed to live forever in the twilight zone of mediocrity, destined to be another promising athlete with unfulfilled potential.

The committed athlete will undertake hour after hour of gruelling training, lifting weights in the gym, sweating on the tartan track, completing lap after repetitive lap in the swimming pool, somersaulting

Housman, Kowalski, Perkins ... Australia's 1500 metres champions in 1996.

on the vaulting horse, throwing medicine balls in dingy gyms, cross training, pushing the body to the absolute limit, communicating with the coach, searching for the elusive 'edge' while trying to achieve the fine line in athletic preparation between physical exhaustion, bodily breakdown and new levels of athletic excellence. However, all of these lonely hours of self-inflicted torture, with a little help from the coach, are useless unless the mind, too, is steeled for the pressures of tough competition.

In the Atlanta Olympiad, Australia, fortunately, had three of the best distance freestyle swimmers in the world in Glen Housman, Kieren

Perkins and Daniel Kowalski. All three were highly committed young men who were prepared to train long and hard to realise their goal. They knew that they had the opportunity to represent Australia, but were also aware that there were no freebies and no guarantees if they wanted to wear the precious green and gold. Like everybody else, they had to pay the price.

These young men were extremely well coached by experienced men who realised the tremendous pressure exerted at the coalface in the Olympic arena. All had been part of the coaching staff in Barcelona.

Housman was coached by former Australian Commonwealth Games swimming representative Michael Bohl; Perkins by the craggy-faced, rat-cunning and experienced World Swimming Coaches' coach of the previous Olympiad, John Carew; Kowalski by hard-nosed former Institute of Sport coach Bill Nelson. All men realised the importance of the Olympic Trials. They knew that competition for the Olympic 1500 metres spot was fierce and that only two Australian gladiators could be chosen. They didn't have to be reminded of Henry Wadsworth Longfellow's celebrated words:

> *Not in the clamour of the crowded street*
> *Not in the shouts and plaudits of the throng,*
> *But in ourselves are triumph and defeat.*

The first shot in the psychological war of the Olympic year was fired on January 4, at the Victorian swimming championships, by the hungry young Kowalski who, denied Barcelona representation by rivals Perkins and Housman, had vowed that it would not happen again. Fiercely proud, Kowalski served notice at the Victorian championships on his more experienced rivals with a sizzling swim in the 400 metres freestyle of 3:52.66. He followed this up by recording the fastest time in the world for 1996 in the 1500 — 15:10.76. This was Daniel's way of saying, 'Boys, I may be the youngest, I may only have enough hair to shave once a week, I missed Barcelona, but I want to go to Atlanta and I intend to get the individual swims in both the 400 metres and the 1500 metres no matter who I have to tread on.'

How would Daniel's more experienced swimming rivals respond four days later at the Queensland swimming championships?

Carew, when pressed, plays his cards close to the chest. His plan evolved around an Olympic agenda so all other influences, as far as he was concerned, were secondary. He shook his head, peered over his not-too-often-polished glasses, and grunted, 'Kieren will be okay as long as he keeps putting in the work and doesn't get sick!'

Carew is coaching the world record holder, the 1500 metres Olympic champion. He has a sense of history and destiny, knowing that only two other athletes — USA's ironman Mike Burton and Russia's great Vladimir Salnikov — have been able to win the gruelling Olympic distance event twice. He is desperate for Kieren to be the third and this has become his driving passion, his obsession — all other swimming events pale into insignificance in his clear-cut thinking, his Olympic agenda. He passed up the opportunity to have Kieren swim at the World Short-course Championships in Rio because he felt short-course racing was not conducive to winning Olympic gold, and declined graciously an invitation for Kieren to race in the NSW championships.

Michael Bohl's response is different. He knows Kieren has denied Glen gold on many occasions but the coach has followed Glen's career as a young boy and marvelled at his natural endurance qualities. A friend and fellow coach, Ian Findlay, was worried about Glen's lack of explosive speed and worked hard to improve it while he was coaching him. This had been done. Now Glen has a dangerous weapon in his arsenal ... speed. Bohl admires Glen's natural buoyancy and the dolphin-like bounce in his stroke when he is technically 'on'. He witnessed first hand the disappointment when Glen was denied the great Salnikov's world record at the National Swimming Championships in Adelaide in 1990, when the electronic timing equipment failed. This disappointment seems to have hung like an albatross around 'the little Aussie battler's' neck.

Now Bohl believes Glen is the best 1500 metres swimmer, but thinks he needs to race well, to lower Perkins' colours on a number of

Above, left to right: Michael Bohl (coach of Glen Housman), Scott Volkers (coach of, among others, Susie O'Neill and Sam Riley) and Bill Nelson (coach of Daniel Kowalski). Right: The crafty Queenslander, John Carew, long-time mentor of Kieren Perkins.

occasions, to get his racing confidence back. If Glen can win, his self-belief will blossom. In self-belief there is power and only with it can our visions become realities.

Bohl's tactics are simple. He will restrict Glen's schedule just a little here at the Queensland Championships, to give him the opportunity to beat Kieren in the 1500.

The scene is set. The racing is sensational. Glen swims faster than

Kieren in the 200 metres. However, they are both upstaged by a talented, annoying upstart — Kiwi swimmer Danyon Loader, who has arrived fresh from a successful World Cup competition.

Loader is on a hit-and-run mission at the Queensland championships to remind the boys that he'll be around come the Olympics and he intends to be among the gold medal action. Loader gets double gold when he disposes of Perkins in the 400 metres, but Perkins beats Housman in the same event.

Next day Perkins sends a message out to competitors all over the world when he swims 7:55.48 for the 800 metres. Glen, as planned, sits in the stands. He watches silently as Kieren grits his teeth and punches the air in exultation at this great time. Glen is now in a psychological clutch situation ...

He must win the 1500 metres or be mentally destroyed by Kieren Perkins!

John Carew looks like the cat who has just swallowed the canary! Kieren is on target for Atlanta! The Olympic Dream looms closer to reality.

Later at these Queensland championships the 1500 becomes an intriguing tactical battle as Kieren leads and tries several times to shake the desperate bull terrier-like Housman. Housman knows he must win, he knows he gains respect by his actions so he digs deep, as only champions can, and he sprints away from a tiring, unrested Perkins in the last 100 metres.

The Psychological Scoresheet:
Housman   1
Perkins   1
Kowalski   1

Let the mind games continue.

Bring on the Trials ...

Act II

There is a time when dreams, talent, discipline and hard work meet opportunity ...

Optus Vision was one of the new pay TV stations in Australia and had done a deal with Australian swimming to televise a number of meets around the country, mainly state and national championships. However, the 1996 Olympic Trials was to be the highlight. Duncan Armstrong, the 1988 Olympic 200 metres freestyle gold medallist, was an integral part of the commentary team. I was asked to join the Optus call, conducting pool-deck interviews at the conclusion of each race. I can tell you, no arm twisting was required to get me on board.

As I was no longer actively involved in coaching elite athletes, I welcomed the opportunity to attend the Olympic Trials as a guest of Optus Vision. After all, the job gave me the best seat in the house. I would witness first hand the joys, heartaches and dramas as they unfolded. It would also give me the opportunity to meet some of the new kids on the block as they made the Olympic swimming team. Furthermore, this close early contact would be invaluable in assisting me in my new role as an athlete liaison officer for the entire Australian Olympic team. I was looking forward to this challenging role of supporting and motivating any athlete who required help.

So it was that on April 21, 1996, after I squeezed through the milling crowd that was waiting patiently outside Sydney's magnificent Homebush Aquatic Centre, I bounced into the new Olympic pool. I knew instinctively something special was in the air.

The Aquatic Centre was lit like the brightest sunny day you could imagine, the lights accentuating the crystal clear pool water. White-clad officials scurried around the newly scrubbed pool deck checking backstroke flags, testing the false start rope, tightening the anti-wave lane ropes that would be used to separate combatants over the next seven days of pressure-cooker racing. Pool staff wheeled out the electronic timing equipment saved for special occasions such as this.

Former Olympians strolled by, expectant, waiting to welcome new members to the club. It was a veritable Who's Who of past

The King ... Kieren Perkins

Olympians at the pool. Many took the opportunity to renew old acquaintances ...

Dawn was chatting earnestly to Bev Whitfield, Munich Olympic 200 metres breaststroke gold medallist (who has since passed away). Murray Rose, resplendent in a new suit, looked as fit as any of the young bulls parading around the swimming pool deck. Visions of his magnificent duels with the great Japanese swimmer Tsuyashi Yamanaka at the Melbourne Olympics and Murray's follow-up victory in Rome four years later flashed to mind. I couldn't help wondering if he would have been able to emulate Dawn's phenomenal record of three consecutive Olympic gold medals had the selectors given him the opportunity to defend his 400 metres title in Tokyo.

Murray had broken the world record while studying overseas at the University of Southern California in Los Angeles. However, since he was not able to swim in the Australian trials in 1964, because of some form of bureaucratic bungling, he was overlooked for selection. His non-selection opened up doors for Bob Windle, who went on to win the 1500 metres, keeping Australia's distance tradition alive.

> *The highest reward for a person's toil is not what he gets for it but what he becomes by it.*
>
> John Ruskin

Big 'Brooksie', Neil Brooks, there to do TV commentary, was chatting to Mark Kerry and Mark Tonelli, two of his fellow members from our gold medal medley relay team in Moscow. Someone yelled across the pool, 'Where's PE?', referring to the fourth member of the illustrious quartet.

Brooksie roared back, 'I think he's meditating with the Dalai Lama.' And they all chuckled good-naturedly as they were reminded of Peter Evans' off-the-wall personality.

You could feel the excitement, taste the atmosphere. The music blared. Something special was about to happen. The musical beat was strong and rhythmical, the lyrics significant ...

Show no mercy ...

Nervous swimmers, normally boisterous and chatty, filed slowly and quietly into the arena, found a quiet spot, and started their stretching ritual before going to their coaches ... they knew it would be do-or-die swimming.

One young hopeful must have anticipated the song as the motto 'Show no mercy' was splashed across the back of his T-shirt. The words had an ominous ring to them — to qualify outright, swimmers needed to finish first or second inside a tough qualifying time, top eight in the world, or sheepishly ask their mates to bring them back a T-shirt from Atlanta. Athletes had had this message drummed into them over and over again in the weeks, months, years leading up to these 1996 Australian Olympic Trials. There would be no exceptions. World record holders, too, were expected to perform within these strict guidelines or stay at home.

Head coach Don Talbot had indicated that he did not want passengers on this team. Deadwood would be left behind. The pressure was on. Perform or watch the Olympics on television.

> *Better to live one day as a lion than a thousand days as a sheep.*

Here was the opportunity to become a member of a very exclusive club, one that will admit you only when you have proved you are worthy, proved yourself on the sporting battlefield.

You may have tasted the bitter gall of defeat on many occasions, but by dedication, by a stubborn refusal to be mastered, by sheer 'guts, determination, and persistence' you are able to drink deep from the revered chalice of victory. Once you've qualified — and only then — can you don the precious green and gold, buy the Olympic ring, and wear the same five rings on your Australian blazer. The racing would be tough. It was no place for the faint-hearted ...

Coaches were nervous, expectant, hopeful; dedication was about to meet opportunity. Some of their charges had spent the past four years preparing for this meet. Some longer. Now was the time to celebrate their talent and show the Australian people just how good they were. Coaches' egos, too, were on the line. Butterflies swarmed internally as they fought back these squeamish feelings in order to appear composed and relaxed, and not pass on any of their feelings of anxiety to their charges. One false coaching move could leave years of training and sacrifices unfulfilled ... ripe fruit left to rot on the vine, unharvested. And, in some instances, the athlete left with emotional scars that will haunt them to their grave because, in the process of chasing victory, they have never been taught that there will be occasions when failure is inevitable — but as long as you have given your very best, it's okay to fail.

In fact, failure, in most instances, is an integral part of victory.

'Fatty' Wilkinson, former Olympian, had combed his stubby moustache especially for the evening. He was relaxed but in earnest conservation with young iron swimmer Emma Johnson. His beady eyes stared deep into hers. Was he trying to hypnotise her as the great Forbes Carlile had done to him many years ago? Was he trying to will her into the Olympic team? She was taking on a huge program, racing

four tough events plus relays over the week; critics were asking whether this was a wise move under such cut-throat racing conditions.

Michael Bohl, oblivious to the pressures of the meet, seemed totally relaxed in his Queensland tracksuit with all his young charges laughing around him. He'd represented Australia at the Commonwealth Games in Brisbane in 1982. But he'd also suffered the anguish and heartache of having his dream destroyed when, after winning a number of national championships in the Olympic year for Moscow, he was later defeated at the trials and missed the 1980 Olympic team. Incredibly, 12 years later, as a young coach, his dream was fulfilled when he marched proudly into the Olympic arena in Spain and enjoyed the opening Ceremony. He had watched fascinated, heart in his mouth, drinking deep from the Olympic fountain, as the crippled archer launched the flaming arrow with uncanny accuracy to ignite the Olympic flame and set ablaze the Games of the XXIV Olympiad in Barcelona.

He'd learned so much in Barcelona and made friendships that would last a lifetime. Now he desperately wanted members of his team to share in that magnificent Olympic experience. I wandered over to chat to him, shook his hand and said, 'Good luck, mate, hope you get one of the coaching jobs again.'

'Laurie, I'd gladly give up my coaching spot to get all of my swimmers on the team. They deserve it, they have worked hard,' was his reply.

I looked at him, he was serious. I was so proud of him unselfishly always putting his swimmers' welfare ahead of his own ambitions — a great attitude, no wonder he had such respect from, such tremendous rapport with, his swimmers. I knew intuitively that one day this young man, one of my former swimmers, would be one of the great Australian coaches.

I looked around and saw Perkins. What an athlete! I recalled his great victories ... Olympic 1500 metres champion in Barcelona ... Commonwealth champion in Victoria in the 200, 400 and 1500 metres. Plus two world records there ... World champion in Rome in the 400 and 1500 metres. Another world record. An enviable record.

Daniel Kowalski, the pretender to the throne, was talking to his coach by the diving pool. However, I couldn't see Glen Housman, the third member of the trinity. My heart beat a little faster in anticipation of the 1500 metres and I thought how cruel it was that one of these great athletes — the first, second and third-ranked swimmers in the world — would have to watch the 1500 metres final from the sidelines in Atlanta.

On the first day of the trials, in event four, the 22-year-old Perkins caused a minor ripple around the pool when he qualified in 15th position in the 200 metres freestyle, the event that he had won four years earlier when preparing for Barcelona. He looked extremely sluggish as he swam seventh in the B-Final in 1:54.00, a time that was slower than the half-way split time in his 400 metres world record and indeed slower than his morning heat swim. This was not a good sign. The press went into a feeding frenzy. Coach John Carew was hunted and hounded by the media.

'What's wrong with Kieren? What's wrong with the King?'

The question was on everyone's lips. The normally solid, calm, taciturn Carew was obviously stressed and at a loss for a logical explanation. Carew mumbled something about Kieren's stroke being off a little but guaranteed he'd be right for the 400 metres on day four. Not so! Day four of the championships saw the biggest bombshell of all. Daniel Kowalski cemented his place in the team with a fine 3:50.60, a long way from Kieren's world record of 3:43.80. A battling Perkins was also passed by tall, tough Maroubra swimmer Malcolm Allen.

Malcolm, raised by his grandmother since he had been a little boy, had dreamed of wearing the green and gold for years. As Perkins struggled, Malcolm sniffed an opportunity and pounced on the out-of-form Perkins. The unthinkable then happened, our Olympic champion, world champion, world record holder, our gold medal hope for Atlanta, had again failed to make the team. The crowd at the pool fell silent. They could not believe it. They were stunned, as was the whole nation.

Kieren now had his back to the wall. Under the strict Australian selection criteria he had to get first or second in the 1500 metres, the most gruelling swim race of them all, scheduled the last event on the

last day, or be left behind. This was a real Steven Spielberg script and I was right among the action.

The press went crazy. Channel 9, who had been taking some of Optus' footage, decided under the circumstances to cut live into *Hey Hey It's Saturday*, hosted by Daryl Somers, to cover the race.

The nation stopped to cheer Kieren into the team. The courageous Perkins attacked the race the only way he knew how ... flat out ... he went straight to the front just as he did in all of his major international victories, daring the field to catch him ... Kowalski trailed him, waiting his opportunity ... Perkins kept the pressure on ... Kowalski played cat and mouse, following, stalking, watching, in control ... just waiting his opportunity.

I walked the pool deck in my commentary position for Optus Vision. I was right there among the drama. My heart beat faster as I willed the world champion to victory. Australia needed Kieren in Atlanta. Kieren held his lead ... he was pushing his body to the limit. I was so close I could see the pain etched on Kieren's face as he came into turn. Daniel sensed his vulnerability and made his move. I lost my composure as a television commentator and started cheering for Kieren ...

'Go, son! Go! Hang on! Fight! Fight! Go son! Go!'

No self-respecting TV commentator should lose their cool and start cheering for one competitor in the middle of a race. But half the nation did the same, caught up in the high drama of Olympic selection. However, my cheering was to no avail. Daniel, well prepared and confident, surged past a tiring Kieren ... the crowd was stunned, Kieren was starting to flounder. I started cheering louder.

Now all eyes turned to Glen Housman, who started to make his move. Would he catch him?

No! Kieren dug deep, held off Glen's challenge and I was filled with mixed emotion — elated for Kieren but sad that Glen, who had been cruelly denied a world record in Adelaide when that electronic timer had malfunctioned, would now watch the Olympic 1500 metres from

HE'S BACK

HAT A RELIEF! Kieren Perkins after last night's swim.   *Picture: DALLAS KILPONEN*

Kieren: I've never been happier to be in the team

By IAN HEADS

KIEREN Perkins last night booked his passage to Atlanta on the oldest quality in sport — true grit.

Perkins dug as deep as he ever has into the qualities that made him a champion — finishing second in a nerve-racking Australian 1500m freestyle final which stopped the nation the way the Melbourne Cup does.

"I've never been happier to be on an Australian team than I am tonight," said world record-holder Perkins after finishing second to Daniel Kowalski at Homebush Aquatic Centre.

The winning time was slow — Kowalski clocked 15 minutes 10.44 seconds — but the capacity crowd didn't care.

Perkins had to finish first or second last night to make the Atlanta Games team. When he touched in 15.11.50 there was a great, collective sigh of relief — especially from Olympic officials, who have planned all along to build the team around his greatness.

Murray Rose, one of four Australian Olympic gold medallists at the pool, called it "the most exciting 'ordinary' race I've ever seen".

Perkins said: "With 200m to go I thought 'this is terrible, I've got nothing left'."

Australia will send a swimming team of 34, including Perkins, to Atlanta.

GUTS AND GLORY: Page 51.

70

the grandstand. It just didn't seem fair that the No. 3 ranked 1500 metres swimmer in the world wouldn't compete in this event in Atlanta.

Next day the papers echoed how the entire nation felt about Kieren with the headline.

'HE'S BACK!'

Kieren would now have an opportunity to defend his Olympic title but, again, spare a thought for the gallant Housman. Helen Keller's words ring so true, sporting defeat is character building in the game of life ...

Character cannot be developed in ease and quiet. Only through experiences of trial and suffering can the soul be strengthened, vision cleared, ambition inspired and success achieved.

Act III

Kieren hauled his aching body from the water and looked up to the stands where his fiancée, Symantha, was sitting. She had tears of relief streaming down her face. Kieren, too, was relieved. The strain and pressure of the past week had been difficult on everyone, particularly with the press so hungry for news, analysing every swim and every stroke and making predictions. Would he make the team? Or would the great Kieren Perkins drift into oblivion? What would the sponsors' reaction be if he failed to make the team?

Now he smiled and waved to Symantha, and she smiled back. He didn't have to worry about any of these things now. He was in the Olympic team and, for now at least, he had the opportunity to defend his title. However, like all great champions, he realised the next race — the 1500 metres in Atlanta — was the big one. He must begin preparation immediately.

Kieren moved to the area that had been set up on the pool deck for post race interviews. This one would be a little easier; he would not have to defend his poor form. Daniel Kowalski, his friend and rival, was beaming and no wonder — he'd had a great meet, qualifying in three individual Olympic events (the 200, 400 and 1500). Kieren shook Daniel's hand, happy for his comrade, but, again as great champions do, he resolved to use the lead-up to Atlanta to work hard. Kieren craved a different result at the Atlanta Olympics.

This was an interview I was looking forward to. During the week of the trials, the Perkins interviews had been tough. The public wanted to know what was wrong and, as a working journalist, I was supposed to probe. However, as a coach, I was trying to temper the interviews to minimise any negative comments or questions that could affect his chances of making the Olympic team.

I have, as have many others, always been a big Perkins fan — right from his very first silver medal, won at the Commonwealth Games in Christchurch, New Zealand, in 1990. There, as a brash 16-year-old, he had chased Glen Housman all the way to register his first memorable sub-15-minute 1500 metre swim. Twelve months later, Kieren's courage was thrust upon the world as he battled the giant German, Jorg Hoffman, stroke for stroke in an epic World Championship 1500 in Perth. Perkins, despite breaking the world record there, had to settle for silver, but he had well and truly arrived on the international swimming scene.

Here at the Olympic trials for Atlanta, my heart was racing. I had just marched up and down the pool deck for the past 15 minutes for Optus, analysing every stroke. Now I thrust the microphone into Kieren's face and asked some mundane question about how he felt. But my mind was reliving his courageous swim. I had prowled every lap with him and saw him spread-eagle the field in the early stages. I'd screamed for him as Kowalski closed the gap and then pounced on Perkins' tiring body. I'd willed him on as Housman, making his own desperate bid for Atlanta, gave chase. And here was Kieren beaming, as he answered easily how great it was to be part of an Australian team for his second Olympics and how he would do his best. Ever the professional, he thanked everyone for their support.

The interview over, still dripping wet, he headed straight to Mr Carew. Good old Mr Carew, so dependable, knowledgeable and strong. He'd have all the splits. He'd analyse his mistakes. But at this moment

Never give in to self-doubt. You have to back your own ability, work hard on fine-tuning your technique, and enjoy the challenges that come your way.

Steve Waugh

Kieren was too consumed with relief and joy to worry unduly about the splits. He was IN! For now that was absorbing his mind.

John Carew's usually expressionless face had the trace of a slight smile. It had been a hard week for him, parrying with the press and trying to stay totally positive for Kieren despite the fact that the champ was obviously not up to his best.

'You did it tough, son, but you're in. Well done.'

'Thanks, Mr Carew.' Kieren smiled.

'I've got your splits.'

'Thanks.'

'I'll show you tomorrow. Swim down, relax and enjoy the time with your family,' commented the ever-clinical Carew.

Kieren walked to the warm-down pool and dived in. He could feel the cool water envelop his body. He moved effortlessly along, close to the lane rope, immersed in the water as his thoughts drifted. Water always seemed to have a therapeutic effect on him, right from day one when his dad had carried him through the door of Mr Carew's pool to learn to swim.

John Carew too was immersed in his thoughts.

It seemed only yesterday, he smiled, as he remembered how Kieren, aged just eight, was brought to the Carew Learn-to-Swim centre. Not long before, Kieren had been playing with his brother, Jarrod, but with boyhood exuberance had run through a plate-glass window and sliced his leg to the bone. All up, he needed the best part of 100 stitches in his leg. A cold shiver ran along John Carew's spine as he

> *After the fight, for a while I was bitter. I had all*
> *sorts of excuses. The ring ropes were loose. The*
> *referee counted too fast. The cut hurt my training.*
> *I was drugged. I fought that fight over in my*
> *head a thousand times. And then, finally, I*
> *realised I'd lost to a great champion, probably*
> *the greatest of all time.*
>
> George Foreman, on being knocked out
> by Muhammad Ali, Zaire, 1974

remembered the horrific scars. He remembered how he had put Kieren on a kick board for the three painful months it took before the eight-year-old could walk properly again. They had been together a long time ...

While Kieran swam down, I sought John out. By now, his mind had snapped back to the present. He was sitting quietly on his own, writing things down and examining Kieren's split times.

'Congratulations!' I called as I got closer.

'Thanks,' he replied, then added, 'he's in, that's all that matters. Now we can plan to win in Atlanta.'

'Do you really think he can?'

'Of course. Laurie, we've had a terrible preparation since the Queensland championships. You just wait till Atlanta!'

'Do you really believe he can win there?'

'Of course!' he replied indignantly.

'Why?'

'He has a great will to win. No, a ferocious will to win ... he can focus ... he knows pace ... he has a very low heartrate, so he has a great motor ... he's quiet ... he listens... he'll do whatever I ask.... I'll make sure he does the training.... and, Laurie ...

'He'll take care of the rest.'

74

I'll never forget how the members of the Australian team sat stunned as Kieren struggled to make the final of the 1500 in Atlanta. He was now in lane eight ... unbelievable ... just 0.23 seconds slower and he would have been first reserve, with no chance of defending his title, reduced to being a spectator wondering ...

What if? ... What if?

Straight after the heat, John Carew raced down from the stands. His heart was thumping. His palms were sweaty ... he could not believe it. Kieren's times in training had indicated to John that the Olympic champion was almost back to his best. John really believed Kieren could win. Tactically, they had planned to get an outside lane, away from the Englishman Smith and Kieren's old mate, Daniel Kowalski ...

But lane eight?

What a disaster!

What went wrong?

John, genuinely concerned, raced to the warm-up pool to find his young charge. He soon learned that Kieren, during the race, had suffered a bad stomach pain, with the cramping of the diaphragm making it difficult, almost impossible, to breathe. Roger Fitzgerald, Kieren's personal physio as well as the Australian team physio, was called and his expert hands found and then remedied the problem.

The experienced Carew pointed out the positives to his champion. He reinforced how well Kieren had been going in training. He expounded the benefits of lane eight; out there he could swim his own race without having any of his opponents sit on him. He reminded 'The King' that he had not even shaved down and that the gold medal was his for the taking.

What went through Kieren's mind in the next 24 hours remains a mystery, but his remarkable gold medal-winning swim had tears flowing all around Australia. Afterwards, Robert Raftery sent me a poem that sums up the performance beautifully ...

THE KEEPERS OF THE FLAME

'Look at the margin now ...
I don't think they'll get him from here!'
And down in the seats in the stadium,
The Australians are starting to cheer.

It's Kieren, lane eight and he's flying,
He's 10 to 12 metres ahead.
And the way that they're cheering for Kieren,
It's like he's come back from the dead.

They'd written him off for the finals,
The chapter had closed in the book.
And the mood in the swim team 'Australia',
Was starting to take on 'that look'.

Then Susie O'Neill in a clincher,
Struck gold in the pool — butterfly.
As Petria circled the silver,
That caused Mullumbimby to cry.

Now down in lane eight burns a furnace
A champion's mind linked to heart.
With tactics refined to the second,
He's maintained the lead from the start.

With a superfish fleet there behind him
He's locked out the demons that spill.
Kieren wants gold for Australia,
And Perkins is in for the kill.

Back in Brisbane the band is still playing,
It's 200 metres to go.
And the fears that we held for the finish,
Have gone with the tide's outer flow.

There's majesty there in his stroke rate,
The torpedo unsheathed is on course.

He's lifting sky high in the stirrups,
And there's a power of war in his horse.

Now the big turbo diesel's just fired,
As a fin set the waters to sing.
The Aussies are hand-smelting silver,
With Kowalski abreast on the wing.

Coach Carew's eyes are now glistening,
Our flags are exploding poolside.
Kieren's now sprinting to glory,
With a raven-haired girl by his side.

It was one of the great 1500s,
The most gruelling swim race of them all.
For the pain wracks the body from 500 out,
And the pain can collide with the wall.

But for now the euphoria's explosive,
Cheers ... scalding tears for a son.
A swimmer, a sportsman, now the master,
World champion ... number one.

Had we just seen a glimpse of the Snowys,
And watched a lone mountain man ride?
Seen the glistening iron mask of a rebel,
Smouldering where Ned Kelly died?

Had we redefined 'Dawnie' and 'Dougie',
In that lesson lane eight had to teach?
Had our kids seen a vision in clear-cut precision,
Felt a courage unborn yet ... in reach?

Now his medal is housed by a mantle of teak,
Baptised by Muhammad of Bill Clinton speak,
And deep in its heart, though it's still just a game,
By the five rings Olympic, burns a bright torch aflame.

The harder the conflict, the more glorious the triumph. What we obtain too cheap we esteem too lightly: it is dearness only that gives everything its value. I love the man that can smile in trouble, that can gather strength from distress and grow brave by reflection. 'Tis the business of little minds to shrink; but he whose heart is firm, and whose conscience approves his conduct will pursue his principles unto death.

Thomas Paine

5 — Atlanta Opening Ceremony
Goin' for gold

The Atlanta Olympic Games Opening Ceremony is almost indescribable. If watching it on TV evokes emotion in the viewer, then being part of the march generates goosebumps for the participant. The thrill that comes from simply putting on your precious Olympic uniform for your first public team parade also defies description, but certainly stirs the soul. The excitement at the initial gathering of the Australian team in our headquarters quadrangle prior to bus departure time for the Opening Ceremony is something that has to be savoured to be appreciated.

The incessant movement of athletes and officials from all nations, some in traditional dress, in the Olympic Village resembles a herd of African wildebeest on their annual migration. Multicoloured buses, mouths agape, used to transport all marchers from the village to the Opening Ceremony, swallow country after country, and then spew them out at a special temporary holding area — the baseball stadium, which was the home of the Atlanta Braves and is situated adjacent to the new Olympic Stadium. This giant 'Braves' stadium will be demolished after the Games. Here, the athletes file by canteens and, ant-like, take a packed meal as they pass. Once inside they assemble, alphabetically by country, and sit patiently. Athletes and officials can watch the Opening Ceremony on giant video screens placed at either end of the holding stadium. Athletes mingle and smile. Others sit and soak up the atmosphere. One area of the stand starts a Mexican wave with little result.

They are waiting to march!

Shelley Oates, K4 paddler, is particularly keen to mingle, so I load her up with a handful of sponsor's pins to swap for me. These pins, unfortunately for her, have the sponsor's name 'Boral' above the Aussie flag and Olympic rings. Traditionally, athletes don't want to swap sponsor pins for country pins so this calls for Aussie ingenuity. A little white lie — 'Boral' becomes the Aboriginal word for 'gidday', meaning 'hello'. These are very special pins and trade like hot cakes as athletes from all nations look for a bargain. Shelley unloads the lot and returns for more. As she mingles with the foreign athletes, swapping the pins, Aussie athletes, in on the scam, walk past, waving to her and calling out 'Boral'. The catchcry for the day in the Braves' stadium is, 'Boral, mate!'

Finally, Australia is called to assemble. Your body tingles, the hair on the back of your neck stands on end, your heart bursts with pride and before you know it, 400 proud Australians march, skip, then run down the 50-metre incline ramp that leads into the Olympic Stadium and onto the track ... a stampede of pride. The 'old stagers', the two,

All

Australian flag bearer Andrew Hoy leads the Aussies into the Atlanta Opening Ceremony.

three and even four-time Olympians, jostle for inside positions closest to the crowd and the TV cameras. All the while you are conscious of the fact that you are from the smallest continent in the world, representing the 18 million Aussies back home, many of whom you know are now sitting transfixed, glued to their TV sets.

On entering the Stadium the combined 'lion's' roar of approval from the spectators explodes in your ears and your eyes are darting from side to side, devouring, feasting, drinking, soaking up the atmosphere, trying to ink it into your subconscious so that this magic moment, this one moment in time, remains ever part of your psyche.

You wonder how proud Andrew Hoy, the veteran of four Olympics and reigning Olympic Three Day Event team champion, must feel marching at the front of our team, carrying the Australian flag. Fleetingly, you sympathise for the big grey, Darien Powers, his competitive companion. The healthy-coated sleek big horse, like all champions, loves the atmosphere of huge parades. On that balmy Atlanta night, Andrew, back straight, flag aloft, astride the prancing horse at the front of our mighty team (the fourth largest at these Olympics) would have provided a memorable equine spectacle to rival even the parade of hopefuls down the straight at Flemington on Melbourne Cup day.

Perhaps in Sydney?

Once inside the Stadium you're fascinated by the modern computerised camera technology. The mini remote-controlled video camera strung high above the arena on four almost invisible wires, high flying like a miniature robotic trapeze artist, whizzes from one end of the arena to the other, back, forward, side to side, focusing on athletes' faces or fans in the stands, capturing the glamour, the grandeur, the excitement, the unity, the moment ... that one moment in time you want to last forever. (But you can't see the amazing camera on rails that will race the fastest men and women in the world down the 100 metres sprint, capturing every straining muscle as they lunge for the tape and Olympic immortality.)

The march continues. You see some old friends in the stands. They've made the journey, Brisbane to Atlanta, front-row seats, standing, cheering, arms pistoning up and down, going crazy ... enjoying being part of 'the moment'. They are waving an Aussie flag from side to side, up and down. You've never seen an Aussie flag move so fast for so long. Their faces explode into a huge grin as they recognise you and the pace of their jumping and waving doubles as they register their delight. You're intoxicated by the moment. You can't help wonder if they paid face value for their Opening Ceremony tickets or bought them off some street scalper for two, three, four or, in some cases, five thousand US dollars.

Finally, the triumphant 'Caesar-like' march is over and you're positioned in the middle of the stadium, waiting, watching other nations in their national dress parade, knowing, soon they will be combatants, competing for Olympic gold and glory. But only a few will ever scale the dizzy heights to victory and you wonder who they will be. Which Australians will be victorious? Who will be Australia's first Olympic gold medallist in Atlanta? Will it be a swimmer, or will that honour go to someone else? Someone who has spent many long, lonely hours honing their skills, persisting in the tough times, knowing in his or her heart that often the only thing standing between athlete and achievement is the faith to hang on and keep going when all seems lost.

For one tiny instant your mind flashes back to the previous night. The incredible singalong on the grassy mounds in the quadrangle at Georgia Tech University (the centrepiece of the team accommodation in Atlanta). Most Aussie Olympians living in the Village gathered there for a final show of camaraderie, to wish each other good fortune for the days to come. You can see the sea of Aussie faces representing all sports — tall basketballers, height magnified as they stand then sit beside tiny gymnasts, boxers chatting to shooters, tennis players sharing song books with swimmers, all before you there on a hot Atlanta night. Sportsmen and women bound together forever as part of the Australian Olympic family.

You remember the diminutive, smiling Nadine Neumann, standing alone, eyes closed, singing the hauntingly beautiful ballad 'Give Me

I hate a good party! This photograph was taken at the Georgia Tech University in Atlanta, as I led a singalong the night before the opening ceremony.

One Moment in Time'. Her team-mates are spellbound in the muggy night air.

Four years earlier, this same girl had dived into a swimming pool, hit her head and broken her neck. However, by some miracle of fate her spinal cord was not severed. She spent months in traction. With nothing to do she watched the Olympic Games on TV. A dream was born that took her on an incredible journey, from neck brace to Atlanta. Incredibly, to qualify for Atlanta in her event, she had to master two of the world's premier swimmers — Australia's own breaststroke world record holders Rebecca Brown and Sam Riley. The task seemed impossible, but belief, desire, attitude, courage and persistence are powerful tools, particularly when shared by people such as Nadine and her coach Greg McWhirter.

These qualities can overcome fear, failure, procrastination and indecision.

Now, here you stand in the middle of the Olympic arena, reflecting on your journey and you wonder how it all came to this ... how a young kid who used to watch Australian swimming legends train

> *Some succeed because they are destined to, but most succeed because they are determined to. Desire is the key to motivation, but it is determination and commitment to an unrelenting pursuit of your goal — a commitment to excellence — that will enable you to attain the success you seek.*
>
> Mario Andretti, racing driver

around his Dad's pool in Townsville now stands proudly among them. The ancient Greek poet Pindar's words ring in your ears.

Just as the sun shines brighter than any other star,
So shine the Olympics brightest of them all.

Then an unbelievable, almost primeval, sound interrupts your thought process. A roar, originating deep inside 85,000 human breasts, slowly rises ... becomes a throbbing crescendo. The home team, the USA, a sea of red and black waving miniature US flags, enters the stadium.

Their flag bearer, double Olympic gold medallist, the giant four-time Olympic wrestler Bruce Baumgartner, marches in front holding the American flag aloft at arm's length. The Sullivan Award winner strides proudly forward, eyes glued straight ahead until he reaches the Presidential party. Only then does he snap his eyes right to salute the silver-haired smiling President of the United States, Bill Clinton. The rest of the US team march casually behind, soaking up the moment as they wave to their adoring fans.

Michael Johnson marches upright, confident, immaculate. The roar continues as the US pride and joy circle all teams like a pride of lions waiting their opportunity to attack. Then the noise grows ... louder, louder, louder ... becomes deafening, threatening to burst your eardrums as the 'Dream Team' enters at the rear. They'd been flown in by helicopter for security ... or indulgence.

You silently thank Robert Raftery for his poem, 'We're Goin' For Gold', which he wrote and sent to you especially for these Atlanta Olympics. In the middle of the Olympic Stadium, as the US team

What an amazing, wonderful sight ... the athletes of the world in Atlanta.

circles, you recite it again for the Australian athletes in the immediate vicinity. It had been well received last night at the team get-together. Tonight, in this atmosphere, 'We're Goin' For Gold' takes on a new meaning.

When all teams are in place, Billy Payne of the Atlanta Organising Committee takes the centre stage and speaks. You are back to reality.

'Rejoice and resolve that these Olympic Games can reflect the hope for a brighter future, a better world. The magical unifying effect of these Games must carry into the next century and create a world unified in peace if we dream all things are possible.'

Next Samaranch, the controversial little grey-haired Spanish President of the Olympic movement, moves forward easily and confidently, and, with a twinkle in his eye, says simply:

I declare open the games of Atlanta celebrating the 26th Olympiad of the modern era.

WE'RE GOIN' FOR GOLD!
by Robert Raftery

It's time ... to turn good into greatness.
It's the biggie, old mates, and we're in it!
It's happened! You're here and you're champions.
There's gold in the wings. You can win it.

You're sittin' out there and you're suckin' in air.
Your heart's in your mouth. I can tell it.
Mates, I'm talkin' to you. It's Laurie! True blue!
There's gold in the air. Can't you smell it?

You've done the hard yards, you're the cream of the crop!
You're a fighter! You're focused, you'll pump till you drop!
Tomorrow you'll churn and the water will boil,
As you rip at the air and you tear at the soil!

Now go out and blitz 'em but be in no doubt
for Australia to win, 'Let the animal out!'
They'll taunt you! They'll fight you! They'll spit in your space!
And I'll watch as our flag paints a smile on your face.

As the cameras engage you and capture that tear,
And your mates all around you erupt in a cheer.
Stand proud, mate, and wear it by the rings and the flames
And cherish your moment of gold at the Games!

But you're thinkin' of home and your thoughts start to roam,
Can't really believe that you're here!
You're on hallowed ground and that magical sound
And the world trembles ... Echoes that cheer!

The announcer takes over, accompanied by a trumpet fanfare ...
Ladies and gentlemen, the Olympic flag will now enter the stadium.
Eight former athletes walk the flag around the track with grace and
dignity. You recognise super-athlete Edwin Moses, the world's greatest-
ever 400 metres hurdler, moving with the spring and ease of a great
black panther. You also recognise Mary T. Meagher, super swimmer,

As that rectangled rag of our great Aussie flag
Rockets above and ... you're there!
You're the pride of the fleet and the world's at your feet
And our anthem's shot blastin' the air.

'Australians all let us rejoice for we are young and free
With golden soil and wealth for toil our home is girt by sea
Our land abounds in nature's gifts of beauty rich and rare
In history's page at every stage advance Australia fair.'

Huh! You reckon we hated you down that long track
And ... at times ... I admit we were on your back!
But mate, I can tell you right here and right now ...
We're as proud as a parent can be ... take a bow.

I don't want to tell you I love you ...
But I'll tell you right now I won't fail yer!
Nor will the crew of that rugged great ship
Parked out the front called 'Australia!'

So go my golden beauties! Don't put your gold on hold!
Now is the moment! This is your time!
And I love you as much as I would you were mine!

Get out there! Get at 'em and rip 'em apart!
With the blood of your country ablaze in your heart!
The medals are yours, mate, to have and to hold ...
So STUFF THE SILVER ...

WE'RE GOIN' FOR GOLD!!!!'

---

who still holds the 100 and 200 metres butterfly world records. They are the oldest swimming world records in the book ... set in 1981! These two US living legends lead the way.

One hundred doves of peace, flying with 100 innocent children, circle the arena, symbolically carrying one for each year of the modern era. Then the voice of Martin Luther King, whose life was cut tragically short by an assassin's bullet, booms through the stadium via giant video screens.

I have a dream that one day the sons of former slaves and the sons of slave owners will be able to sit down together at the table of brotherhood. I have a dream that one day this nation will rise up, live out the true meaning of its creed: we hold these truths to be self-evident, that all men are created equal.

The announcer calls:

On the eve of the Centennial Olympic Games we look back to honour some of the Olympic heroes who represent the achievements of all athletes of the past 100 years.

A hush falls over the huge gathering. Living Olympic legends are about to be paraded on a central stage. One by one, they're introduced. The Aussie contingent voice their approval as our own Dawn Fraser, Olympic gold medallist in Melbourne, Rome and Tokyo in the 100 metres freestyle, is presented first. You feel proud to be an Aussie. And you wonder how this woman who was never beaten internationally in her pet event, who broke 39 world records, who was the first woman to break the minute, who held the world record for eight years after her premature retirement, must be feeling.

The announcer calls the other living legends on stage, one after the other ...

- Bob Beamon, USA: the man who leapt into immortality in Mexico City, 1968.
- Mark Spitz, USA: superfish, seven gold, seven world records, Munich, 1972.
- Nadia Comaneci, Romania: little Miss Perfect, Montreal, 1976.
- Teofilo Stevenson, Cuba: heavyweight boxing legend, three-time gold medallist, 1972, 1976 and Moscow 1980.
- Carl Lewis, USA; would be trying for his fourth consecutive gold Olympics, having started with four gold at Los Angeles, 1984.
- Greg Louganis, USA: diving great, double gold in 1984, double gold again in Seoul, 1988.
- Vitaly Scherbo, Russia: six gymnastics gold, at one Olympics, Barcelona, 1992.

The oldest living Olympic gold medallist, a sprightly 97-year-old Yugoslav gymnast, Leon Stukelj, is the last to be called forward. He wanders out, loses his way and is directed to the stage. He bounces up the stairs and once on stage jumps and clicks his heels, is applauded by the legends and wins the hearts of all spectators and athletes in the stadium.

You ponder: What will the US do to top Barcelona's flaming arrow to light the Olympic flame, which was first lit in Berlin in 1936 and is now kept at Mount Olympia in Greece? You look up to where the flame will burn. It looks so much like a McDonald's chip packet — large fries — the resemblance is uncanny. Then you're jolted back to reality ...

Al Oerter, four-time Olympic gold medallist in the discus, appears with the torch. The flame has arrived! He passes the torch to local hero, boxer Evander Holyfield, who runs by, two ears intact, to pass the torch to the first-ever Greek female gold medallist, 100 metres hurdler Paraskevi Voula Patoulidou — here is recognition of Greece's place in the Olympic century. But Holyfield doesn't let go; together they run on, clutching the precious flame, savouring the moment. Janet Evans, Olympic swimmer, takes over and runs proudly to the rostrum, hair flowing freely behind. Will she light the flame that will burn high above the arena for the next 16 days?

Suddenly, as Janet Evans stands, torch aloft, a dark, unrecognisable, almost eerie figure appears from the shadows on the rostrum and shuffles ever so slowly towards her ... a hush falls over the entire stadium. Someone whispers 'It's Ali!' Muhammad Ali, Olympic boxing gold medallist and former heavyweight champion of the world ...

Ali grasps the torch ... now riddled with Parkinson's disease he stands ... shakes uncontrollably for some time ... before moving forward, almost stumbling with the torch, to light the flame.

Tears flow freely down the cheeks of thousands of athletes and spectators as they are touched by Olympic magic ... the flame falters then seemingly travels magically through the night sky to the keeper of the flame ...

*It's Ali!! The hush that grew as we realised who would be lighting the
Olympic flame is something I will never forget.*

While we were entranced by the spectacle of Muhammad Ali and the Opening Ceremony at the main Olympic Stadium, an hour and a half drive in good traffic from team headquarters in Atlanta another group of Aussies, the rowers and kayakers, were holding their own opening ceremony. They were gathered in our own Aussie sub-village at Dahlonega, a former United States gold mining town which is close to the rowing venue at Lake Lanier. Would the choice of this gold mining town be a good omen for this tough, focused Australian rowing group? Time would tell.

A week before the Opening Ceremony, the Australian rowers had held a meeting. They looked at the implications of attending the Opening Ceremony, the lateness of the finish, the time to clear the venue, and the time they would be in bed as a result. They decided that although they would love to attend, in the best interests of team performance they would not participate — for total team harmony it would be all in or none in.

In the pursuit of excellence, hard decisions and sacrifices have to be made if you want the best possible results. The Australian rowers were committed to excellence and therefore unanimously voted to bypass the Opening Ceremony ... a tough decision. To the ordinary person at home it seems almost inconceivable that athletes who had suffered for so long to make an Olympic team, who had sacrificed so much, who had dreamed for years of marching proudly into the Olympic stadium with their Aussie team-mates, would now, on the eve of fruition, pass up the opportunity to march ... the very celebration of all their achievements and sacrifices. However, for committed athletes striving for lifelong dreams and goals, such decisions are not the imposition or hardship that many would imagine them to be, but merely a reality, a milepost on an athlete's journey to excellence. Obstacles encountered along the way test the resolve but, in the final analysis, these are merely impediments to conquer, so that when they sup at the banquet of success the victory wine tastes so much sweeter.

These winners can appreciate disappointments and have tremendous empathy for people such as Abraham Lincoln, whose persistence shines in his stormy career ...

- 1832 lost his job.
- 1832 defeated for legislature.
- 1833 failed in business.
- 1834 elected to legislature.
- 1835 his girlfriend died.
- 1836 had a nervous breakdown.
- 1838 defeated for speaker.
- 1843 defeated for Congress.
- 1846 elected to Congress.
- 1848 lost nomination for Congress.
- 1849 rejected for Land Officer.
- 1854 defeated for Senate.
- 1856 lost nomination for Vice President.
- 1858 defeated for Senate again.
- 1860 elected President of the United States.

After the decision had been made not to march in the Opening Ceremony, the coaches held their own meeting. They felt that to let this special occasion pass without official recognition and celebration could have a negative effect on the team. But if they could somehow use the occasion intelligently, it would add a new dimension to the strong team morale that had developed slowly and then intensified as they toured together through Europe. This spirit had been fortified even more when they assembled with the entire Australian Olympic team for final team uniform fittings and collection in Athens, Georgia.

The Athens assembly culminated with the final team dinner, which, although lacking the dynamic feel of the dinner held in Frankfurt, before the Barcelona Games four years earlier, had its moments. A 40-strong gospel group, resplendent in long white robes, gave a rendition of *Waltzing Matilda* that lacked any real Australian passion. However, the place came alive with a vengeance when a local rock band started belting out the beat and the rowers to a man commandeered the dance floor. Noel Donaldson, coach of the Oarsome Foursome, capped off a memorable evening by stage-diving to the driving rock music. Noel's performance was the undisputed evening highlight — I only wish I'd thought of it. The rowing morale was strong; in fact, they were one of the tightest-knit groups in Atlanta.

> **For the resolute and determined
> there is time and opportunity.**

It was, therefore, important that the coaches organise something memorable so as not to leave the team flat or deflated because they could not march. After much argument and brainstorming, the coaches decided they would have their own opening ceremony. The athletes were gathered and informed that headquarters had decreed they were going to have their own celebration. It would be held in the university quadrangle, before moving onto the oval. They would all be required to dress in their full Olympic march-out uniform for the occasion. Initially this met with minor resistance from the troops, but soon all were resigned to the fact and joined in the fun.

While our rowers busied themselves dressing up in the precious team uniform, coaching staff (who, days earlier, had crossed two state borders to purchase fireworks not for sale in the state of Georgia) worked on the university oval, preparing their own Olympic pyrotechnics display. Soon all was ready. The march began.

Rowing head coach Reinhold Batschi now became the Chef de Mission and led the way. The rowing team purred with delight as he good-naturedly mimicked our own Chef and former Olympic cox John Coates' peculiar walk — nothing is sacred from the Australian sense of humour.

What followed was a hilarious fashion parade, the fireworks display, an early night and Olympic memories that are etched into their subconscious —shared and treasured by this special group of people who had decided that nothing was going to prevent them from making Australia the No. 1 rowing country in the world. In their four-year quest they had competed against fellow Australians who held the same goals, striven for and maintained the highest standards of training and attitudes necessary for success ... and won the right to compete. Now they realised how futile their efforts would all be if they put the whip down in the straight.

Reinhold Batschi had identified 18 months earlier, in a pre-planning

Great Britain's Steven Redgrave (left) with his Coxless Pairs partner, Matthew Pinsett, after winning gold in Atlanta. Redgrave had now won gold at four straight Olympics, having changed his preparation in '96 after seeing how the Aussie rowers were going about things.

Allsport

trip to Atlanta with other team officials, a need to be close to the rowing venue if we were to maximise the performance of our rowing team. This would avoid the daily grind of the long, hot, uncomfortable, energy-sapping bus ride that all rowers who stayed in the village were required to make to the competition venue, usually in hot uncomfortable buses on hard plastic seats. How right he was! For those who stayed in Atlanta central, the journey often took more than an hour and a half as inexperienced drivers became lost or stuck in the Atlanta snarl.

The Australian Olympic Committee agreed and planned accordingly, organising accommodation at the nearby university. A dietitian was

> *Excellence is never an accident; it is well
> thought, well planned and well executed.*

engaged to check on the university menu, to see if it contained the necessary nutrients for a group of athletes involved in hard training and racing. This proved to be a masterpiece in strategic planning; Australia was the only rowing team to organise accommodation outside of the village. The AOC were happy to bear the extra cost of such accommodation until the rowing competition was over. Only when they had competed and the job of trying to be the best rowing nation in the world had ended would our rowers join the rest of the Australian team in the Village.

When British rowing legend Steve Redgrave saw the living and travelling arrangements organised by ACOG (Atlanta Organising Committee), he took a leaf out of the Australians' book and immediately moved out of the Village and closer to the rowing venue. He was not prepared to jeopardise his quest for a fourth consecutive Olympic gold.

Not only did our Olympic committee organise accommodation, but Robert Thornton, the administration director (who had been to Atlanta for pre-planning half a dozen times in the 12 months preceding the Olympics), rented 10 air-conditioned comfortable mini-vans so that our rowers would be totally independent. In addition he canvassed all homes along the lake's edge for a place to park these vans. A house within 100 metres of the entrance was found and rented. At times these places became a home away from home and weary rowers waiting to go back to the university would flop on lounges and enjoy a relaxing half hour watching television or having a cuppa.

This planning, the meticulous attention to detail in its execution, along with the total commitment by all members of the close-knit Australian rowing team all contributed to making them our best-performed Olympic rowing team ever, with two gold, one silver, and three bronze medals. Through total teamwork and a total commitment to excellence we became the No. 1 rowing nation in the world.

Crew rowing is the ultimate team sport. All the team members are in the same boat, which will perform only as well as their perfectly co-ordinated effort makes it. The Olympic final is won by the best crew, regardless of the individual excellence of any one athlete in the field of boats. The athletes in the crew must compete fiercely against one another to make it, and then they have to pull together in a race.

Canadian women's rowing team

6 — Part of a Whole Team
Working together is success

Since our rowing team, by living in Dahlonega, was so far removed from the bulk of the Australian team for the first week of competition, John Coates, the Chef de Mission, felt it was important that they believed that they were not being neglected or deprived of anything because of this isolation. He wanted to emphasise that this was an advantage not a disadvantage. Although they were an hour and a half from us they were still an integral part of our team and had a significant role to play in total team performance. Mr Coates insisted that the athlete liaison officers do things to try to mould them into the larger Australian team fabric.

John Devitt, former Olympic champion and assistant Chef de Mission, was our team leader and he appointed swimming legend Michael Wenden and me to this task. We made sure that the rowers received daily copies of 'The Boxing Kangaroo', the official daily newsletter of the 1996 Australian Olympic team. This daily newsletter was researched and put together by Greg Campbell and Jim Webster, media liaison officers for the team. In addition, Michael made daily phone contact with the rowing manager to see if they needed anything. Any request was dealt with quickly.

On one occasion, Michael and I took a day trip to Lake Lanier, the rowing venue at Gainesville, Hall County, to meet and greet the rowers and watch them go through their training paces. We went by the ACOG transport system.

Oh joy! Now I understood why our rowers weren't staying with us.

On that trip, Michael flashed his video camera at everything that moved and I was given a great lesson in Olympic rowing history.

'Did you know rowing made its Olympic debut at the Stockholm

*An illustrious group of Australian Olympic champions in Barcelona, 1992
... (left to right) Sieben, Armstrong, Devitt, Elliott and Wenden.*

Games in 1912?' he told me, while shoving his damn camera right in my face.

'No!' I stammered.

'Who won Australia's first Olympic rowing gold and where?' he then asked, video camera still pointing straight at me. I was starting to feel a little uncomfortable. If my rowing ignorance was captured on camera he could totally embarrass me at some later date. And knowing Michael with his quiet little chuckle and quirky sense of humour ... one day he would.

'Turn that camera off!' I raised my voice. 'I don't want my ignorance captured on video.'

'You should read your handbook then, shouldn't you?' he teased, then answered ... 'Bobby Pearce, 1928, Amsterdam,' then gloated, 'and ... for your information ... he won the single sculls again four years later in Los Angeles.'

'Michael! Please turn that camera off,' I pleaded. Normally I love a camera, but Michael was making me squirm.

'... And in Amsterdam he stopped to let some ducks swim in front of his boat,' he continued.

'Michael, turn the camera off,' I pleaded once more. But Michael was having fun.

'Who was Australia's next rowing champ?'

'I don't know ... please, Michael.'

'Merv Wood, 1948 gold, 1952 silver.' He was enjoying my ignorance.

'Peter Antonie and Stephen Hawkins won the double sculls at Lake Banyoles in Spain,' I ventured, trying to sound knowledgeable.

'Yes. But when did we win our first medal in the men's eight ... and ... what colour was it?' he kept up the embarrassing barrage.

'The Oarsome Foursome won in Spain,' I continued, trying to change the subject to something I knew.

'Yes, but answer the question. When did we win our first medal in the men's eight ... and what colour was it?' he kept niggling.

'Michael you win, now turn that camera off.'

Two Aussie sporting heroes, Gillian Rolton and Michael Wenden, in Atlanta, not long after Gillian had ignored a badly-injured shoulder to help our three-day event team triumph for the second straight Olympics.

The word win was magic to his ears. He turned the camera off and, with his peculiar little wry smile and a twinkle in his eye, announced, 'Helsinki 1952 ... you'll have to smarten up on your Olympic history ... 'cos tomorrow I'll be asking questions on double trap shooting and 25-metre rapid-fire pistol ...

'Be ready.'

'Look at that!' I whispered. The bus had just turned a corner and the magnificent 20,000-seat grandstand stretching over Lake Lanier came into view. It was breathtaking ... of course, Michael turned his video back on.

As we crossed a bridge the Oarsome Foursome, silhouetted against the grandstand, rowed majestically by. The long, tedious, 88km bus ride had been worth it — just to see these four men skim across the glassy lake's surface. I watched spellbound as, led by stroke Michael McKay, they moved seemingly effortlessly across the lake, long blades dipping and disappearing in perfect unison before reappearing dripping water at the other end. These men had something special. They had developed teamwork to an art form. They moved in perfect symmetry ... they knew that their success depended on the support of each other and the biggest stumbling block to this success was ego. Noel Donaldson, the little redheaded stage diver responsible for moulding their egos into one tight team unit, worked on the Henry Ford motto:

Coming together is a beginning,
Keeping together is progress,
Working together is success.

The bus pulled up. Michael and I checked our bags through security.

'Meet you back here in an hour,' he said.

'Okay!' I replied as I wandered down to the lake's edge to catch another glimpse of the Oarsome Foursome going through their paces. As I sat there watching and idly tossing small stones into the lake, I wondered if these four men, whom the selectors had shown so much faith in, could repeat their magnificent Barcelona performance. I knew how hard it was to refocus once you had achieved. They had been beaten at the Australian championships. Many experts had written them off

*The Oarsome
Foursome at the
'96 Olympics,
after successfully
defending their
coxless fours
title. Left to
right: Nick
Green, Drew
Ginn, James
Tomkins and
Mike McKay.*

Sport: The Library

as 'yesterday's heroes', but the Australian rowing selectors had shown
enormous faith and courage by selecting them for the men's coxless
four.

Drew Ginn was brought into the four to replace Andrew Cooper,
who felt it would not be fair to the team if he were to remain in the
four as the 'fire in his belly was not as strong'. He didn't want to be
the weak link in the chain, knowing that any team is only as strong as
its weakest link. He would watch and cheer for his former team-
mates instead.

When the Foursome had finished their workout and rowed to shore,

> *Do something. If it doesn't work do*
> *something else. No idea is too crazy.*
>
> Jim Hightower

I casually went down to pay my respects.

'Good workout fellows?' I questioned.

'We're on fire,' answered Mike and they all nodded accordingly. You just knew they were close to greatness ... they just had 'the look'.

'Can I help you get the boat out?' I asked.

'We'll be right,' answered Nick Green.

'Yeah, we've done this a thousand times,' added James Tomkins, the unlikely-looking banker who, during his career, like team-mate Mike McKay, had won the King's Cup 10 times.

'James, I wonder if you guys can help me,' I questioned. 'I really want to get even with Michael. He's been giving me a hard time with his rowing knowledge ... making me feel inadequate.'

'Well, that's not like you, Laurie,' grinned James.

'No ... so I figure if I can get some prize information on some rowers here in Atlanta I can turn the tables ... but I need your help.'

'Sure,' he replied. 'What about asking him which three rowers have three Olympic titles?'

'He'll never get that,' said Nick. 'I don't even know it myself.'

'What about asking who is Steven Redgrave's rowing partner at these Olympics?' chimed in Drew Ginn, who until now had been silent.

'Thanks,' I said. 'This is just the sort of information I need. I'll make Wenden squirm yet. He'll be sorry he tangled with Laurie Joseph.'

Armed with this knowledge I made my way up the hill towards the large hospitality tent, perched high on the lake's edge, for a cool drink. In this heat, you really need to keep your fluids up, particularly athletes, if they are to avoid dehydration.

Aussie comedian Andrew Denton (centre) and entertainer Steve Vizard (far right) entertained us at a team barbecue on Day 12 in Atlanta. And among the people they met afterwards were two stars of the Australian rowing team, coxless pairs champions Kate Slatter (to my immediate left) and Megan Still, and me!

'See you tonight at the team dinner,' called Nick as I waved goodbye.

Michael was in the distance, talking to some other rowers, still waving the video camera around. I would bide my time. I would get him. I would make him pay.

Two hours later we were at the rowers' village. The spirits were high. Section manager Andrew Guerin asked Michael and me to say a few words to the team. I was a little scared. This would be a tough audience. They were already totally focused; the last thing they wanted was some fools from outside coming in trying to motivate them. I ate dinner in silence, wondering what would be the best approach. Michael spoke first. They were respectful but fidgety ... my heart raced a little faster. I made a last-minute decision — my time at the podium would be real brief and I would try to involve them somehow. A friend, Robert Raftery in Brisbane, had faxed me some poems, one done especially for the rowers, I would perform one. I walked to the microphone, took it off the stand and started the poem.

BUCKET OF GOLD

You've come this far my champions,
From the land where it seldom rains,
With your kitbags full of kangaroos,
And a throbbing in your veins.

You knew when you came you were in for a fight
'Cos there's gold in Olympic Atlanta tonight.
The hockey's amazing ... the beach volleyball just might!
And down at the pool it's a magical sight.
All this pomp all this power ... we're as high as a kite
'Cos there's gold in Olympic Atlanta tonight!

Our kids, mate, I'll tell yer, are 10 feet tall
They're 'goin' for gold' and they're in for a haul.
The enemy's here with their gold diggin' picks
But I know you kids, you're smart little tricks.

The spies have flown over and they well-near carked it!
They spotted our dragline out front where they parked it!
Now the whole world's out checking our paraphernalia
'Cos there's a fear that the dark horse might just be Australia.

Our great Aussie nation has built her foundation
On mateship, merinos, and gold,
And that ship with the treasure ... we've got her full measure,
And the key to the lock's in the hold.

Aussie mateship's strong and be sure it won't fail yer
So fill up your swag with gold for Australia
Bright shiny nuggets and once that you've filled her
Let's all link arms and waltz with Matilda.

Here, I started singing *Waltzing Matilda*. Not in my wildest dreams could I have imagined the response. Everyone rose to their feet and started singing *Waltzing Matilda*. I called one of the Stewart twins, who were members of our rowing eight, to the microphone to sing solo the verse:

Down came a squatter mounted on his thoroughbred
Down came the troopers one two three.

He messed it up completely! I couldn't believe it. I thought Paul Keating was the only one who didn't know the words to this classic Aussie song. The team went berserk with whistles and laughter. I snatched the mike back, gave him a good-natured biff over the ear for his ignorance. The team went crazy again. His brother slapped his side in glee, taking delight in his brother's embarrassment. The team responded with gusto. It was not the greatest rendition of Banjo's song I've heard but it was certainly the most raucous. I waved and sat down, glowing, smug in the fact our visit had been highly successful.

Now I only had to get Michael back to be totally fulfilled.

We left the dining hall. Michael left his precious video camera behind. I picked it up. Now was my big chance ... I had waited all day for this moment. I trained the camera on the back of his head and put it on auto focus.

'Michael,' I said innocently.

'Yes, Laurie.' He turned, I held the camera still.

'Who is Steven Redgrave's coxless pairs partner, and, if he secures the gold, which two great European single sculls winners' records will he surpass?' I asked.

'That's easy! His partner is Matthew Pinsent!'

'As for the Europeans,' he continued, 'I think you'll find that Yvacheslav Ivanov of the Soviet Union and Pertti Karpinnen of Finland have won three single sculls titles each.'

'Ahh! How ... eh ... how do you spell those names?' I asked meekly. The Oarsome Foursome had got me as well ... I would have to wait another day. The bus trip back to the Village for me was a long and tedious one.

Michael smiled all the way.

*Whether you think you can, or
whether you think you can't ...
you're right.*

Reggie Jackson

7 — Life's a Beach ... Volleyball
Kentucky reigns!

Stephen Anderson, coach of beach volleyball duo Natalie Cook and Kerri Pottharst, walked briskly into the athlete services office and caught my eye.

'Laurie, I heard you and Herb are available to help anyone who needs it here in Atlanta,' stated the 32-year-old African-American beach volleyball coach from Louisville, Kentucky. Anderson had been employed by the WA Institute of Sport to prepare the girls for their assault on Olympic gold in Atlanta.

'Sure, mate. How can we help?' I replied, warming to his easy manner and dazzling smile.

'Can we get together?' he asked.

'Sure, glad to. How can we help?' I repeated.

'I want you to speak to the girls. I've done all I can but they need to believe in themselves more,' he said.

'Well belief really comes from being prepared for competition and, seriously, mate ... only you know if the preparation has been satisfactory.'

'They've prepared great ... I've told them a hundred times they can win ... but coming from me ... I think that they've heard it so many times ... they just can't get their teeth into it. They just can't comprehend it.'

'Herb's the one to talk to about belief,' I replied easily.

'That would be good. Do you think he could spare some time to talk to the girls?'

'I know he would but ... maybe you and I and Herb should get together first to clarify exactly what you would like us to reinforce to the girls. This way we'll all be pulling in the one direction. I think that's very important.'

'Anything you say would be fine,' he replied graciously.

'No, no, no ... our role is to support the athlete and the coach. We are merely a tool for the coach to use to squeeze a little extra out of your charges. We don't want to usurp any of your authority. Our role is, and must be, supportive, and ... only if the coach requests it. It's very important that you retain total control over your athletes.'

Steve Anderson, the driven Kentucky-born coach of Australia's women's beach volleyball team, Kerri Pottharst and Natalie Cook.

'Okay! When?'

'I'll speak to Herb and get back to you. What room are you in?' I asked.

'I'm on the second floor above admin ... end room ... closest to McDonald's ... leave a message under the door ... I'm off to Atlanta Beach with the girls for training now,' he answered easily.

'Atlanta Beach? I didn't know we were anywhere near a beach here in Atlanta.'

'We're not! They've just named the volleyball competition arena Atlanta Beach. It's about 32 kilometres away in Clayton County.'

'Why don't you go with him Laurie?' butted in John Devitt. 'We're okay here at the moment and it'll be a good opportunity for you to meet Kerri and Natalie.'

I didn't need any arm-twisting, I was happy to get out of the office. I set off for the buses with my new-found friend.

'How do we get to the venue?' I asked as I increased my pace to keep up with Stephen. However he'd seen the girls waiting at the bus stop and hurried towards them.

'Come and meet the girls,' he said, ignoring my question. 'Hey girls, this is Laurie, he's coming to watch us train.'

'Hi girls,' I waved.

'We know Laurie, everybody knows Laurie,' they answered, making me feel very comfortable.

'So ... girls, how long to the venue?' I asked again, since Steve had left my question unanswered.

'It's a way by bus. Nice, though,' said Kerri.

'It's called Clayton County International Park ... great trees ... real woodland environment ... heaps of outdoor beach volleyball courts, three man-made lakes,' Natalie told me. 'There are two main stadiums there. Center Court seats 8000 spectators while Court Two seats 3000 with total seating capacity for 11,000 ... it's just great, wonderful to be part of it all.'

> *If you think you can then it is possible
> but if you think you can't you are climbing
> the mountain of failure and defeat.*

'It's even better if you get a medal,' I added. I felt I just couldn't let the opportunity go by without adding my little two cents' worth.

There were nine on the bus — two British players and their coach, a Cuban player sitting at the back of the bus, a Canadian medic and us. We sprawled out, one to a seat, like clothes on the floor of a teenager's room. In our little group, Stephen, the coach, and I sat closest to the front of the bus and twisted around, one leg half-cocked over the seat and one arm running along the silver rail on top of the seat. This way we could see and talk to the girls.

They were both smiling and, as they chatted, it was obvious they were happy.

'We play those Pommie girls first,' said Natalie trying not to look at the girls but nodding her head towards them.

'I feel sorry for them,' I replied with a little laugh.

Natalie gave me a mischievous look, then grinned, 'You used to coach me, you know.'

I was stunned. I looked at her, I couldn't believe it.

'When?' I questioned.

'I came to one of your hell camps at Christmas for a couple of weeks,' she explained.

'You went to one of the Christmas camps on the beautiful Gold Coast?' I teased incredulously.

'Yeah, it cured me of swimming! At that camp I decided to play volleyball.'

'I'm sorry, I can't remember.' I felt a little embarrassed at not remembering.

'Oh, it's okay, I was only eight and you must coach hundreds of little grommets. You'd remember Mum, though.'

'Oh, who is your mum?' I enquired, thankful that she didn't pursue why I couldn't remember her.

'Beverly Chapman from Ayr.'

'You're kidding!'

'No.'

'Of course I know your mum — she used to swim with my wife.'

'That's right,' she answered.

'Phil McLeod used to coach her.'

'Yes, Mum still talks about Mr Mac.'

'She was a breaststroker?'

'Yes.'

'Small world,' I said, shaking my head. I could still see her mum healthy — tall, slim, attractive, full of fun. The type of young woman that stops young men from missing training.

'How come an American is coaching our girls anyway?' I turned to Steve, changing the subject.

'Ask them,' he answered, nodding towards the girls. The girls looked at each other and giggled.

'You tell him, Nat,' smiled Kerri.

'We auditioned him,' laughed Natalie.

'You what?' I questioned, not quite believing what I was hearing.

'Well, when Kerri asked me to partner her on the World Championship series circuit we needed a coach and, when the Western Australia Institute of Sport said they would fund one, we conducted our own auditions.'

'How did you do that?' I asked, fascinated.

'We placed an ad, and while we were on tour had coaches all over the world take us for a training session,' added Kerri.

A happy threesome ... Natalie (left) and Kerri in Atlanta with one of the Aussie team's athlete liaison officers.

'Yeah, Steve won hands down. He was by far the toughest coach ...' chipped in Natalie good-naturedly.

Steve blushed. The girls enjoyed his discomfort and I was enjoying the banter.

The bus passed by a large security fence. Inside, a wide, cobbled pedestrian road lined with flagpoles flying the national flag of all competing nations split two huge man-made lakes.

The lakes were alive with water birds, swans gliding majestically, ducks feeding, heads down bottoms up, oblivious to the passing traffic. The road ended at a large blue-tiled building with the mandatory giant American flag fluttering on top. This was the public entrance to the competition courts.

We continued to the athletes' entrance. The security gate swung open and two burly uniformed guards climbed aboard to check accreditation once more. The gravel entrance road wound through a lot of dogwood pines up to a demountable building almost hidden among the trees.

As we alighted from the bus there was another security check. All bags were passed through X-ray machines. Both Kerri and Natalie picked up their bags, walked to the drink station and filled their drink bottles, before choosing two pieces of fruit from a large basket that nestled invitingly in the far corner. I thought I'd get in on the act, too, and pocketed two bananas for later.

Outside the building a long wooden ramp zig-zagged through the sweet-smelling trees down to the eight beach volleyball courts. Once at the bottom, the girls sauntered over to the notice board and checked to see which court they'd been assigned for practice. I followed at a respectable distance, a keen observer.

I was impressed with their professional approach. When they arrived at the court the Brazilian No. 2 pairing were finishing their practice session. Our girls ignored them and went systematically about their own preparation. Natalie and Kerri separated. Both spread out colourful sarongs on the clear white sand and each went through their own stretching routine in readiness for the practice.

I wandered down to the end court to watch two of Australia's entrants, Anita Spring and Liane Fenwick. They were having a friendly practice with an Italian pairing. I caught their eye and gave them a wink to let them know I was supporting them. They smiled quickly, but then it was back to business. When they'd finished I had a brief conversation with them before heading back to check on Kerri and Nat.

Quickly, I struck up a conversation with one of the court supervisors.

'Enjoyin' the Games, mate?' I quizzed.

'Sure, guy,' drawled the sunburnt supervisor with a generous supply of zinc plastered all over his nose.

'The Brazilians look good,' I observed.

'They do ... but I have to say these Aussie girls are real intense. Every time they come here to practise they mean business. I watch all the teams but your girls are the most intense.'

'And the coach?' I inquired.

'He's tough. He really works them.'

'Do you think they'll get a medal?' I continued.

'Maybe ... maybe not,' he answered, but that was no comfort to me.

Steve bounced onto the court as soon as the Brazilians' practice time was up. He was stripped to the waist, the skin on his well-formed six-pack glistening as the sun danced on his sweaty torso. I pulled out my camera and played tourist as he put the girls through their paces. He gave them no respite as they boosted and spiked. He ran them to all corners of the court through the soft sand. The girls were exhausted. Their towels were soaked with sweat and they gulped down litres of water to quench their almost insatiable thirst. It was tough going and he showed them no mercy. I was impressed and words I used to imprint on the fertile minds of my young charges when I was coaching rang in my ears ...

Only the pain of a hard workout can save you the agony of defeat.

Their agony was finally over when Steve called a halt to the workout. I wanted a photo of the coach and his two athletes together, so I called them over to take the shot. But Kerri was hot and exhausted and started to hyperventilate. I thought it best to put a rain check on the photo as she needed to be helped from the court to an empty chair. Steve was visibly annoyed that she could not stand a few extra moments for the photo and, as she was being helped off, he spun on his heel and stormed off. Kerri slumped on the chair, utterly exhausted, breathing heavily with the towel draped around her shoulders. Her elbows rested heavily on her knees, her cheeks cocooned between her hands. She was totally spent; she had given her all to the practice.

I watched Steve grab his shirt and march angrily towards the bus with the sweat rolling down his back in great droplets. I chased him.

'Steve!' I called.

'Yes!' he grunted over his shoulder.

'Steve, what's the matter?' I quizzed.

'Oh, I'm so angry and disappointed with Kerri. She should be tougher. It's three days till the Opening Ceremony and she's too tired to stand for 30 seconds to get a photo.'

> *To win without risk is to*
> *triumph without honour.*

'Sometimes there are circumstances ...' I ventured.

'Look, Laurie,' he said as he wiped the sweat from his face with his shirt, 'I want these girls to win gold and for that to happen they must believe and they must have no weaknesses. I see this as a weakness.'

I could sense by the emotion in his voice that he, as a coach, was desperate for victory. This, of course, is the first ingredient for success because without hunger the coach won't go the extra mile and as a result the athlete will lack something in preparation. A hungry coach can transfer that burning desire to his athletes. However, from experience, I knew that if that hunger is not tempered with positive reinforcements to sustain the athletes it can kill their enthusiasm. I just had to speak.

'I agree, Steve! ... But, let's be honest ... those girls have just completed a gruelling workout in this unbelievable heat ... you should be happy.'

'I'm happy. But why show weakness right at the end?'

'Steve, look ... can I, as a coach myself, be brutally frank?'

'Sure.'

'You need to give those girls some positive reinforcement ... some praise for the good things they do. That was a fantastic workout, but not once did I hear you congratulate the girls. They worked their butt off for you there today.'

'Laurie, it's just three days to the Opening Ceremony ...'

'Right, so the coach's job is nearly done. Soon you'll be out of the equation. The girls will be on their own. They'll be out there in the middle battling for points.'

'That's why I need to keep polishing their skills.'

'I can't agree. Your job now is to make these girls independent and strengthen their belief in their own abilities. You can't play the game

for them. Let go ... build these girls up ... give them some praise ... make them feel good.'

'Maybe ... but I know how good these girls are and I want them to win.'

'So do we all ... but honestly ... you can't teach them new skills with three days to go. Concentrate on reinforcing the skills they already know. Talk to them about the little things that can improve their performance ... things like rest ... good food selection ... use all resources to give the girls positives, positives, positives. You yourself hit the nail on the head when you told us you want them to believe in themselves.'

'That's why I need you and Herb to talk to the girls.'

'We'll gladly do that, but realise you have the real power. These girls chose you as their coach. They believe in you!'

'You think so?'

'I know so. Remember they chose you as their coach over all others. Remind them of the great workouts they've done. Have them draw competitive strength from the preparation you have given them.'

'It makes sense. I guess I need a bit of help, too. Tell me honestly what you think.'

'You have to let go now. You can't have these girls in a state of psychological dependency. You now must provide stability in a strange environment. Make the girls feel good. Help them to relax. Let me ask you another question ... are they a good pairing?'

'Yes!' he answered emphatically.

'Well tell them!' I jumped in, then hit him with another question.

'Why are they a good pairing?'

'Well, Natalie is tall, she captained the Australian juniors indoor volleyball team in 1994. Her agility at the net is incredible. And, when you combine that with Kerri's backcourt experience and brilliance — she played on the Australian Indoor women's team for

While Kerri and Natalie were out on the court playing off for the bronze medal, back in the Olympic village a proud group of Aussies was cheering them home.

over 10 years, plus she played in Italy for a couple of years — it's a formidable combination.'

'Tell them!' I almost screamed. 'Give them independence. Independence is the key now ... a deadly dependence could rob them of victory ...'

There was an awkward silence before I went on.

'Mate, act cool, even if you want to tear your hair out, 'cos your frustrations won't help them now.'

'Thanks! I'm glad you came. It's just I know they can win ... and I get so frustrated when they make a mistake.'

'That's understandable, but everyone makes a mistake. Even Michael Jordan occasionally misses a three-pointer. Everyone I talk to has told me what a fantastic job you've done on the girls' fitness and skill level.'

'That's true, their fitness is great and their skills are as good as any team in the competition.'

'Forget about the mistakes, start talking about other things.'

'Like what?'

'Positives! The good training sessions ... their victories ... the way Natalie spikes, the way Kerri serves ... I don't know, you know better than me. Make them respectful of their opponents ... but not fearful. Have them understand they are world class. Maybe show them a video of the best victories. Give them responsibility and I know they will respond.'

'Thanks!'

'Show a bit of faith in the girls.'

'Faith?'

'Yes, faith! Faith in your athletes.'

'I do.'

'Faith that you've worked them hard.'

'I have.'

'Are you, as a coach, satisfied that you have given personally 100 per cent?'

'Yes.'

'Are you satisfied that you have imparted the technical skills needed for success in international competitions?'

'Of course!'

'Are they fit?'

'You know they are.'

'Well, just let go. One more question. Have these girls kept to a commitment of consistent high-quality preparation?'

'Yes! They have worked consistently and they have worked hard.'

'Then let go! You can't hold their hand on the volleyball court. Show faith in the girls. Give them responsibility. I'm sure they will respond.'

'I know they are capable but I don't know if they believe. What can I do to help? I don't want to be useless.'

'You help by simply being there and giving them the positive reinforcements that will give them the belief in their own abilities. Tell them they look good. Check to see that they are eating well. Check to see if they are getting enough rest or drinking enough fluids. You still can exert a tremendous influence on their final performance.'

'You're right, I know, but it's hard to let go.'

'You've just got coach's nerves. The work's done. Enjoy the Olympics and help your athletes relax.'

'I still want to get Herb to speak to the girls.'

'Sure, I'll arrange it. When?'

'Tomorrow before lunch. We get back from training at 11.30.'

'I'm sure that will be okay. I'll see Herb. Let's say 11.45 in the athletes' lounge.'

'Thanks,' he said and slowly walked up the hill towards the bus.

I waited in the shade of the trees. Soon the girls appeared, still utterly spent.

'Well done, girls!' I said.

'I don't think Steve is too happy,' commented Kerri.

'No. That's not right. I've just been talking to him, he's real happy,' I countered.

'Why doesn't he say so?'

'Well he believes you girls are capable of winning gold. I think that's why he's so intense. Forget about training, let's go home and relax.'

We all wandered to the bus, each engrossed in our own thoughts.

Later that day, I contacted my mate Robert Raftery, back in Australia. I consider Robert to be a modern-day Banjo Paterson, and asked him to write a poem especially for the volleyball girls. He faxed me back the following:

LIFE'S A BEACH VOLLEYBALL
(For Kerry, Nat, Laurie, and our new Kentuckian mate)

Mates, we know what it's like hitting beaches
And wading in sand to the shore
A great nation was christened as the sands, blood red, glistened
From the bullets and bombs of a war.

It was there that we found a raw courage,
As our tall battle standards were torn
A young bloke ... reached out for a donkey
And the spirit of Anzac was born.

And soon in a circled arena
Our modern day soldiers will stand
And the world will come down to their beaches
Feel the thunderous swirl of its sand.

The Kentuckian coach you have chosen
Has moulded your style into power
So Kerri and Nat imagine that
You're Aussies primed for this glorious hour.

Imbued with compliance and splendid defiance
Offspring of the Anzacs you stand
Strident and tall, 'Life's a Beach ... Volleyball'
As you spike for gold in the sand.

Herb's meeting with the girls the following day was inspirational, as he remembered and related his own preparation, his own fears as an athlete and the philosophy of his coach Percy Cerutty, of total commitment to preparation.

He reinforced for the girls how their great preparation with their hard taskmaster coach could only lead to victory. It was, as Percy would say, a 'remorseless march towards the inevitable'.

Herb suggested that the hardships they had endured under their coach would only serve to strengthen them in their quest for Olympic gold. He urged the girls to start projecting positive body language and self-talk by continually reinforcing the positives among themselves; comments such as:

I deserve the gold — I have worked hard
Ipso facto: it is inevitable.

He spoke of how Percy had him walk in a quiet forest or listen to music to gather mental strength. This became a powerful emotional reservoir when he raced.

I sat and listened. Herb had these young women hanging on every word. Percy would have been proud of him.

He spoke of the great Al Oerter, four-time Olympic gold medallist, and related how under extreme pressure he was always able to dig deep for that superhuman effort when most needed.

As soon as he'd finished, Steve, the girls and I went to lunch. No one spoke. All were saturated with positives, Steve and I convinced the girls would be fighting for gold.

Steve had asked me to organise a room for the girls to watch some of their best international matches on television, so immediately after lunch we headed for the University of Georgia's mini-theatre. The four of us were dwarfed in this room. It was fantastic; the only thing missing was the popcorn and ice-cream.

We scrutinised each match, replaying each time they won a great pressure point. An hour and a half later the girls left in no doubt they had the credentials to topple the Brazilian world champions. They believed ... without belief there is little or no chance of victory.

Steve and the girls bonded. A young coach had learned. The preparation was done. The belief was there ... now only the competition arena could give them the opportunity.

Over a week later, as Kieren Perkins prepared for his assault on Olympic gold, a group of Aussies gathered in the athletes' lounge to cheer each point as the girls fulfilled their promise with an Olympic bronze medal.

Well done, girls!

Party time! Australia has won the women's beach volleyball bronze medal!

When an archer misses the mark, he turns and looks for the fault within himself. Failure to hit the bullseye is never the fault of the target. To improve your aim, improve yourself.

Gilbert Arland

8 — Herb
The remorseless march toward the inevitable

I lay quietly on my back on top of the sheets in the small university room, arms folded, staring at the ceiling. I was thinking accommodation for the Atlanta Olympics could best be described as cramped, clean and comfortable. The room boasted two beds, two desks, two study lights, two wardrobes and very little floor space. It was typical crowded university campus accommodation.

It was after midnight. I never got to bed before midnight in Atlanta ... just too busy, organising things for athletes to make their job of achieving a personal best performance here easier. My mind was racing, going over the day's events of jobs well done and planning for tomorrow. I heard a scratching at the door, someone fumbling with a key.

'The door's open,' I called. The door slowly opened, a crack of light streamed in from the hallway and Herb tiptoed in after it.

I first met Herb Elliott at the Barcelona Olympics in 1992, when he was seconded to the Australian Olympic team in a trial run to see if the presence of some of our more successful former Olympians could be used as morale boosters for the new breed. The aim was to aid the team's performances, to give the athletes that little extra, the edge, that may be the difference between gold and silver, or even making the final or watching it from the stands. The move proved to be a masterstroke by the Australian Olympic Committee, an outstanding success. Herb, the great Dawn Fraser, whose reputation precedes her, and Seoul track and field gold medallist Debbie Flintoff-King joined forces to help create an environment that would assist athletes to perform at their very best. Each complemented the other, each was well respected as a great athlete and, more importantly, as a great person.

The great Herb Elliott in Atlanta, with his wife Anne and the bloke Herb shared a room with in the Olympic village.

'How's Anne?' I asked. Anne is Herb's beautiful wife and he'd been to visit her at The Days Inn Hotel in downtown Atlanta, opposite the Fox Theatre, where a big contingent of Australians was staying.

'She's fine, mate. I'm sorry to wake you.'

'No problems. You didn't wake me, I've only just got in myself.'

'I nearly stayed the night,' Herb declared. 'She gets a little lonely.'

'You should have,' I responded.

'But my roomie would have been a little worried on his own.'

'Don't worry about me,' I said. 'I'm a big boy, I'll be okay ... and I understand if your husbandly instincts get the better of you.'

I didn't see it coming in the dark but I felt the pillow hit my chest almost the second I'd finished speaking. He was quick.

'That'll be enough of you, young Laurie,' he said good-naturedly.

Herb got undressed in the dark, not wanting to disturb me any further.

He was always being considerate and unselfish like that. Great principles. It made me wonder how he could have been so aggressive, self-centred, ruthless and determined on the running track ... maybe he was not being considerate at all, maybe he just didn't want me to see those old-style 'Reg Grundies' he wore — I'd been ribbing him about them. I smiled as I thought about it.

'Don't you want me to see those fancy undies of yours,' I teased.

'I feel completely at home in these undies!' he retorted.

'Why don't you get rid of those undies and get into something more modern and daring?' I persisted.

'They're oldies but goodies,' he shot back.

'Yeah, but mate, the long sides ... the long sides.'

'Hey! You don't discard something because it's old, particularly if it's functional ... like Percy's training methods — some of these modern-day coaches could well afford to look at some of the things Percy did with us,' he answered.

'Herb?' I raised the inflection in my voice to question him further.

'Good night, Laurie,' he cut me off. 'See you in the morning.'

As I lay there in the dark I thought how strange that Herb should mention his great mentor and coach, Percy Cerutty, as we discussed long-sided old-fashioned underpants. Percy must have had a huge influence on his life. I lay there for five minutes, immersed in my thoughts, looking into the inky darkness and enjoying the silence of the night. Finally, I could contain myself no longer.

'You still awake, Herb?' I asked.

'Go to sleep!'

I thought how lucky I was to be actually rooming with an Olympic champion ... an Olympic Champion ... how good is that ... and a legend to boot ... the time he ran in Rome 1960 for the 1500 metres was sensational, 3:35.6, a world record.

What made Herb Elliott so superior?

What really gives a champion that edge, that indefinable 'it' that makes them stand out, totally successful, not only in the athletic arena as a competitor but also in life and in business?

Was it 'the man' himself? Was it the mentor? In this case, Percy Cerutty? Was it a combination of people and circumstances?

How big a part did Herb's madcap mentor coach play in his successes and the 17 sub four-minute miles in the days when four-minute miles were a bit of a rarity?

These questions plagued me.

'What was Percy like?' I quizzed.

'Go to sleep. It's 10 to one in the morning and we have a big day ahead of us tomorrow,' Herb said. I could hear him roll over.

'No ... really? What was Percy like?' I asked, now desperate to find out something about a man I had always admired as Australia's greatest track coach. 'Was he as mad as the press made out?'

'Percy was a genius. Now go to sleep!' he growled.

'When did you first meet him?'

'At my school, Aquinas, in Western Australia. Brother Murphy, the track coach, organised him to visit,' Herb replied politely.

'What were your first impressions? I've heard he was a bit off the wall.'

'Yeah!' You could hear the smile in Herb's voice as he remembered his old coach. 'I can still see him now ... a bronzed, lithe, grey-haired old man, looking as fit as a 30-year-old and stripped down to a pair of shorts. He pranced and skipped and waved his arms on our school oval and prattled on about flying. One of the boys dug me in the ribs and giggled. I was embarrassed for the old bloke but I was impressed by his fitness. And what he was saying all made good sense ... it was just the way he was demonstrating that made you wonder about him.'

'But how did you come to train with him?' I asked.

'I guess it just evolved. He was in Melbourne. Dad took us to the Olympics there in 1956. I was just captivated by Kuts' running

Disciple (Herb) and mentor (Percy Cerutty) on the sandhills of Portsea.

performance and it fired me up to pursue athletics. I knew that if I wanted to be the best I would have to go to Melbourne ...

'You just do what you have to do if you want to be successful. It just seemed a natural progression that I trained with Perce,' he yawned.

I thought how often outstanding performances of many of the great sportspeople, such as the great Russian distance runner Vladimir Kuts, ignite the tiny spark lying dormant in many of our youth, challenging them to pursue their dreams.

'I bet Portsea was fun,' I continued. I'd read how Cerutty used to run his charges through the sandhills on the Victorian coast. I was wide awake and keen to talk, even though Herb was tired and obviously reluctant to get into any deep and meaningful conversation. I was not about to give him any peace.

'Yes, it was ... but it was incredibly ... hard ... no ... 'stoic' is a better word and it fits in better with Percy's philosophy ... Percy taught a way of life.'

'I once went to see him at a seminar at the University of Queensland. He impressed me, he seemed so intense,' I challenged.

'Percy believed in what he was doing so fervently. He couldn't suffer fools and he hated half-heartedness. He demanded you give body, soul, every passing thought to athletics, always striving for perfection.'

'He seemed a little ... ahh ... crazy?' I suggested cautiously.

'Life certainly wasn't dull around Percy, he was wonderful company. I remember one time in Europe at one of those boring, dull functions they invariably used to have after competitions. During one particularly tedious speech Percy stood on his head on the lawn in the middle of it all ... the audience were stunned, they didn't know what to make of it. It certainly made for a memorable afternoon. Another time, at an instructional athletic clinic at the University of California in Los Angeles, I remember him taking the microphone to address the

crowd after many of America's top coaches, who were overweight and some were smoking cigars, had spoken. Percy electrified the arena as he berated these coaches, calling them pompous clowns who had no right to teach students in that manner. They were fuming with anger and embarrassment but they had heard the truth.'

'What other incidents like that stick in your memory with Perce?' I asked, keen to keep him going now that I had him loosening up.

'In Ireland once, after John Landy had broken the Irish mile record, at a civic reception — a garden tea-party actually — during the speech which, as I mentioned before, were invariably stuffy and boring, Percy's silver-maned head appeared above an eight-foot high partition. The boys spotted him ... with a crazy look Perce started pulling faces. The audience and the mayor started laughing ... suddenly the box on which he was standing gave way and he crashed, pulling the entire partition down on top of him. Perce jumped up and started doing push-ups and shadow boxing, and the audience went into hysterics ... that will live with me forever. Things were never dull around Percy.'

'Amazing!' I chuckled. 'I remembered him prancing around, carrying on and calling on volunteers to take their shoes off and run about like animals at that seminar when I was doing my Physical Education diploma.

'He was a real teacher, he loved to show people how to run.'

'Was he big on technique?' I asked, trying to keep this fascinating, enlightening conversation rolling.

'Yeah ... but ... he helped me not so much by technique but by releasing in my mind a power that I only thought existed ... for me he became a real mental mentor.'

'How?' I asked. I was soaking up every word, captivated by this wealth of knowledge discharging from the bed opposite.

'Percy was an emotional person. He was able to harness and transfer that emotion to other people.'

'Give me an example!' I was on a roll ...

'Well, on days before my important races he would go onto the warm-

131

up track and run four laps so hard that he'd stagger to the finish line, find me and, with saliva running from his mouth and eyes bulging, say:

"You may run faster but you won't run harder."

'I remember him pushing me aside in the gym and shaming me to lift heavier weights. He would never ask anyone to do anything he hadn't done himself. He was great, he explored the limits of the mind and demanded by the strength of his personality you do the same. He taught me to take my body to places I never thought possible. He opened my mind to possibilities.'

'Wasn't he sick himself as a younger man?' I asked. This was better than any university degree course in psychology or any seminar the so-called motivational 'gurus' put on as they lecture tour the country. This was real life motivation.

'Percy's own life was an inspiration to me,' Herb continued. 'His struggle for achievements in the face of physical handicaps ... you know that he had a nervous physical breakdown in 1939?'

'No!' I lied, but I did not want to stop this outpouring of valuable information. 'Tell me,' I ordered.

'In his enforced absence from his job as a telephone technician he read and started a physical living regime that he reckoned would kill or cure him. He changed his diet, his exercise pattern, his whole life. He started a marathon career at 48 and was the Victorian record holder by 50 — that's open all age, not just 50-year-olds. He is one of the few Australians to run 100 miles under 24 hours. So I felt if I didn't punish my healthy young body as he did his older one I'd abhor myself. He was just an amazing man ... a little eccentric though,' Herb chuckled as he remembered his mentor.

'What else?' I was engrossed.

'Oh, just a whole range of little things impressed me about Percy. Like when he was young he had a great fear of heights ... Percy decided to conquer this, so every day he'd go to the pool and force himself to climb the diving tower a little higher day by day until he finally could jump from the highest one.'

Herb in the 1500 metres final in Rome, remorselessly marching to his inevitable gold.

'A great mentor. I think everyone needs a mentor,' I stated, but it was more an implied question.

'Thrust against pain and eat natural foods, become a "Stoat". Percy used to tell me, "Pain is a purifier." It has changed me from a cigarette smoking introvert to this fine specimen you see before you,' Herb continued. I laughed.

'What's a Stoat?' I questioned.

'Percy postulated that Stoats were nature lovers, they have an unswerving devotion to an ideal, they associate themselves with their primeval source by going to the sea. Once a month, we used to have to go for long hard runs on the beach at Portsea then plunge naked into the icy ocean.'

'You're kidding! What else?'

Herb wins the gold by 20 metres, smashing his own world record by almost half a second.

Allsport

134

'Stoats are special people. They stand for hardness, toughness, they maintain their mind and body at a high pitch by getting sufficient regular rest, at least eight hours' good sleep each night ... which reminds me, good night, Laurie!'

I was shattered Herb wanted to go to sleep. How could he? This was so interesting.

'No, Herb! Just finish off this bit first,' I pleaded. I was like a little kid enjoying a bedtime story, knowing it was well past bedtime but trying to extend the pleasure of the moment.

'Stoats will not be found in social places after midnight. In fact, Stoats should be asleep by midnight. Good night, Laurie.'

'No Herb, just finish Percy's creed, pleeeeeeease,' I begged.

'He believed only the cultivated appreciate beauty,' Herb went on. 'Only the pure can understand purity, only the strong can measure their strength, and only the self-disciplined can command genuine respect ... you don't cast pearls to swine ... fix your goal and work for it, Percy used to say.' Then Herb added, very firmly, 'Mate, I'm getting a little tired, I suggest we continue this conversation tomorrow.'

How lucky was I to be able to be intoxicated by these precious gems. I wondered why Australian track and field officials wouldn't ask Herb to share his vast experience, to share Percy's philosophy and intensity, with our future stars. No wonder he'd advanced to the position of head honcho for Puma in America. No doubt the skills he had acquired during his athletic career were not wasted and had helped him in his remorseless climb up the corporate ladder.

'Did you like Percy's unrelenting intensity?' I pressed.

'I loved his intense prodding to get me going. He used to shame me, to cajole me, to inspire me — but there comes a time in your career where you actually reach a point of no return as you chase your goal. Once I reached this stage that was it. There was no stopping me. I had no other choice. It became my destiny. I think when athletes reach this point they realise there are no shortcuts and ... if they want that elusive edge over their opponents they must have that burning inner desire to succeed ... this inner desire comes long before they step out onto the running track, for without that inner drive you are like all the rest. You don't have what Percy called *the remorseless march towards the inevitable*.'

'Why?'

'Well, you've laboured for so long, sacrificed so much, that you can't go back. You must reach your goal and trample on anyone who tries to stop you. No one will or can stop you.'

'True,' I whispered, 'but what keeps you focused when you've made it?'

'Once you have made it, it's tough. When you're sitting on top of the world you need the prodding again to ensure you don't fall off your perch. Certainly, I felt I needed Percy's inspiration, his nagging, his continual reminding more than ever leading into the 1960 Rome Olympics. When you're on top you sometimes feel you've made it. That's why you need to refocus goals immediately after achieving one.'

I could hear him yawn again but this was great coaching education, so I added, 'I think young people in particular need to be continually reminded of the evils of complacency and the dangers of believing your own press clippings or television stories.'

'Yes! But you really have to have respect for the person who is prodding you or it becomes a nag,' returned Herb.

'Well, I'm sure that's one of the main reasons Kieren is so successful. He respects "Mr Carew", as he calls him. John as a coach is nowhere near as flamboyant as your Percy but he is a realist who knows that success does not happen without a tremendous amount of hard work, pain and sacrifice and, as a result, is continually reminding Kieren of this fact — particularly in the face of Kieren's growing media and sponsorship commitments.'

'I can sympathise with Kieren at the moment. He must be under a tremendous amount of pressure ... media expectations so high ... beaten at the trials ... struggling for form.'

'Oh, I think being beaten at the trials, although not pleasant or

Debbie Flintoff-King, her husband Phil (the Australian track and field team's coach) and Michael Wenden among the crowd in the main stadium in Atlanta.

palatable for him, is probably a blessing in disguise ... sometimes we need a good uppercut to get our mind back on track,' I suggested.

'I feel sorry for him missing the 400 metres swim,' I continued. 'The way he demolished the field in Rome at the World Championships was unbelievable. Total control from the first stroke. I've never seen an athlete control a world-class field like that before. Maybe the defeat at trials in the 400 was just the tonic he needed for success here. How often has failure been the fertiliser of success?'

'Were you scared going into your 1500 metres in Rome?' I changed tack.

'Not so much scared but prepared to confront the butterflies in the old tummy full on ... I used to race my opponents in training all the time.'

'How?' I asked.

'Oh, as I was running up a hill I would imagine them breathing there on my shoulder so I'd just push even harder ... I always won in training, I never gave in. I think good training builds confidence and character, and gives you the courage to face those fears as you remorselessly march towards the inevitable. Now, Laurie, put a sock in it. We need to sleep or we'll be useless tomorrow.'

There they were again — Herb's often-repeated famous words of wisdom: 'The remorseless march towards the inevitable.' I thought

*Opportunity rarely knocks on your door. Knock rather
on opportunity's door if you ardently wish to enter.*

B.C. Forbes

about them and about Kieren's huge challenge in the days to come. I mused out loud in the dark.

'I've been watching Kieren train lately, he's starting to show a bit of form again ... his training times indicate he will put up a mighty fight in the 1500. It's going to be a great race. I think he's starting to regain his confidence again.'

'You know it takes a tremendous amount of mental concentration to race at Olympic level. You have to block out all thoughts of your opposition and focus entirely on your own race. Mental concentration fatigues. Now good night!'

Herb rolled over and left me to my thoughts.

A week later I sat in the Olympic Stadium in Atlanta fiddling with my new toy, a mini-disc recorder that I had purchased in Australia with the express purpose of interviewing all our Olympic champions in the hope that they might reveal the secrets of their success. I could not get it to record. I started to tighten my jaw and grind my teeth. This was the telltale sign that I was becoming increasingly frustrated, angry at my inability to make it work. The modern term, I think, is 'stressed bigtime'.

'I hate new toys that don't work. I hate cars that don't work, in fact, I hate anything that doesn't work,' I muttered to myself. I put on the oversized headphones, forgetting the instructions given to me by my youngest daughter, Emma, before I left home, 'Don't wear them, Dad! They make you look like a nerd, Dad! People will think you're dumb.'

'For heaven's sake put that thing away and enjoy the track and field, the Olympics have finally started!' declared Phil King, a close friend and head coach of the Australian track and field team. He was sitting beside his wife, armed with a pair of binoculars so that he could command a view of the whole stadium.

'No! I won't let it beat me. I won't! Why won't this thing work? Pass me the instruction book again, please, Herb. It's got to be something real simple.'

'Relax, Laurie, enjoy the spectacle,' chipped in Herb.

'I know I'm not the most technical person in the world but why won't this thing work? Testing, testing, hello, hello, here we are at the track and field ... testing, testing, hello, hello, please let it work this time.'

'Put that thing away and enjoy the track and field,' ordered Phil.

'Not yet! I won't let it beat me. Put this carrying case under your seat please, Herb.'

'Here give me a quick look at it,' ventured the great Herb Elliott, my room-mate, who sat beside me waiting the running of the men's 1500 metres. Then he promptly took the mini-disc recorder off me.

'Who do you think will win the big one?' I ventured, now that my toy had been confiscated.

'Morceli! He let himself get boxed in in Spain. I don't think he'll let that happen here!'

'What about you, Phil?'

'Morceli, he's too good! He's the class act in the field.'

The competitors lined up for the 1500 metres.

'Forget the mini-disc. I'll get this fixed for you tomorrow. I want to watch the race!' said Herb and packed up the recorder.

Morceli won. No world record. I looked at the time on the big electronic scoreboard. Herb's time in Rome 36 years ago on the old running surface was faster. It just intensified my respect for Herb Elliott the man, the athlete, who, with his madcap mentor, Percy Cerutty, made both life and track and field a remorseless march towards the inevitable.

Next day Herb fixed the mini-disc.

He put a battery in the microphone.

A champion is someone who gets up when they can't.

9 — Anna and Katrin
A kite flies high in the winds of adversity

It was just a few short months to the Atlanta Olympics. I could hardly wait ...

I wonder what it looks like. They reckon it's going to be more practical this time, something we can wear when the Games are over. I hope so — all my other uniforms, including the beautiful 'babypoo yellow' blazer from Seoul 1988, are just taking up space in the far left-hand side of the wardrobe, keeping moths fat. There is a real need for a smart uniform for Olympians to wear to the numerous functions after the Games. Something that doesn't make you stand out like a sore toe would be preferable. The reason many athletes only wear their uniforms to the Opening Ceremony and then put them in mothballs is that they are so unfashionable, 'uncool'. Not to mention the fact that people can see you coming like a lit-up Melbourne tram on a cold, dark winter's night.

No young athlete, or old fart for that matter, wants to be accused of being a poser, so the team uniform, which should be a source of great pride, is left to languish in the cupboard gathering dust ... something fashionable you could wear with pride would be just perfect.

I interrupted my thought processes, put the car blinker on and turned sharply into the car park at Palm Beach Currumbin Olympic swimming pool. I was here to collect my precious Olympic team uniform. I'd been to Sydney the day before to launch Telstra's Atlanta fundraising phone-in for Olympians and Paralympians, so I couldn't collect my uniform when everyone else had. I smiled when I thought about the function ... It had been a fun day and it gave me a chance to meet a couple of Atlanta team members.

Jimmy Walker was there — K4 paddler, nice bloke, great biceps,

Shelley Oates, proudly Aussie!

learned to paddle in the lifesaving movement. Gutsy, great team man. Another kayaker, Shelley Oates, was there too, flashing the best smile you could wish to see. Miss personality plus! Talk about guts and ability to focus; what a determined young woman ... been through hell to make the Olympic team. I can't believe she used to be on a netball scholarship with the AIS until she wrecked her knee. John Elliott, from Kookaburra, who'd organised the function for Telstra, was telling me that when her netball dream was dashed she decided she'd go to the Olympic Games as a kayak paddler ... amazing! ... fancy learning to paddle a K1 in Canberra in the middle of winter.

When I queried Shelley about learning to paddle she told me that when she first started she spent more time in Lake Burley Griffin freezing than she did in the boat. Once home she'd spend hours in front of the heater rugged up, rubbing numb hands, teeth chattering, clicking like an old Victa mower, thawing out before returning for another dunking in the afternoon. Just a super effort in human persistence.

It never ceases to amaze me the incredible lengths people will go to in chasing their dreams, whether it be in sport, the arts, business, or even academic achievement. It appears to me, the common thread in all cases is desire — the desire and the determination to succeed. It's that burning desire and determination that keeps the dream alive and keeps people driving relentlessly, beyond normal human capacities, towards their goals, even under extreme discomfort and often seemingly insurmountable odds.

My mind started racing again. I still couldn't work out what John

> *We are what we think. All that we are arises with our thoughts. With our thoughts, we make our world.*
>
> Gautama Buddha

was talking about when he said Shelley was worried that her place on the Olympic team was in jeopardy. To me, her selection was a mere formality since she was part of the winning K4 team at the national selection trials.

Wonder what that's about ... surely they've named the Olympic kayak team by now ... I'll never be able to understand selectors ... I'll ask Michael ... I finally met Dennis Green ... great ... what a legend in kayak paddling ... carried the flag for Australia, too ... how about that ... gee, the boats have changed ... that was a great idea displaying boats from Dennis' old kayak to Jimmy's new, you beaut, superlight, streamlined Olympic kayak

My mind kept racing, jumping, remembering.

How about that paralympian sprinter kid? What's his name again? I must find out, got to follow him at the Games. Gee it's interesting, the new technology on the artificial legs for speed running ... too bad I can't get a technological flipper ... yeah, a technological flipper for our swimmers would be sensational.

Before I knew it I was there. I parked and walked quickly into the pool. Michael Wenden greeted me. He had picked up my uniform for me the day before in Brisbane. Michael, of course, was one of Australia's former Olympic heroes, 100 and 200 metres freestyle world record holder and dual Olympic gold medallist at altitude in Mexico. He is now an integral, hardworking member of the Australian Olympic Committee.

'Laurie, can you give Anna Wood a ring?'

'Who me? I hardly know her.'

'Yes you! I spoke to her yesterday and ...'

'Who me?' I interrupted. 'Michael, I just came to get my uniform.'

'Yes you! You can contact her at the physio section of Bond Uni.'

'Who me?' I repeated.

'Yes you! It's about time you started to pay your way and earn your keep as Athlete Liaison Officer for the team,' he smiled.

'You are going to be one of our main troubleshooters with these athletes in Atlanta ... so, I feel it's time to get to know a few more of them.'

'Okay, okay, what's the story?' I questioned.

'I spoke to her yesterday when I picked up our Olympic uniform. She and her K2 partner are a little stressed by rumours floating around in the kayaking community now about selections. She wants to talk to you.'

'Haven't they finalised selections yet? I thought they did that immediately the trials were over.'

'No they don't select like swimming. They have their own formula.'

'But surely they pick the winners at trials?'

'It's not that simple, there are all sorts of combinations in kayaking. Anyway, here is an opportunity for you, as our Olympic liaison officer, to troubleshoot, put out some minor bushfires and put these girls' minds at ease ... maybe even contribute to their winning a medal.'

'I'd love to do that ...Yep ... I'd love to contribute but I don't want to big note myself ... What do I say? Hi! I'm Laurie Lawrence I'm here to solve all your problems, come talk to Uncle Laurie.'

'Don't be stupid! Can you please give the girls a ring?' he was starting to get a little impatient. 'See if you can find out just what the problem is and we may be able to sort out a problem before it arises?'

'No problems.' I replied.

I wondered just what the national kayak selectors were doing. It seemed to me to be another case of officials playing ducks and drakes with athletes' careers and aspirations. The men's team for Atlanta had already been submitted to and accepted by the Australian Olympic Committee, but the women, after four long years of dedication, pain and sacrifice chasing their golden dream, were still waiting on tenderhooks for their names to be sent to the AOC for ratification. This apparent stupidity, lack of communication and procrastination, I felt, had the potential to destabilise the team. It could jeopardise not only the medal chances of two of Australia's most dedicated and best-credentialled paddlers, Anna Wood and Katrin Borchert, but also those of the K4 girls, who, too, had sweated long and hard for a chance at Olympic glory.

Maybe this had something to do with Shelley's insecurity?

I grabbed my bag of goodies, called a quick thank you to Michael, and hurried to my car. As soon as I sat down in the car I reached for my mobile phone. I find if you don't start working immediately on the task once you are committed to it often it can be two weeks or even longer before you get round to starting.

Katrin Borchert (left) and Anna Wood, Australia's K2 500 kayak team in Atlanta.

Anna answered the phone in her bright voice, her Dutch accent clearly evident. We arranged to meet at 4pm at a restaurant not far from where she worked at the university.

'Can I bring Katrin?' she added.

'Sure, see you at four. Bye.' I hung up the phone and wondered what the two girls wanted.

Anna and Katrin, who are training partners on the Gold Coast, have a very special and close relationship. This friendship has been forged in the blood and the sweat of the training arena and the tears which flowed as a result of the tragic suicide of Anna's husband, Steve, an Olympic bronze medallist. This senseless suicide left Anna a young widow with an Olympic dream and a two-year-old fatherless son. How often in life are we strengthened by human tragedy and that indomitable human spirit burning deep inside our souls which says 'hang on' when there seems to be nothing left to hang on to, or 'climb higher' when the mountain seems unconquerable, or 'try again' when all seems lost. But we do ... and, by sheer persistence, we emerge stronger, more capable human beings for the experience. This tragedy and their common quest for Olympic glory had bonded Anna and Katrin like twin sisters.

Their K2 pairing originally came about by accident. They were hastily thrown together as a pair and paddled the K2 for Australia at the World Championships in Germany in 1995. Katrin, a beautiful, tall, blonde German was now a naturalised Australian. A product of East Germany's sports school system, soon after migrating to Australia she became Australia's fastest K1 paddler. Anna, who was born in Holland, married Australian Steve Wood and she too became an Australian citizen.

During the 1995 World Championships their K2 combination took shape and they amazed themselves and other Aussie team members when they paddled faster and faster through heats and semi-finals, culminating with a magnificent sixth place in the final, just 1.7 seconds behind the winning boat. This was the highest-ever placing by Australian female kayakers in a senior international competition and the closest time margin of any Australian combination to the winning boat. Since it takes the best paddlers in the world time, sometimes years, to develop style, rhythm, balance and understanding for international successes, this magnificent performance underlined the girls' tremendous potential and labelled them as a definite medal chance for Australia in Atlanta.

They could see themselves as medallists in Atlanta. They believed in themselves and their kayaking ability, and belief in any sphere of human endeavour is paramount for success. Once our eyes are opened to the possibilities of success, then opportunities take tangible shapes and enable our visions, our dreams, to become realities. Virgil put it very simply and strongly when he wrote:

They can ... because they think they can.

I knew their preparation must have taken a huge battering on November 23, 1995, when Steve suicided and left Anna with a little red-headed bundle of energy. Most people would buckle to the enormous pressure of being left with a toddler and shattered dreams. However, where there's a will there's a way, and Anna has that steely Dutch determination; she is a fighter. She realised her dream must not die. She hung an old sign above her bed to keep her focused:

A kite flies high in the winds of adversity.

Katrin moved into the lonely house with Anna and Jordan, to make it more practical for them to pursue their shared Olympic dream.

The long hours in the boat, the agony in the gymnasium, Katrin's unselfishness in doing extra household duties to allow Anna time to give Jordan all the love and attention he needed, seemed to have paid off when the pair blitzed the field in the K2 at Olympic trials, winning by a whopping three seconds. This sent the Australian kayaking fraternity into raptures, predicting gold for the girls in Atlanta. The girls showed their versatility at the trials by narrowly being beaten in the K4. Katrin, the best female K1 paddler in the country, false started in the K1 and was disqualified. However, Anna, her soul mate, won the gold from teenage world junior champion Jacqui Mengler. The sacrifices of training seemed to have paid handsome dividends, the score was on the board, so I wondered what the problem was, and why the girls would want to see me. I pondered again if it had anything to do with Shelley Oates still not knowing whether she was in the Olympic team ... surely they knew the team by now ... nationals were finished ages ago ... What's the problem? What's the delay in selection? Is there a hidden agenda? Is politics about to rear its ugly head in Australian sport again?

These questions would be answered soon enough.

I pulled up outside our home and loaded myself up with the uniform. I could hardly wait to try it on. My wife Jocelyn greeted me at the door.

'Finally got them.'

'Yep. Can't wait to try them on.' I walked quickly into the room and threw the suitbag of clothes on the bed and dropped the carry bag of other goodies beside the bed. Jocelyn, one step behind me, scooped them up, unzipped the carry bag and hung them up.

'Try them on,' she enthused.

I grabbed the blazer first and stared at the gold pocket. It was beautiful. The gold thread sparkled on the dark cloth. The embroided Olympic rings sat nicely under the Australian crest. The words 'Atlanta 1996' under the rings said it all. I looked at the three gold buttons on the front. The crest and rings were embossed on these too. Three similar buttons on each sleeve set it off. It was a very smart blazer. You would be proud to wear this anywhere.

'Try it on,' my wife enthused.

I did. I swam in it. It was big. It looked as though it had been measured for Steve Kettner, our heavyweight weightlifter. I couldn't believe it.

'Try the slacks on,' she said disappointedly.

I did. They were big. I swam in them too. They must have been Steve's as well.

'You're not wearing them,' she insisted. 'I'm sick of you looking like Mickey Mouse.'

'They'll be alright,' I teased. 'I'll tighten the belt.' I pulled the slacks up under my armpits. They were huge.

'You're not wearing them, they belong to Mark Bradtke. Get them off!' she ordered.

'The tie fits,' I joked.

'Didn't you get measured for your uniform?' she asked impatiently.

'Of course, I did. You know I drove up to Brisbane months ago to get measured by that tailor in Queen Street.' I was getting defensive, she was getting aggressive.

'Do you think I'm stupid?' I added.

'No! But I know you ... anything will do ... and I won't have you going to the Olympics with baggy clothes, looking like the village idiot.'

'The tie fits,' I joked again.

'Don't you care how you look? You'll be on TV. The kids will be watching. You ring the Olympic Committee right now and get this rectified!' she insisted.

I went into my office and phoned Tracey Johnstone, who was in charge of coordinating all the team clothing.

'Tracey, Laurie Lawrence.' I chatted.

'Yes, Laurie.'

'Tracey, my uniform doesn't fit.' I felt sorry for Tracey. It must be a nightmare for her fielding complaints about uniforms from a team in excess of 500 people. 'What can I do about it?'

'Don't worry, pack it all and bring it to the team assembly in Athens, Georgia. We'll sort it all out there.'

I would have to wait to see how smart I looked in my new Olympic gear.

At 3.30pm I headed for my rendezvous with Anna and Katrin. It was only a 10-minute drive to the restaurant, but I really loathed being late. I guess I got this habit from my father, who was a stickler for punctuality. Inevitably, I was early, so I sat in the car, watched the

Concentrate all your thoughts upon
the work at hand. The sun's rays do
not burn until brought to a focus.

Alexander Graham Bell

surf, marvelled at the power, and waited for the girls. Anna was first to arrive. She got out of her car, went to the back seat and unbuckled a healthy little red-headed boy, clean, impeccably dressed and obviously well loved and cared for. She hoisted him under one arm, looked both ways and walked quickly across the street.

'Anna,' I called.

'Oh, Laurie, thanks for coming,' she enthused.

'No problems,' I replied.

'Katrin won't be long.'

'Where do you want to sit?' I questioned.

'Let's sit out here so Jordan can wander a little and I can keep an eye on him.'

'Fine. Now, how can I help?' I questioned again.

'Wait for Katrin,' she instructed. 'She's an important part of the team and I want her to have input too.'

Soon after, a tall athletic woman bounced across the road. Her hair was cropped short, ideal for the Queensland climate. I cast my coach's eye over her as she broke into a jog to avoid an oncoming car. She was in good shape. She saw us, smiled, looked at her watch, breezed over and said, 'Just made it.'

I introduced myself and asked, 'How can I help you?'

We sat around a small table. Anna leaned over and said, 'Well, where do I start ... you know my husband killed himself.'

It was blunt and to the point. I nodded. She looked at Katrin as if to get approval and then poured out the background of his tragic suicide, which had left not only the canoeing fraternity but also the Olympic family in a state of shock.

'I've come to terms with it ... but now my main aim is to look after Jordan,' she said and nodded to the little boy with a crop of freckles and red hair, a legacy of his father. As I sat there listening I couldn't help but admire the mental strength required by this young woman to accept what had happened and refocus on the future.

Then Katrin spoke, 'Laurie, we think the selectors are trying to rob us of our K2 pairing at the Olympics. We want you to help us.'

'Do you deserve the K2?' I asked.

'Yes!' they chorused in unison with the strongest conviction in their voices.

'Why?' I asked.

'We won the Olympic trials easily,' Katrin pointed out.

'And we have been training with and against each other ever since they paired us at the World Championships last year,' Anna went on.

'Laurie, we know we are the best and we can win a medal,' Katrin enthused. 'We have built a very special team chemistry and relationship.'

'Katrin knows me and I know her,' said Anna.

'Okay, what's the problem then?' I asked.

'You see, we've just toured Europe with the Australian squad, racing in Belgium, Italy and Hungary.' I listened intently. She checked on Jordan and continued.

'We got third in the final regatta in Hungary against the world's best, just 0.7 second behind the winning boat. This was the one the selectors said was important. It showed our tremendous improvement and indicated that we were on track for a medal in Atlanta.'

'Laurie!' Katrin interrupted. 'I think the problem is we paddled too good in Europe.'

'How can you paddle "too good"?' I questioned.

'Well, while we were there ... for training we thought it would be good to do some extra racing,' Katrin explained.

'That makes sense to me,' I said.

'At all the regattas we got girls from other countries who weren't paddling to team with us in the K4 ... Jordan don't. Come to Mummy.'

'Yes,' I listened.

'Well we beat the Australian K4 team in every regatta ... now the selectors want to take us out of the K2 and put us in the K4 to strengthen it.'

'Seems crazy to me. Why?'

'We don't know. We think it has something to do with funding ... a

Katrin (left) and Anna on the waters of Lake Lanier during the '96 Olympics.

K4 success is worth more than a K2 success.'

'Are you sure?'

'Well ... That's the only thing we can think of,' said Anna.

'We don't want to paddle the K4. We have trained hard for the K2. We have developed a great understanding as we have strived towards our goals,' said Katrin.

'Yes,' chimed in Anna. They were in rhythm even now. 'We've worked hard. We know what excellence is about. We are continually striving to improve ourselves by doing more, by trying to go the extra mile, and now these people want to shatter our dreams.'

'This has been our dream for a long time, Laurie. We don't want to stop or change now with the job only half done. We have sweated, sacrificed and suffered pain, and we feel we don't deserve all the rumour mongering that is currently floating around the country. All we want to do is race the K2,' added Katrin.

'Well, I'll see what I can do, girls. No promises. I think the best way is to get the media on side. Channel 7 has the Olympic rights. I'll ring "Fordo", he might be able to help.'

We stayed for another hour or so chatting about their aspirations and what they had endured to this point. This only strengthened my resolve to try to help them.

David Fordham was contacted. He did a great story that was aired on Seven's Sunday morning sports program. The girls were ecstatic, but the battle had only just begun. Even though these two girls had proven they were the best and were the obvious choice in the K2, they had a real fight on their hands.

I crouched low and dipped my head as I dragged myself out of the mini-bus that had transported us from Atlanta Airport to Athens University. It was here in the University surrounds that we would cement relationships with other Australian team members, be briefed on the Atlanta Olympic Village and complete our team uniform outfitting. Here we would have a chance to check sizes and exchange uniforms that did not fit.

Two small trees surrounded by tables and chairs offered little shade but dominated the square that led to the living quarters at the University. Anna and Katrin were relaxing at one of these tables.

'Why aren't you girls on the lake?' I joked.

'We're okay. We haven't got our canoe here but we're working out in the gym. We're keeping fit, don't you worry,' smiled Katrin.

'Did you resolve the K2 issue?' I asked casually.

'Not yet! But we're still fighting! We are gonna get the K2! It's ours!' replied Anna, with steely Dutch determination.

'They are leaning towards pairing Shelley Oates and Yanda Nossiter in the K2, which will stuff all our plans,' said Katrin.

'When will they tell you? It's getting a little late isn't it? After all it's only two weeks to the Opening Ceremony,' I said.

'Yes, it's a real strain not knowing what we are doing, but we must do the K2 … it's our dream and we won the trials,' said Katrin.

'Yes! It's a worry we could do without at this stage in our preparation,' added Anna.

'If there is anything I can do to help give me a yell,' I said, but I was powerless, really, as this was an internal decision that had to be addressed by team management.

'We'll be okay, we won the trials, we deserve that paddle. We'll keep fighting,' said Katrin.

'Talk to you later,' I said.

They waved and I struggled off with my port. I checked into the room, but my mind was occupied with thoughts of how this mess had to be having a detrimental effect not only on Anna and Katrin but on members of the women's K4 as well. I knew from past experience with world and Olympic champions how important clarity of purpose is in the success of an athlete. It enables them to focus exclusively on the job at hand. This, I believe, heightens their chances of success.

Over the next week and a half the girls kept up their insistence and desire to paddle the K2. Finally team management decided the best way to settle the issue was to give the girls a time trial. A time was set, over a full second inside the girls' best-ever time. This time would really test their ability, but many felt it was just a token gesture to placate the girls.

When the time was first mooted the girls were shocked but

philosophical. They felt it unfair that they had to paddle such a difficult time just to prove their competence for an event that was rightfully theirs, but if this was what had to be done then they would do it. It was just another obstacle in the march towards their goal.

Just a few days before the Opening Ceremony the girls paddled their way into K2 selection with a magnificent time trial.

A little over a week later I cheered myself hoarse as all their hard work was rewarded and they paddled into third place for a bronze medal behind the Swedish and the German pairing. I was delighted for the girls.

Time passes, we all get engrossed in our own everyday aspirations and sadly now my contact with the Olympic family is more often through reading newspapers and seeing them on TV.

However, I was at one of my many speaking engagements, this time for the Jenman Real Estate Group, when, as luck would have it, I spoke after another Olympic kayak paddler, Andrew Trim, who is silently sponsored by the Jenman group. I sat there, enthralled, as I listened to Andrew reminisce on past successes and expound on his hopes for Sydney. This was a dedicated young man. Later, in private,

Andrew Trim, Yanda Nossiter and Danny Collins at the '96 Closing Ceremony.

> *Clarity is truly power. When you have
> clarity about what you want, it gives you
> the strength and courage to achieve it.*
>
> Marcia Griffin

I made arrangements to have lunch with him and Danny Collins, the giant Tasmanian and Andrew's K2 partner. Given the opportunity, I'm sure Danny could hold his own in any woodchopping event.

The lunch was basic but the conversation was enlightening. These two young men, both on the 'OJOP Program' with Australia Post to give them the best opportunity for Olympic representation, were obviously on a mission for Olympic gold in Sydney.

They studied the lunch menu carefully, choosing food that would enhance their training.

'You guys are serious,' I remarked casually.

They both nodded before Andrew looked me in the eye and said, 'Laurie, we went to Barcelona. We were bronze medallists in Atlanta. We know what the Olympics are about. We really don't want to waste our time going to Sydney if we can't give the gold a real shake.'

As we sat and spoke about their plans, their training, the coaching support from the great John Sumegi as well as the total support of their wives and employers, I knew these young men were indeed seriously joining the Sydney gold rush.

The waiter cleared the table, big Danny grinned and ordered more bread while I enquired with genuine interest about their female counterparts.

'How are Anna and Katrin going?'

'Sensational!' replied Andrew.

'They won the World Championships K2 500 as well as the K2 1000,' added Danny.

'Awesome,' nodded Andrew, with respect in his voice.

'You're kidding. That's great. They're well positioned for Sydney then,' I said.

'You're not wrong,' said big Danny as he devoured two more slices of dry fresh bread.

We finished the meal, and I left the lunch inspired and vowed I'd attend some of their early morning training sessions as well as making contact with the girls.

I stopped at the Palm Beach 7-Eleven for some fresh batteries for my mini-disc recorder on my way out to Tallabudgera Valley. As I drove at regulation speed along the narrow bitumen road that snaked through the lush green fields of the valley I was engrossed in serious thought about the questions I might ask Anna about her current aspirations and desires.

I had seen and spoken to her at a couple of Olympic functions but in her typical modest way she had not mentioned the scalps she and Katrin had under their belts after the recent World Championships. She had not mentioned how theirs was the best performance by any Australian paddlers, male or female, at these championships.

I was so preoccupied in my thoughts as I drove through the picturesque countryside that I cruised past Anna's turn-off. In fact, I was three kilometres up the valley before I realised my mistake. A quick phone call and a strategic backtrack soon saw me driving into a large gravel driveway, with a little freckled-faced four-year-old waving me in with a toy plane. Anna appeared at the doorway and with a cheery smile guided me into the lounge room.

'I think we'll talk in here,' she said with that unmistakable Dutch accent, 'Dad's mowing the back in the tractor slasher.'

'Wherever suits you,' I replied easily.

Jordan looked me up and down quietly before declaring, 'This is Bugs Bunny.'

'Well you'd better get him some carrots,' I replied.

'Put Bugs to bed now Jordan,' Anna said firmly and, miraculously, he obeyed.

'I thought you were going to retire after all that drama in Atlanta?' I asked.

'Well, 1996 was going to be my last year but I reconsidered because I was sure I had a few years left in me. Also, I didn't want to let Katrin down ... We got two silvers in '97, then two golds in '98 ... now with two golds in my pocket I feel I have to make a commitment for another two years.'

'You think you can win the Olympic gold?'

'Well, I'd like to think so, but you can never be totally certain ... you have to be realistic ... 'cos you never know what happens. I got knocked off my bike and broke my arm six weeks before a major competition once ... but these sorts of setbacks make me even more determined.'

'The sacrifices you make help you appreciate the victories even more?' I questioned.

She didn't answer but stared out the big glass window as if dreaming. Then she looked me squarely in the eye.

'I want gold at the Olympics. It's the only thing missing from my collection.'

There was no doubting her sincerity.

'You need Katrin though.'

'Of course.'

'Is she as keen as you?'

She laughed.

'You don't know Katrin — she lives kayaking. She is the perfect partner for me. Totally consumed and dedicated.'

'Why?'

She looked at me as if I'd uttered some profanity and answered.

'We want to be the best in the world ...'

'And ...'

'We totally support each other ... we don't want to let each other down ... we certainly don't want to be beaten by the Germans, particularly Katrin, as she is ex-German.'

'What about you?'

'Same ... I've been competing against them all my life... there's no way.'

So you've got a bit of that Dutch mongrel in you.'

'Yes, stubborn,' she laughed. 'We're both like that ... if we are going to do something we want to do it to the best of our abilities.'

'You train hard?' I asked matter-of-factly.

She looked at me, horrified, before answering, 'There's no use going on the water and saying, "Oh, I'm tired, I'd better go off now." When we go on the water we train 100 per cent. It's 100 per cent commitment, every session, there's no doubt about that.'

As a coach this gave me a great feeling. I remembered how many of the great champions I'd coached — Holland, Sieben, Wickham, Armstrong — would regularly drag themselves from the water exhausted from total concentration and effort.

'No pain, no gain, eh?'

'Right! Every session we're going for it! No use wasting my time out there ... I've got better things to do with my time if I'm not 100 per cent committed ... I could go down the beach with him or do other things,' and she nodded to Jordan, who was flying his plane around the lounge room, making the appropriate noises.

'How do you keep the intensity up every session?' I quizzed.

Anna with Jordan after taking the bronze on the final day of competition in Atlanta.

'Katrin and I push each other ... and ... we love to train with the guys in our club. I try to keep up and every week I crawl a little bit closer.'

I thought of Australia's first female cycling gold medallist, Kathy Watt, who before her historic gold in Barcelona had decided to train with the men.

The men became her benchmark. Once a week she raced them in a criterion at the local cycling club — round the track for an hour trying to drop the opposition before that last desperate sprint to the finish. In addition, Kathy rode the Dandenong Hills once a week ... the unforgiving Dandenongs that helped spawn the gold medal for the great Debbie Flintoff-King. Kathy would spend five tedious hours in the saddle, with four male companions setting the pace, as she forced herself to hang on and not give up.

'They like that?' I enquired, coming back to reality.

'Oh, they are looking over their shoulder,' she laughed, 'but they are a great bunch of guys ... always good humor ... a few jokes on the water ... they're really supportive ... they're committed themselves, and training is fun.'

'It's fun training with the men?'

'Oh yeah! We make sure the men go in front of us and we try to keep up. We do occasionally. It makes us train hard.'

> *For the resolute and determined
> there is time and opportunity.*

'That's important?'

'Of course! You can't hope to be the Olympic champion if you don't prepare well. A solid preparation gives you confidence at race time, so we train 100 per cent every time.'

Just then Jordan moved in, plonked himself on his mother's lap and started to squeeze her lips and turn her face towards his.

'Mum, Mum, Mum ... I want a drink!'

She immediately went to the fridge and poured him a fruit juice. He gulped it down and went on playing.

'Sorry, I have to look after this little fellow,' she said with a smile.

'That's fine!' I answered and my admiration magnified for this young widow, a mother, a world kayak champion who still held down a job as physiotherapist at Bond University to support her young son.

'Is it hard to juggle being a working mum and a world champion?' I queried.

'Oh yes, but I want to keep my career. I studied four years for it ... I love my job ... I love paddling ... I love training and I love being a mum to Jordan ... there's never enough hours in the day but somehow I'll manage.'

'Do you sleep at all?' I asked, tongue in cheek.

She laughed.

'I try to sleep eight hours, which is often not very realistic. Sometimes I don't get home till 6.30 at night, then I have to cook dinner, put him to bed, do the washing, cleaning, whatever ... I don't waste any time ... sometimes in the mornings when I get back from training I work on minutes ... three minutes for a shower ... two minutes for breakfast ... two minutes to make the lunches ... I'm very structured ... I'm organised ... I'll be right.'

I thought of the many modern-day professional athletes who have financial support and back-up teams to help them achieve their goals. And the many others who whinge because they don't have support. Yet this woman, who had already endured enough heartache to cripple most people, continues to organise her life without fuss so that she is able to achieve her dreams.

Time passed so quickly as we discussed the support of friends, how she felt her basic drive comes from an intrinsic love of her sport that has kept her competing at an international level for 15 years. We spoke of the support of people like Lorraine and Bob Evans, who had become like second grandparents to Jordan. We also discussed the teamwork between herself and Katrin and the different roles they each played in the boat; how she sets up the stroke and rhythm and Katrin supplies the power and drive, and an urgency to get to the finish line during the last 200 metres.

I came to fully appreciate their commitment for Olympic gold, but my coach's instincts worried about complacency creeping into their training now that they were the world champions.

'Any danger of you losing that drive now that you are world champions?' I questioned.

She looked aghast. 'Absolutely no danger! I have never won Olympic gold, that is the only medal I don't have so it's a great incentive for me to keep going. I'm not going to waste my time! I'm not going to float along for two years and see where we end up. When we line up for the final we don't take prisoners! Definitely not! We want to be ready!'

'Do you two really believe you are going to be the Olympic champs? I asked simply.

'Of course!'

'And if you don't?'

She smiled and looked me squarely in the eye and replied, 'Laurie, if that's the worst thing that happens to me in life I'll be okay.'

Then a little boy called, 'Mum, let's go get a doughnut.'

You play from the shoulders up —
it isn't all important, just 90 per cent ...
and it may be more than 90 per cent.

Arnold Palmer

10 — Rowdy
The long road
to a fast start

The year was 1981. Ambrose 'Rowdy' Gaines walked slowly across the Auburn University campus in Alabama, USA. His head was down; gone was the confident gait and the spring in his step that he had during the Olympic trials. The Moscow boycott had scarred him deeply. He had to lash out at something to vent his anger and frustration so he kicked at stones, sticks, leaves.

It was lucky Rowdy didn't own a cat.

He headed towards the University's Athletic Department, where head coach Richard Quick had his office. Rowdy hesitated ... he didn't want to disappoint Richard ... Richard had been so good to him.

'I hope Richard's in his office. I really need to talk. I can't bottle up this frustration inside myself any longer,' he mused out loud, moping along, kicking more stones and continuing the conversation with himself.

'How could they do this to us? They call us Olympians ... they select us to represent USA, but we aren't allowed to go ... it stinks ... why would politicians do this? Why? Why? Why? I've never seen one of them at the pool at 5am in all the years I've been training. Don't they know what it's like to dream, to plan and to work hard towards a goal no matter what the cost? We've trained our whole lives chasing this dream, waiting for the opportunity to represent our country at the Olympics, and the rotten government pulls the pin because Russia invades Afghanistan. It's not fair.'

His thoughts flashed back to the present.

'How am I going to tell Richard I don't want to swim any more?'

His paced slowed and his thoughts wandered again.

I know I could have beaten Jorg Woithe in Moscow ... 50.40 seconds ... what a pussy ... that's so slow ... I swam 50.19 at our trials and I went 49.61 twice leading up. I could have beaten that time, I know I could. Why would President Carter do this? What's his motive? What does it prove? ... Wish he'd kept farming peanuts ... The troops are still in Afghanistan ... still shooting guns ... still killing each other. The only people Carter hurt are we athletes ...

He sure has wrecked my dream.

He slowed even more as he approached Richard Quick's office. Richard had been father, brother and friend to him. Rowdy remembered the first year training at Auburn, he had kicked him out for not performing in training, for not giving it to himself, not working hard enough. How did Richard put it?

'Not doing yourself justice, son, too soft on yourself, better go home.'

Just a simple statement. Funny how some things stick in your mind. Soft wasn't in Richard's vocabulary. Rowdy smiled to himself as he thought of the great coach. No wonder he admired him so much ... with Richard it was 100 per cent or nothing. He turned to retrace his steps ... it was going to be hard to tell him.

'I'll tell him tomorrow,' he thought. 'Yes, but what would Richard do in this situation?'

He could almost feel the coach's presence there, the firm grip on his forearm as he looked at him with those clear blue eyes, saying: 'Son, don't procrastinate ... it only gets harder ... if a job's to be done, just do it.'

He stopped, turned, and went back towards Richard's office to face the music. He'd learned so much from swimming — responsibility, integrity. He had to face up to his problems, and the sooner the better.

Soon he was outside Richard's office, his heart pumping as though he was in his first national final. He knocked tentatively on the office door.

'Come in!' returned a muffled voice from inside. 'You've caught me eating a sandwich.'

> *Not in time, place or circumstance,*
> *but in the man lies success.*
>
> Charles B. Rouss

'I'll come back tomorrow,' he responded quickly. What luck! This would give him one more day to prepare.

'Don't be silly,' laughed Richard.

'Richard, I ...'

'Rowdy! Sit down, son! To what do I owe this pleasure? Training doesn't start till Monday!' he said as he put his half-eaten sandwich on the table.

'Richard, I ...'

'You son-of-a-gun, you look great! You've been running haven't you?' Richard picked up the sandwich and set about finishing it.

'Richard, I ...'

'Rowdy, what is it?'

'Richard, I just can't swim this year!' he finally blurted out.

'Why not, son?' Richard was surprised. He threw the last bit of his sandwich into the bin to give Rowdy his full attention.

'Richard, those politicians! They robbed me of my dream! The boycott stole my dream! I ... I ... just don't think I could swim this year. I just can't face the training ... and face the ... well, everything we go through ... you know.'

Richard leaned forward and looked the young man squarely in the eye.

'Rowdy, I'd like you to think about something. You're the captain of this team. You're a Senior. You're the school leader and we need you!'

'Yes ... but ... but I feel so bad, Richard! I just feel so bad. I can't ...'

'Son!' Richard interrupted, 'It's time you stopped feeling sorry for yourself ... forget the boycott. Refocus.'

Rowdy Gaines — favourite for the 100 metres freestyle Olympic gold in 1980 until the US boycott, Olympic champion four years later in Los Angeles.

Allsport

'It's not that easy.'

'I know, but consider this ... consider throwing your energies into the team — work for the team, give yourself to the team ... have a couple of goals, but really try to have a positive influence on the team ... not just by scoring points, but more importantly by your encouragement and by making everyone on the team feel better. Use your experiences and seniority to influence the team. Rowdy, we really need you. Make this, your senior year, a real, fun, positive one for both you and the team.'

'I s'pose ... I could take a different approach. It might be fun.'

'It will be fun ... another thing. Get your grades up ... start thinking about the rest of your life, not just swimming. You should try to be the best student you can. Get ready for life after swimming. Remember you can't eat gold medals.'

'Okay, I will.'

'Oh, no you won't! I don't want anyone around this team with negative vibes! You go home, young man! Come back next week. I don't need your answer right now. You just go home, think about it for five days, then come back with the answer that is going to be best for your future. Don't make a hasty decision, just to please me. Son, I want you to do what is best for Rowdy Gaines ... but I know you have so much to give this team. Come along ... learn a little more about life ... learn about supporting giving and sharing ... be selfless ... do a Mother Teresa.'

Richard watched the troubled young man walk out of his office. There was much more to coaching than just supervising workouts. You need to be a friend, an adviser, a psychologist, a sculptor, a planner — moulding young people's lives for the future. He hoped the association with his team-mates, the bonds and camaraderie built over the years, would be sadly missed by Rowdy over the next five days and it would draw him back to the pool like a magnet.

This was his strategic masterplan. If it worked, the young man might go on to great heights; if it failed, at least he could sleep easily knowing he'd tried.

'Those politicians,' he thought, 'why did they boycott? Why? Why mess with young people's lives? Those Aussies are smart, nothing stops them. They've been to every Olympics since Athens 1896. I would have given my right arm to take our boys to Moscow!'

Five days later, a blonde-headed, tracksuited, determined young man with a towel slung over his shoulder was first to the pool, even before the coach. When the coach bounced into the pool for morning practice, Ambrose Gaines turned to him and said simply, quietly, and determinedly ...

'Richard, I'm ready.'

And he was. He'd made the commitment and nothing was going to stop him. He threw himself wholeheartedly into his studies, his training and into supporting his team-mates. He stopped feeling sorry for himself. He refocused his goals, which are the most important things for success in sport, life and business. You can't live on memories. He trained even harder. He made straight As at school. The NCAA championships were both a personal and a team triumph. He set two American records in the 100 and 200 yards freestyle. He led and encouraged the team to its highest-ever NCAA placing, which would have been even higher except a key swimmer got really sick the day before the meet.

One week after the NCCA championships, coach Quick, fearing his star performer was going to retire, organised a time trial and Ambrose Gaines broke the world record for the 100 metres freestyle. It was a brilliant piece of coaching by Quick. Rowdy was back! Quick's philosophy had taken a disillusioned young athlete to the pinnacle of success, a world record, and in most difficult circumstances — by shifting his emphasis to something other than his own need to perform — by asking him to contribute something of himself to the team. By encouraging his team-mates, Rowdy became an integral part of the team and, unknowingly, started to perform better himself.

Ambrose 'Rowdy' Gaines retired happy ... or so he thought. But fate deals us strange hands in the game of life.

After the summer nationals, when no American had swum very fast, the urge to compete again began to build again for Rowdy Gaines. He thought the flame had died, yet he still felt cheated, unfulfilled. The flame still smouldered deep inside and could only be extinguished by drinking deep from the Olympic fountain. He'd been world champion, but had been denied the opportunity to compete at the Olympics. He could stand it no longer. In the fall he marched into Richard's office and demanded:

'Richard, I want to make a comeback! Los Angeles seems the perfect place!'

Richard sat back, pleased but stunned, and looked at the determined young man.

'Rowdy, hang on!'

'Richard, I'm serious!'

'Rowdy, you have to analyse your reasons for coming back. You need

> *Anyone can wish for something — and most people do.*
> *But only a few know that a definite plan, combined*
> *with a burning desire, is the only way to get there.*
> Australian women's hockey team collection

to enjoy the process ... I'll repeat this ... You need to enjoy the process of trying to accomplish your goals, whether you reach your goals or not. You have to do it unreservedly and not be a bitter person if you don't reach your goals. You can't be bitter if you are going to put in this time and effort and don't win an Olympic gold medal or, God forbid, don't even make the US team. Don't forget, you are not the same athlete you were at 19 years of age in Berlin. You were awesome there ... just awesome ... unbeatable ... now the German Albatross, Michael Gross, has surfaced ... remember that he beat you in South America and, at this stage, he's favourite for your events ... you have not been training the past 12 months.'

'I've been keeping fit.'

'Hold on, I haven't finished. This has to be an enjoyable experience.'

'Richard, don't you have faith in me?'

'I do, but I want you to be totally aware of what you are doing and, more importantly, I want you to swim for the right reasons ... because then you will give of your best.'

'Richard, it's eating my heart out ... I know I can win. Help me ... I have faith in you. I have faith in my ability, I know we can do it. I'll go to my grave wondering if I don't give it my best shot.'

'Okay. Okay. Rowdy, look ... my thoughts are that this has to be an enjoyable experience, otherwise you will get to hate this great sport — and you've accomplished too much for that to happen. You know people talk about arrogance, confidence, but the most important thing about sport is that it should be real fun. If you have fun many other benefits will follow. I want you to swim again for the sheer enjoyment, not just because the US boycotted. You have to put in some long hours, so if you are not getting the thrill of the challenges I throw at you during training then ... Rowdy ... you won't make it, so don't do this to yourself.'

Two years later, after a lot of hard work and lots of fun days, Rowdy found himself in the 100 metres freestyle final at the Los Angeles Olympics.

The US trials had been extremely hard racing, both physically and psychologically. Rowdy had been relegated to second place there by Mike Heath. He didn't enjoy getting beaten one bit but at least he was off to the Olympics. Surely the US couldn't boycott the US but, then, those politicians are silly enough to do anything. Yes, he had made the Olympic team, but he was not in the same form as the year of the boycott when he had been at the peak of his career. He had expected to win four gold medals in Moscow. Four years on, the second-place result at trials dented his confidence. Although he was still the current world record holder he was not the self-assured athlete of 1980.

Mike Heath, on the other hand, was supremely confident and in good form. He was the fastest qualifier of the 67 nominees for the Olympic final.

Rowdy certainly had experience on his side. However, for an experienced athlete, he wasn't handling the pressure too well. He had spent a nervous afternoon trying to relax by watching Woody Woodpecker cartoons on TV. Luckily, fellow American Tracy Caulkins, the women's medley champion, strolled by, and a chat to her helped relax him a little and convinced him that he may not need that loser's speech he'd prepared, where he would graciously congratulate those swimmers who'd beaten him. He had helped many of his team-mates in the summer of 1980; those selfless acts could not go unrewarded and now it was payback time ... an Olympic team-mate was there in his time of need.

Finally ... the evening of the finals. Rowdy was being introduced to his home crowd. He was waving, but he seemed to be outside his body. The roar was deafening, he was trembling, he let the noise wash over him like a soothing ointment. He closed his eyes and soaked

it in, savouring the moment. He'd done the hard yards, he'd visualised this race a thousand times, he wanted it so badly. He remembered Richard's words, 'relax, enjoy yourself, this is a celebration of talent'. Soon he would be on automatic pilot. He turned to take off his track top, and there was Richard smiling, confident, waving. Their last-minute conversation flooded back ...

'It's going to be a quick start, be ready!' his coach had told him.

'Why?'

'The starter is that clown from Panama.'

'Who? Good old Frank?'

'Yes, Frank Silvestri. They call him "Quick draw" Silvestri.'

'Isn't he the same guy that started at the Pan American Games in 1983?'

'Yes ... you remember ... he was so fast people were getting left on the block. The US team actually put in a protest to ban him from starting.'

'He's starting our race?'

'Sure, he was starting this morning. He's up to his old tricks. So be ready ... it's going to be a quick start ... a real quick start!'

'Will I use the track start?'

'Of course! But you won't have time to step two feet to the front of the block as you normally do ... just step straight into your track start ... soon as you're down, GO! Don't wait, I promise it will be a quick start. He's mad, ready or not, he pulls the trigger. You'll be half a body length in front before they start. They'll panic. They'll never catch you.'

By the time the whistle went for the start Rowdy had his goggles on. He was ready for a quick start. Sure enough, just as Richard had predicted, it was a fast start. Rowdy exploded out of the blocks using the track start as planned, and, as Richard had predicted, he was half a body length in front immediately.

Heath and Australia's Mark Stockwell, his two main rivals, were not prepared for a fast start and were immediately playing catch-up, rushing their stroke just a little. Rowdy had stolen a march! He was determined no one would catch him now and powered down the first lap, Stockwell in pursuit.

A perfect turn saw Rowdy driving home to win in 49.80. The pro US crowd went wild. Mark Stockwell was the silver medallist, in 50.24. Rowdy leapt from the pool, straight into the arms of his exuberant coach, who yelled in his ear, 'Way to go for a fast start.'

They jigged, laughed, jumped, hugged, gave high fives and the crowd thundered a standing ovation.

Stockwell, meanwhile, was seething with anger. Feeling he'd been cheated of Olympic glory he punched the electronic touchpad, ripped his cap off in disgust, jumped out of the pool and headed for the Panamanian starter, firing a verbal protest as he went. Australian team manager, big Terry Buck, was right behind to calm and support. Terry lodged an official protest. The Australians in the stands were stunned. Protest dismissed.

I left the stands, boiling inside, and went to the TV viewing room set up by the television network. I wanted to confirm it for myself. That was a false start — Gaines had jumped the gun. The television replay would prove beyond doubt that Mark Stockwell and Australia had been cheated of a chance of a gold medal.

I set up the race on the TV monitor and replayed it over and over again. While I was engrossed in this, Randy Reece, coach of fourth-placed Mike Heath, came into the viewing room, muttering through his black moustache something incoherent about a false start.

I like Randy and consider him to be one of the best coaches in the world. He is innovative, dedicated, knowledgeable and tough on his swimmers, a deadly combination. He viewed and left still muttering. I stayed on replaying the race. Finally it dawned on me ... Gaines did not false start. He got a perfect fast start because he was down and ready. We Australian coaches had not done our homework on Frank Silvestri. Richard Quick had.

I replayed the video again. Mark Stockwell had missed the start because he was not down quickly enough. In fact, the gun had gone

By failing to prepare we prepare to fail.

while he was still going down — he was six inches from his starting position. I watched Mark Stockwell slowly inch back Rowdy Gaines' lead down the first length and speed into the turn ... if Stockwell can maintain this, I think, he wins ... they both flip fast but Rowdy obviously out-turns Mark ... I cringe ... Why?

I replay the turn several times and suddenly it dawns on me ... Rowdy uses his legs hard off the wall, Mark does not. There is no white water at Mark's feet out of the turn, whereas Rowdy is aggressive — the white foam at his feet indicates the power he puts into his driving kick to the surface. Another basic coaching error, I think to myself. These turns have to be practised perfectly in training over and over again until they become automatic responses under pressure. The coach is the swimmer's eyes. As coaches we have to be aware of all the things that go into a successful athletic performance and we must insist on the correct execution during training. If we don't put our swimmers under the same pressures in training that swimmers are going to experience during competition then as coaches we fail; we are hoping to win rather than planning for victory.

Just then Richard Quick floated into the TV room. I jumped up, went over and held out my hand.

'Richard, Rowdy didn't break. He got a perfect start. You out-coached us. Just too smart!'

'Thanks Laurie, that means a lot to me,' he answered humbly.

I turned and walked out, but as I left I couldn't help myself.

I turned ...

'Richard!'

'Yes, Laurie.'

'The Mean Machine is going to show you white water in the relay.'

I just had to have the last word.

The best thing in life is doing
what people say you cannot do.

Walter Bagehot

11 — *Summer*
Great expectations

When I wandered into the warm-up pool in Barcelona, Richard Quick, now US head women's swimming coach and, of course, an Olympic gold medal coach, was consoling a superbly fit, young, female swimmer. She was dressed in US swim costume, with her towel slung over her shoulder and her tracksuit top tossed on the stars-and-stripes team swimbag beside her feet. All of a sudden, for no apparent reason, she burst into tears and buried her head into her hands. Richard acted quickly, he put his arm around her shoulders, just as he'd done hundreds of times over the years with swimmers he'd coached. The TV cameras zoomed in ... Olympic drama!! They love the emotional or sensational ... they prefer to call it realism. Richard saw the cameraman out of the corner of his eye and spun round, gesticulating widely, and exploded.

'Get the hell out of here! This is a private conversation! Put that camera away! You vultures put such high expectations on our young men and women. Then, when they don't reach the unrealistic achievement levels you've placed on them, you crucify them just as quick. Now leave us alone!'

'Oh fair go, Richard!' said the cameraman continuing to shoot.

'Get out of here!' Richard raised his voice, put his protective arm around the young swimmer and led her to a quiet section of the pool, a 'no go' area to the prying eyes of the press.

I watched as he spoke earnestly with the tanned young athlete ... reassuring her, soothing her, preparing her mind for another day. I was enthralled. Slowly her demeanour changed, soon she was smiling.

I couldn't help but wonder ...

> *I'm a survivor ... I believe that no situation*
> *is beyond repair ... half the battle is the*
> *stress you think you're under.*
>
> Ian Botham

What was he saying ... this bloke must have a way with words ... maybe I can learn from him.

I waited until he was packed up ready to leave the pool. As soon as he moved, I moved.

My heart beat a little faster. I'd seen them do this on TV. I timed my walk to meet him at the gate, so that I could sit with him on the bus. I felt a little like one of those rock-and-roll groupies but I figured, what the heck, at least I might learn something.

'Richard! How are you?' I said, surprised as I just happened to meet him at the gate.

'Laurie! G'day mate,' he ventured, attempting Australian slang. 'You're late at the pool?'

'Yeah. Just watching,' I replied. 'Which reminds me, who was that young girl crying with you back in the warm-up pool?'

'Oh, that's Summer Sanders, a tough young kid ... swims medley and 'fly!'

'Feeling the pinch?' I asked casually.

'Yeah! High expectations from the press! They're fools, they want a hero but when the kids don't quite measure up to their writings they want to let a little blood.'

'Funny, the Australian press did the same thing to Steve Holland at Montreal 1976,' I shot back. 'They really crucified him for his bronze medal, even though he'd swum a personal best and inside the old world record ... third just wasn't good enough for them. It's really sad ... they deserve better.'

'I know, your country and mine, they set our athletes up to fail. Half of these journalists have never ever competed, they really don't understand the psychology of competition and of doing one's best. Laurie, you can't do better than your best,' he said.

'Right!' I answered. 'But nowadays, with the spotlight on our young athletes, the understanding and handling of the press plays an important part in their success. They have to be able to handle the pressure created by the press.'

'You bet! Janet Evans is a perfect example of this. In Brisbane in 1987 she let the press dominate her and she was beaten by your girl, Julie McDonald. But, in Seoul, that Brisbane experience really helped her ... it made her realise she had to concentrate on herself and forget the press.'

'I guess. What you're really saying is you can't control other people, so why waste precious time worrying about them, it takes away from your performance.' I was trying to sound intelligent and knowledgeable.

'Yes, and that's exactly what Janet did in Seoul.'

'She was awesome in Seoul! I've never seen a woman dominate an event so easily!'

'True!' he nodded.

Summer Sanders, during the 400 metres individual medley in Barcelona.

Allsport

American swim coach Richard Quick at the 1999 Pan Pacs in Sydney.

Allsport

'Four minutes:3.85 — one of the greatest swims I've ever seen.'

'I agree!' he said.

'I'd like to coach a woman to break four minutes.'

'Now that would be something, but Laurie that is pipe dreaming.'

'It'll happen, Richard, you mark my words ... but Richard, I'm more interested in the pressure on Summer because I saw her crying. What pressure was put on her to perform here by the press?'

'Oh they expected gold,' he answered, 'and not just one!'

'As if these swimmers haven't got enough to worry about with the Chinese girls swimming out of their brain ... not to mention the steroids innuendo.'

'Yeah! But our press wrote Summer up as a five gold medal prospect. Can you believe it? A five gold medal prospect! She barely won the 400 IM at trials ... barely won it. And she was never ever going to beat Chrissy Ahmed-Leighton in the 100 metres 'fly ... hell no! The press wanted a golden girl ... and ... what you have to remember about Summer is that she didn't even think she was a cinch to make

the team. She was happy when she made it in one event but she made it in four, plus the relays. That's when the press jumped onto this "golden girl" tag.'

'Is that what she was crying for in the warm-up pool?' I was anxious to find out what he said to calm her down.

'Look, this girl is incredibly tough and courageous ... for the last six days, because she has been dominated by the Chinese, our press have been wanting her to say that she's a failure. Can you believe that?'

'You're kidding!'

'I'm telling you the truth. You should hear the questions at the press conference. You would swear they were working for China.'

'Sometimes I can't believe the press.'

'They tried to make her ... honestly ... feel bad after the 400 IM because she hadn't won. You know what she said to me ... Richard, I've just won an Olympic medal. I've never won an Olympic medal before. I've just swum my best time. It's a new American record. I've never set an American record long course before. I'm happy, I've got more races to go and I'm looking forward to racing.'

'That's great! What an attitude!'

'You know they did the same thing after the 200 IM! She did another lifetime best, another American record, and they canned her again.'

'What?'

'Yes! And her answer to the press was exactly the same. I did my best ever, I think I won.'

'She's tough!'

'She's tough all right. Sometimes she is so tough she's dumb. You know at our trials she was out in 1:01.47 in the 400 IM.'

'That's fast!'

'Yeah, but dumb. She died bigtime. Her last 100, I reckon I could have beaten her, she looked terrible, she needed a taxi ... the piano was on her back bigtime. In fact, she barely got home. "Skip" Foster tells the story of how he was driving his team back to the hotel after the final session, and he's got a group of guys laughing at how bad she died. Well, he pulls the bus over the side of the road, looks over the back seat and berates them. None of you people would have had the courage to stay in and fight, he says. You'd have all given up. You'd have hurt so bad you'd have stopped trying. She showed courage. Half of you would have got out of the pool. He was real angry, and drove off in silence.'

'But Richard, what was she crying for in the warm-up pool?'

'Oh, just the continual hammering by the press,' he answered.

I must confess here to having a dual motive, in trying to ascertain what was hurting Summer Sanders and how Richard Quick was handling the situation. I was genuinely sorry for the way this fine athlete was being treated, but I was also keen to discover exactly how the pressure was affecting her, because Susie O'Neill, our Australian girl, had to race her the following day. If there was some weakness we could exploit to Susie's advantage, I wanted to know about it.

'Tomorrow is the last day ... the 200 'fly is her best event and she still hasn't won a gold. The press want to know why,' Richard continued

'They can be cruel,' I said, angry and 'fishing' at the same time.

'Do you know what she said to me when she started crying?'

'No what?' This might be the information I wanted ...

'It brings tears to my eyes ... she just said, "Richard, I'm okay ... I just need to release the emotions." In all that time of emotional release not once did she feel sorry for herself. She simply said "I'm going to swim a hell of a 200 'fly tomorrow ... I'm really looking forward to racing ... I just need to cry to get it out of my system ... I know I'm going to do another PB."'

My heart sank. This girl was looking forward to racing and she was

Summer by the pool (left), where she feels so much at home, and surrounded by the world media (below), where things are not always so friendly.

Both pics: Sport: The Library

> *For the resolute and determined*
> *there is time and opportunity.*
> Ralph Waldo Emerson

confident of a PB. She would be a formidable opponent. Not to mention the Chinese. Susie was going to have the race of her life ...

'Laurie, I put my arm round her to comfort her and straight away those vultures, the press, start the camera as though she is crying for losing ... nothing could be further from the truth ... so I abuse them, take her inside and we both shed a few tears. I tell you, Laurie, she is going to be real tough in that 200 'fly tomorrow. She wasn't crying because of weakness ... It was just a release of emotion ... a way of getting ready for tomorrow ... she's going to be tough.'

That was not what I wanted to hear. Still, Susie was a racer, and she was in good form. It would be a great race, may the best girl win. That's what the Olympics are all about.

'What instructions would you give someone like that before they race, Richard?'

'Summer's not a real technical person ... she needs to swim with rhythm ... so I don't want to complicate things too much with split times and strategies ... you can see by her attitude to the race tomorrow she is confident of a PB, so I'm just going to reinforce this and get her to savour the Olympic experience. If she does this she will be hard to beat even if the Chinese are on steroids.'

'Really! Do you believe they are on steroids?'

'Laurie, they're cheats!' Richard was starting to get agitated.

'They are big girls aren't they?

'They are not girls, they are monsters! It's a disgrace! They are a scourge on our sport. They are cheating good, honest hardworking athletes out of their rewards. We have to stop them.'

Richard was visibly perturbed by this subject. I had clearly touched an open nerve.

'Maybe their talent identification is better than ours and they just work harder. Look at their runners. Ma Juren, the coach, makes them run a marathon every day at altitude. Maybe they are not on steroids. Maybe they just work harder than our girls,' I challenged.

'Laurie!' he exploded. He was really, really angry. 'If you believe that you believe in the tooth fairy.'

'Richard, you have to keep an open mind.'

'No way!' he exploded again, even louder. Three athletes seated in the front of us turned around. 'It's the old East German system all over again! Why aren't their men so damn good if they have such marvellous talent ID and such great training programs? No way Laurie! No way.'

'Richard, I just ...'

'Look,' he interrupted, 'I have four female athletes on this team and I just want them to have a fair opportunity to get a medal ... no cheats.'

The three athletes in front turned around and spontaneously applauded.

'Angie Westercreig [a US butterfly swimmer] is 27 years old, her first Olympics, she deserves to have a fair shot at a medal!'

'Angie's in your program?' I wanted to change the topic before the veins in Richard's neck burst. 'What's she like?'

'Olympic Village!' the bus driver called. The trip back from the pool seemed to fly ... I couldn't even remember getting on the bus.

'I'll go and see Bernie, Susie's coach, see if she's going to be ready for tomorrow. Wonder what Bernie's instructions will be? Gee, it's going to be a great race,' I thought.

Next day Susie put up a great race. She led Summer and the Chinese 'flyer for three quarters of the race before fading and collecting the bronze.

Her Olympic gold would have to wait!

Nothing in the world can take the place of persistence. Talent will not; nothing is more common than unsuccessful men with talent. Genius will not; unrewarded genius is almost a proverb. Education will not; the world is full of educated derelicts. Persistence and determination alone are omnipotent.

Calvin Coolidge

12 — Susie's Story
An insight into a champion

I'd been wanting to sit down and have a good yarn with Susie O'Neill for a long time. I'd admired and watched her progress from a skinny 15-year-old who narrowly missed selection for the Seoul Olympics to bronze medallist in Barcelona to Olympic champion in Atlanta. I'd nicknamed her the 'Smiling Assassin' because of the tradesman-like way she demolished her opponents in the pool, and her ferocious competitive spirit. Her easy smile, short-cropped blonde hair, clear skin, casual dress and bright eyes gave no outward sign that she was Olympic champion. She could easily have been the girl next door.

She breezed in with her cheery smile and sat down opposite; I turned on my mini-disc recorder and spoke first …

'Susie, you remember when you were a little girl and how you got involved in swimming?'

'Sure, as a family we always went to the beach at Christmas and I spent lot of time in the water. Later, in our school swimming program, I showed some talent in the water. When I started winning some races Mum took me to the local pool and I started swimming a couple of mornings a week.'

'Was Bernie your first coach?' I asked, completely at ease in her company.

'Yes, Mr Wakefield had a group at the pool called his "Super Sevens", who swam for an hour.'

'So Mum's the culprit; she got you involved in all of this?'

'Yes, but it was fun and I really only swam for health and fun.'

'Tell me about those early days with Bernie and his Super Sevens?'

'Oh, swimming was really, really fun. We swam from seven to eight

The big video screen at the Atlanta Olympic pool closes in on Susie O'Neill during the presentation ceremony after the 200 metres women's butterfly.

in the mornings. I suppose that's why he called us his Super Sevens. We had 45 minutes of swimming and always the last 15 minutes of games and squeals and cheers.'

'What games?'

'Oh, relays, water volleyball, really fun things. I couldn't wait to get to the pool each day. Around the pool we used to play touch footy, throw the frisbee or bounce on the trampoline. It was so much fun.'

'Isn't swimming fun now?'

'Yeah! Swimming is still fun but it's not the same as it was when I was little.'

'Tell me about your family, your mum?' I questioned.

'She's a housewife, and helps Dad with his business.'

'And your dad?'

The mighty oak was once a tiny acorn.

'Dad's a doctor ... an eye specialist ... he's pretty good,' she said and she laughed good-naturedly.

'C'mon, no touting business. I want to know more about your early recollections of Bernie Wakefield and the Super Sevens.'

'Mr Wakefield taught me to love swimming. You'd think if someone was training really hard for 14 years they'd get sick of it. Mr Wakefield made me not get sick of it even though I've been training for 14 years now.'

'Bernie loves the sport of swimming, doesn't he?'

'Yeah. He didn't expect me to come to many sessions ... he made me appreciate going fast and always added fun things that stimulated me and made me want to come to the pool more often.'

'Great! Bernie's always been a bit of an innovator with his coaching methods, particularly with young people. Tell me, how old were you when Bernie took you to your first national titles?'

'I remember it was the National Age Championships in Hobart, Tasmania.'

'What do you remember?'

'How freezing it was in that outdoor pool, and winning the 100 metres backstroke.'

'You won the 100 back? Look out Nicole!' I joked.

'Yeah, I swam backstroke because I always used to stop in my freestyle races. I didn't like my head in the water. I used to get really scared and stop. I'd win the 100 backstroke at State titles but never finish the 100 freestyle.'

'Doesn't sound like a real good start in the swim career of an Olympic butterfly champion.'

'Oh, butterfly was worse! I didn't do too much butterfly. I hated

Susie in Barcelona, where she gained bronze in the 200 'fly.

racing butterfly. I used to get that feeling when you go out in a big surf ... that claustrophobic breathing feeling.'

'I never knew our Olympic champion used to be a scaredy cat as a little girl!' I said. 'But tell me, how old were you when you went to your first open nationals?'

'I was 14,' she answered. 'It was the 1988 Olympic trials for Seoul in Sydney.'

'That's right, you were close to making the team.'

'I got second in the 100 metres butterfly — 62 point something seconds.'

'Did Janet Tibbits beat you?'

'No! Fiona Alessandri from Western Australia.'

'You were unlucky! I think they should have taken you to Seoul.'

Susie smiled.

'You should have been a selector ... I wish they had taken me. I would have been to three Olympics by now. I don't think they wanted to

take young people on that team ... I was only 14 ... but I guess my time wasn't that fast ... I think they should have taken me, though.'

She laughed. It was genuine and unpretentious, and I remembered just what a great role model this young woman is for our youth.

'Do you think it would have helped you?' I continued.

'Oh, definitely!' she replied easily. 'It would have helped me in Barcelona. It was so much better in Atlanta having been to an Olympics before. I felt really relaxed.'

'More experience?'

'Yeah! I think everyone should go to an Olympics before they go to their proper Olympics,' she laughed, '... the one they want to win in.'

I pricked up my ears and, surprised by her assessment, asked, 'Didn't you want to win in Barcelona?'

'Oh, I wanted to win all right. I just don't think I really believed.'

'Was winning a distant wish?'

'I'm really not sure. I remember I swam under the minute for the 100 butterfly with Mr Wakefield the year before and I thought I was a chance in the 100 'fly.'

'I remember Bernie was quite sick at the Olympics. Did that worry you?'

'No, Mr Wakefield was really professional — he never let on he had health problems. I didn't know.'

'Well, what was the belief problem?'

'I think a number of things made me lack confidence. I changed to racing the 200 butterfly about six months out and I wasn't ranked in the top whatever, so I wasn't as confident as I was in Atlanta ... I remember turning in Barcelona with one lap to go and thinking, "Oh my God! I can win this!" Then, when Summer Sanders came up and the Chinese girl, I thought, "Oh no, they are going to pass me ..."'

'A negative thought came to your mind. You would never do that now?'

'No!' she answered emphatically.

'What would you say if someone came up to your shoulder now with 25 metres to go?'

'Get lost... No ... I don't know. Hopefully I'll never be in that position. I'll make sure that when I race I'm well prepared ... barring sickness or injury, that is.'

'It's interesting, isn't it? Interesting to see what goes through people's minds when they race.'

'Yeah ... obviously, I'd be a lot more confident now because I know the sort of training I've done for the 200 'fly... so if someone was to come up I'd feel I was fitter than them ... or as fit anyway.'

'That's really the key isn't it, confidence and belief?'

'Yes! Now I know they're not fitter or better than me, whereas before I had self-doubts.'

'You've gained confidence?'

'Yes. Before, I think it was a bit of inexperience, and I'd think they were heaps fitter.'

'Do you think in the early days it was a lack of racing the 200 fly that caused lack of confidence?' I asked, keen to explore the thought processes that occur in champion athletes.

'Yes, I had my first 200 metres 'fly in January the year of the Barcelona Olympics ... because I hadn't raced the 200 much I had that little doubt in the back of my mind ... I thought the other competitors were heaps fitter than me. I really didn't believe.'

As a coach, it seemed almost inconceivable that the Olympic 200 metres butterfly champion had never raced the event until she was 18, particularly in the days when there are State championships held for nine-year-olds over the Olympic distance.

'It's really hard to believe that you were almost 19 before you raced the 200 butterfly. What made Bernie say to you, "You're going to train for the 200 'fly?"'

'I think he saw an opening. First, to get into the Australian team ... I

> *If you always do what you've always done,*
> *you'll only ever get what you've always had.*
> *Be daring — try something new.*

mean, there was Hayley [Lewis] and Julie [Major], but they sort of hadn't improved for a while and, internationally, there was an opening as well ... Mr Wakefield didn't think they were that fast.'

'So it just happened? He steered you into it?'

'Yes! I used to be like a sprinter and hate the 200, but Mr Wakefield talked me into it.'

'He's a smooth talker, old Bernie,' I said, and I thought then how important her decision to concentrate on the 200 butterfly was in her swimming career.. In this event, as I write, she has been undefeated for four years and is still improving, as she slowly inches up on the longest-standing world record, held by Mary T. Meagher.

Coaches or mentors have a huge responsibility in guiding young people in life and in sport, as calculated, experienced decisions often have far-reaching repercussions.

She went on ...

'Yes. Before I left him he was trying to talk me into swimming the 400 metres freestyle.'

'The 400 free? That wouldn't be a bad idea. You could be good at that.'

'Oh, it would kill,' she said and laughed. I thought it ironic that she should talk about pain when she already tackles an event that makes the body scream in pain.

'Would you think of swimming the 400 free?' I asked.

'Yeah, I've given it some thought. I mean, if I look at it intelligently ... I've got a lot more chance in the 400 freestyle than I've got in the 100 freestyle internationally,' she answered.

I could almost hear her old coach talking.

> *Take away love and our earth is a tomb.*
> Robert Browning

'Of course,' I replied, 'you have natural speed and ... I believe you have to swim in events that you can win, or at least be competitive in ... why else are you swimming if you don't want to win?'

'That's right ... but the 400! At this stage I haven't wanted to do the training for it ... it's hard ... besides, I love the 100 because it gives me the chance to swim the relays.'

'Fair enough, but you swam the 400 free at trials, didn't you?'

'No! I swam it at the State championships in January.'

'Was it the NSW championships I saw you do the 400 freestyle?'

'It could have been. I was swimming quite a few just for training.'

'Just conditioning?'

'Yes.'

'After the World Championships in Rome you parted company with Bernie Wakefield. Why?'

'I was very disappointed with my results at the 1994 Commonwealth Games and, two weeks later, at the World Championships in Rome. I hadn't improved in two years. I felt stale ... as a squad we moved to Chandler and I absolutely hated that pool to train in.'

'Why?'

'After being at Hibiscus and playing touch footy and having fun, Chandler seemed too serious. It wasn't fun. I was just going through the motions.'

'Well, you have to swim so many laps as a swimmer, it must be fun. You have to love it.'

'Yes I do ... but now I was Mr Wakefield's oldest swimmer by far ... I was stale ... most of my swimming partners were young kids.'

'Oh, you didn't have any playmates any more?' I teased. She laughed.

I went on. 'Basically, you didn't have any real friends in the squad. Bernie's kids were just too young to communicate with?'

'Yes, and one of the things Mum and Dad had always said was if you ever stop enjoying the sport that's the time to retire.'

This same sentiment which gives an insight into Susie's intrinsic love of her sport was expressed by her in an article written by Fiona Chappell in the *Sunday Mail*, on September 27, 1998, where she was quoted as saying:

You also hear of many older swimmers who lose their hunger. If ever I stopped enjoying swimming I would retire. It was interesting reading about Debbie Flintoff-King and how she started to run for her family and her sponsors after becoming the 1988 Olympic 400 metres hurdles champion. When that happened, her heart was no longer in her sport, and consequently she didn't perform at her best. She now wishes she had retired directly after the Olympics.

It was becoming plain to me that real success will come only if you really love what you are doing, because only then will you put in the work and time required to be successful.

'So you moved to Scott Volkers. That was a good move,' I continued.

'Yeah. I loved training outdoors and now I had people my own age to train with. I didn't feel like a granny any more.'

'It was refreshing?'

'Yeah, I mean I respect and thank Mr Wakefield ... I wouldn't have got to where I am today without his support and coaching.'

'But it was time to move on?' I was fascinated as to what kept driving this young girl on towards her almost predetermined destiny of Olympic gold.

'Yes!'

'When you left Bernie, did you still dream of winning Olympic gold?'

'Yes, but after the World Championships I felt I had three options ... retire, change sports, or change coaches ... and when I changed coaches I was aiming to win at the Olympics. There was no looking back.'

This simple statement to me is the No. 1 ingredient for success. You must have a goal to shoot for! But, as I'd told my young charges hundreds of times, a dream or goal is useless if you don't have an accompanying plan for how you are going to achieve that goal, so I asked: 'You had almost two years with Scott before Atlanta Olympics. Did you plan the two years leading up to the Olympics with him?'

'I can't ever remember sitting down and saying, "I want to win." The first thing that happened was that I enjoyed the different training. I enjoyed the company of Sam [Riley], Elli [Overton], Angie [Kennedy] and the older swimmers.'

'Swimming was fun again? You got the old spark back?'

'Yes, I loved it. It was really good training with all the older people. It was good to measure myself against someone my own age. It was just great to see how hard they trained. It also gave me a yardstick as to how I was going ... when you train with young people all the time you are always good ... sometimes you sort of lose perspective ... you think you are better than you are.'

'You must have a benchmark, mustn't you? Whether it be the clock or a person. You have to continually monitor what you are doing, measure your progress. What do you think helped you most?'

'Seeing the older people train made me realise I could do so much better. I just knew I could improve so much. Just being in that environment was so motivating for me.'

'Give me an example!'

'Well, I watched Sam. She had beaten the Chinese. She had won the World Championships and broken the world record. She could back up after each hard training session and perform again. It was unbelievable. I had never seen that sort of thing before.'

'She went hard every day?' I quizzed.

'She did some unbelievable sets and she could just do them day after day. This was very motivating for me. I would be hard at it by the end of the week ... but I saw Sam doing it so I knew it was possible.'

'You couldn't last the week?'

Preparing for gold in Atlanta. Coach Scott Volkers is in the foreground.

'No ... it was frustrating, but I figured if Sam was the world champion, watch and learn from her.'

'How did you do it?' I kept probing. Just as Susie had learned from Sam, so future generations of young swimmers could learn from her. The pupil could become the teacher.

'First, I decided to hold my quality set together better and longer, because when I first arrived there to train I couldn't sustain the work intensity for the entire week.'

'So your aim was to learn from the world champion and make a conscious effort to hold your quality training up for the whole week?'

I thought of something my Dad had said when I was a kid: 'You know, son, you can eat an elephant. You just take a little chunk at a time.' But enough of my musings; Susie answered simply.

'Yes.'

'Were you doing more intense, quality work every session?' I continued.

'Yes. Not as many recovery sessions as I was used to with Mr Wakefield ... always something hard in each session ... but I knew it was possible because I could see Sam doing it.'

'Perhaps that's why you could swim hard over a whole week at the Olympic Games and still perform at your best on the last day.'

'I guess ... but now I was training harder every session than what I was used to when I was the best in the squad.'

'The training environment really helped you up the intensity of your training?'

'Yes!' I was training consistently harder but enjoying the camaraderie of the senior athletes around me. We were all in it together.'

'You had no recovery sessions? I asked.

'Oh, we still had sessions where we swam aerobically to recover but there appeared to be more elevated heart rate sessions and quality sessions.'

'Did Scott put together a long-range plan for you? I asked.

'I can't remember having any long-range plan. Rather, I just started

> *It is not enough to say you'll get there or even wish you'll succeed. Take action every day toward achieving your goal.*

training to improve for the next meet ... Scott recorded everything we did. He was my coach now and I trusted him. I really just concentrated on doing the best I possibly could at each training session.'

She was expounding the wisdom of someone twice her age and I really didn't know whether to concentrate on faith in the coach or doing your best. I went on.

'It's important to have faith in your coach ... and have a record of what you're doing?'

'Oh yes! A record allows you to look back on your training, particularly if it's been a successful phase leading into a major competition.'

'Most elite swimmers I know keep a log of what they've done. Have you kept a log of all the work you've done?'

'I did for a while but I just got sick of it. Then I moved to Scott.'

'He keeps the log?'

'Yeah. That's the good thing about Scott. I just leave all the coaching decisions to him. I just turn up for my training session and go home ... I work as hard as I can while I'm in the water. I do the very best I can then try to forget about it. I don't write it down, or look back over it, or worry about if I have improved. You know generally how you are going. I really trust Scott's judgement. What's the use of having a coach if you can't trust him?'

'It's become a real partnership, hasn't it?'

'It has to be if you want to be successful. I really don't know anyone who has made it entirely on their own. You need a good team around you.'

'Apart from trusting Scott implicitly to do all that organisation for you, do you control the other things that make you successful? Things like diet and rest?'

'You need a support team. My parents, although they were never pushy, they've never ever owned a stopwatch, have always encouraged and supported me. They never took family holidays until after the Queensland State titles in January each year ... and they showed me, by example, the value of hard work.'

'I'll ask you more about that later, but tell me, what was your first major meet with Scott?'

'It was the Pan Pacific Games in Atlanta, 12 months before the Olympics.'

'And the result?'

'I did all my best times.'

'That would have given you a great boost of confidence.'

'Yeah. It was good. It sort of vindicated my changing coaches. I dropped two seconds in my 200 'fly, which had been stagnating for a couple of years. I felt great about my swimming. It was exciting and stimulating to see myself improving again.'

'Once you can see your hard work is paying off it really motivates you to keep going, doesn't it?'

'It sure does!' she laughed.

'Was it at those Pan Pacific Championships that you were actually ahead of Mary T's record with 50 metres to go?'

'Yeah, I think in most of my 200s I'm ahead of the world record at the 150. I was at Barcelona as well.'

'Really? Well why can't you break the world record?'

'I'm not sure. It's the one thing I haven't got yet. Guess I have to be fitter.'

'Do you think about breaking Mary T's world record?'

'I'd like to one day break that world record. It would mean so much because that record has been there so long.'

Susie in KL in 1998, when she became the most prolific winner of gold in Commonwealth Games' history.

'She was a legend of a swimmer, wasn't she?'

'Yeah. I have thoughts about it in training. But I don't have thoughts about it when I swim or anything like that. It would be good to have another focus. I think you need that if you want to keep improving. I mean, I've won an Olympic gold but I've never broken a world record.'

'The record would be nice, special. It has stood the test of time, there since August 1981,' I said.

'Yes. Sometimes I think I'm close and other times I think I'm a long, long way away ... 1.2 seconds.'

'I know, but on your own admission you improved two seconds in one year ... I mean ... the world record is possible. It's there. The question is do you want to do it?'

'Yes ... I suppose I'd like to but I don't want to really go around telling everyone I want to break the world record.'

> *The barriers are not erected which can say to aspiring talents and industry 'thus far and no farther'.*
>
> Ludwig van Beethoven

She was so modest.

'I know I'm close but I just can't seem to sustain the pressure in the last 25 metres. I guess I'll have to work harder,' she observed.

'Maybe, but all I'm saying is you can't do something if you don't want to do it. That's No. 1, isn't it? You have to want it first ... the desire is paramount.'

'Yes, well this might give me another aim. After the Olympics I need a goal. I need a focus ... That's the only way I'm going to stay interested.'

'Most champions have a support team. You mentioned your mum and dad earlier. Were they helpful?'

'They have been great. I was thinking about moving out about six months before the Olympics ... they really talked me out of it ... they are so logical ... I'm really glad I didn't now. They just did everything to make things easier for me. Like washing, cooking my meals ... little things that take time ... posting letters ... little things make it so much easier to concentrate just on swimming.'

'Do you have any brothers or sisters?'

'Yeah, I have an older brother, a doctor, he's married and left home. I also have a younger sister.'

'Do you get on well with your younger sister?'

'Pretty well. Catherine's driven in what she does too. She's in third year medicine ... she's just a studyholic ... it's weird that what I do with swimming she does with university. Sometimes we fight, just like all sisters, but we get on pretty well most of the time.'

'Do you think these habits, like your sister's studyholic habits or your trainaholic habits, are qualities that have been passed down to you from your parents?'

'Definitely. They both have high work ethics so I'm sure we get it from them. It's funny, Wayne Smith always says, I can't understand how you've achieved. You've got a good family life ... you're well off ... everything is laid on for you, how can you swim so well? Why do you work so hard?'

'Wayne's a journo, he loves a good scoop?'

'Yes, but that's the dumbest question I've ever heard. My parents are successful because they work at it and they have set a terrific example for me and my brother and sister to follow. Everyone is born with talent in some field or other — it is how you use that talent. I never just achieved in the pool, and a doctor's degree just didn't fall into my father's and brother's laps. After the Olympics, you see, lots of people do well but never come back. They seem to lose interest in swimming and forget about the hard training.'

It was refreshing to hear a young woman speak with such wisdom and humility. So it was no surprise to me to see her magnificent achievements at the Commonwealth Games in Malaysia. Her results were spectacular — a fabulous 2:06.60, inching closer to Mary T's world record of 2:05.96, as well as eclipsing the great Michael Wenden's record of most gold medals ever by an athlete at the Commonwealth Games. Financial rewards and endorsements are now a *fait accompli* so, in this modern day of athlete greed and grab, how refreshing was it to read Susie's quote in Fiona's Chappell's article, post Malaysia:

If ever I stopped enjoying swimming I would retire ... I never want to swim for money or for the financial benefits I can get out of the sport. I'm determined to be driven by a love of the sport.

This simple love of the sport, the great parental example, support from friends, and now a supportive husband, creates an environment that helps ensure success as she pursues her goals. It also reinforces my own conversation with Susie, who has disciplined her whole life towards swimming and winning.

Bring on Sydney 2000!

RECIPE for LIFE
Dream ...
Plan ...
Work ...
Persist ...
Refocus ...

Peter Antonie

13 — Hail Antonie!
The legend of Australian rowing

When their breath's like a blowtorch igniting your ear
And the slash of their spikes are closing and near
Reach down mate to levels your bodies resisted
Go to plateaus the Gods and the greats know existed

Robert Raftery

Mostly from afar, I had come to regard Peter Antonie as a bit of a legend. However, I wanted to find out a little more about Antonie the man, not only to eulogise this great Australian rower who is so highly regarded by his peers, but, more importantly, to learn from him some success principles for life.

So I arrived in Melbourne, armed with my mini-disc, keen to find out what makes him tick and how and why he has remained one of the top rowers in the world, representing Australia uninterrupted for almost 20 years.

On this marathon journey he won a world lightweight single sculls championship in 1986 before his crowning glory, Olympic gold in the double sculls in Barcelona with his young Tasmanian partner, Stephen Hawkins. In fact, in winning the double sculls gold they became the first lightweight pair in the history of international rowing to win Olympic gold. Now that lightweight rowing has been included in the Olympics, it is an achievement that will more than likely go unchallenged in sporting history.

I had intended to pad up this story a little, talk about his bulging biceps, his fine intellect, his sensational quads or even the great little bustling Italian restaurant where we had a pasta lunch and the staff spoke reverently to 'Mr Antonie'. But such a light-hearted approach

One of the most passionate, most committed and most knowledgeable Olympians of them all ... Peter Antonie.

could not do the man justice. So sit back and enjoy, word for word, the text of our conversation, which expounds a great man's recipe for life ...

Laurie Lawrence: First question, Peter! What makes Peter Antonie tick?

Peter Antonie: Oh, I could say that when I first found the sport of rowing, basically I was a small kid. I had to beg to row, and I was lucky to get into the program at the school I went to... and, from that day, when I had my first row, I knew I'd found something that if I stuck at it, put a lot of energy into it perhaps, some day, something might happen. And it grew ... and I loved it ... and I've loved it ever since ... I've done a lot of work in it ... and ... I wouldn't trade it in for anything.'

You could feel the passion in his voice and I thought to myself how Peter's great love of his sport may be the key reason, indeed, the major ingredient for his longevity in rowing. But, more importantly, I believe his genuine love ultimately led to Olympic gold, for without a deep love or passion for your sport or work you are not going to put in the time or commitment that is necessary for success. Fascinated, I asked about his early sporting prowess for I thought one day I may be able to use this vital information to help motivate some other small kid with big dreams.

LL: Did you always row? And ... what sports did you play as a kid?

PA: As a kid? I found Aussie Rules pretty difficult ... I didn't enjoy it 'cos I was struggling ... I played rugby. I enjoyed rugby. I never touched the ball all season but I brought down more big blokes than anyone and won some sort of trophy for team commitment. Even though I never touched the ball all season I felt I made a real contribution to the team. I played cricket ... once at the wicket this ball turned a metre ... I didn't know what to do with it. Finally, when I found rowing, I found something I could do ... then I found I could try hard and get better ... and then ... get good ... and there's something I really know now — it's good to be good.

LL: Is this inner drive 'to be good' what motivates you?

PA: Yes, I think so ... but I've enjoyed it over all these years because it's good to be good ... I really like it and now I realise I love the competition ... although it's really stressful.

LL: Stressful?

PA: Yes, stressful. However, I realise you have to get stressed out, otherwise you're not going to go well ... that's me anyway.

LL: When do you reckon you first showed potential?

PA: In my own mind, the first day I ever got on the water. Someone else might say look at that tiny little scrawny kid and he's not going to do anything ... but I think from starting in the lowest crew in that school ... and I mean ... the lowest crew in that school in the youngest age group in that school, I kept on building on that every single year ... and I feel that's still happening, I'm still building.

This is now the 22nd year I've been rowing and I feel for some reason I've always managed to build on last year ... and even though I was fortunate to be at the top of the Australian standard as a lightweight in my second year out of school, at 18, I feel that as the standard rose around the world ... and ... as Australian standards rose ... I rose through the ranks of that into sculling, which is a different discipline, and I progressed into heavyweight rowing. Things that, as I said earlier, I couldn't dream about started to actualise. I managed to keep moving ahead all the time. Times in rowing improve like times in any sport and I reckon I've managed to improve ahead of that and ... I'm proud of that because it's been hard.

Here we both laughed spontaneously and I marvelled at how this man just set himself simple goals to improve an incremental portion each year. He admitted that it had been hard, yet speaking to him you could feel from the tone in his voice how his personal dignity and pride was important, and this inherent inner pride had a huge impact on his success. Eager to explore whether this personal pride also extended to national pride I continued ...

LL: What did it feel like when you first represented Australia?

PA: Oh, back in those days, that was 1977, I was in a lightweight four with two world champions who had won the world title in 1974. My attitude towards rowing with those two blokes was shut up, listen, learn, do everything you're told. Which I did. I believed that at that time I was in a very, very professional outfit even by today's standards and ... we got together and that crew was formed with the goal in mind to win a world title. Two of us were 18 years of age, which is extremely young for rowing, 'cos the average age is about 28, I suppose, for high-class performance. So, as soon as I was selected into that boat, I had the attitude and the desire to win a gold medal ...

so when we went away, we went away with one goal in mind ... to win. The two guys I was rowing with — they were not there to do anything else except win.

LL: Who were they?

PA: They were world champions already and they were very tough on themselves and us. We did a lot of good over there that year. We won everything except the last race, which we lost by one second after leading for the majority of the race by a huge margin. I blew up ... and I've never forgiven myself ... and I vowed to never stop until we won. I look back at that loss, after winning everything in Europe that year, and ... I was devastated ... silver not gold ... but ... I'm glad it happened.

LL: Why?

It seemed every time Peter spoke he spelled out interesting gems of sporting knowledge that could be stored and shared with future young athletes.

PA: It kept me hungry. It taught me that nothing is certain and, more importantly, it's taught me to value winning. Winning is good.

LL: When did you finally win that elusive World Championship?

PA: I won the world lightweight single sculls championship nine years later, in 1986, then it took me six more years to win the Olympic double sculls in 1992. It's been hard, real hard, but I'm so proud of what I've achieved and, more importantly, I've loved every minute of it. I love rowing ... I love the competition ... I could do without the stress but I love to be the best, and I know being the best involves some stress and a great deal of pressure, so you just have to learn to deal with it.

The reverence in Antonie's voice indicated to me his great love of rowing. Perhaps this, too, was one of the key ingredients to his longevity and phenomenal success in the sport. An athlete, or for that matter anyone who craves success in their chosen endeavour, must have a genuine love of what they are doing. For without that love they will not be prepared to spend the long lonely hours required for success.

LL: It took you nine years. Did you ever think of giving up on your dream to be the best in the world?

PA: There were some tough times but ... no, never ... I just kept trying to get better and continually worked towards my goal. It was easy 'cos I love to row.

LL: What was the fuel that kept that desire alive? Did you have Olympic aspirations?

PA: Yes, but I was a lightweight, so ... in 1980 no Olympics ... that was tough ... I guess in 1984 I was a lightweight, so ... no Olympics again ... I rowed at the worlds in a lightweight eight and a lot of us got crook ... we came second last, holding off a fast-finishing Japan, which is not real good in rowing terms.

LL: Didn't you feel like giving it away then?

PA: I was mad ... that evening I was sitting in the hotel bar brooding ... most of the rowers were there. The world champion single sculler lightweight, Biana Eltang, Danish guy, good friend of mine, was sitting there ... and ... being the world champion for the second year in a row he looked very comfortable, very relaxed ... and I thought, I want to be in his shoes. I've got to be the world lightweight single sculling champion — by myself — then I'll know if I'm any good or not.

I was enthralled. Here I was, locked in Peter Antonie's office in the ANZ building in downtown Melbourne, and he was just relaxing and relating the ups and downs of his great career — the dreaming, the goal setting, the persistence in the tough times. To me, this was coach's heaven.

LL: What did you do about it?

PA: I thought to myself, righto, put in a big year ... a real big year ... so I came home and increased the intensity of rowing, and I reckon everybody in the country has followed suit since then. We were training two to three times a day ... sessions of everything — running, rowing, bike riding, gym, the works ... and I said to myself if this doesn't work I'll be a cyclist.

LL: A cyclist? What, do a Kathy Watt? You know she started out as a cross-country and distance runner, don't you?'

PA: Yes, good eh! ... And I reckon I could do a Kathy! I thought I'll give up rowing and take up cycling because I reckon I'd be suited to it 'cos I'm fairly light in upper body, good in the legs and good aerobically.

LL: I'm glad you didn't.

PA: Me too! But that year I absolutely dominated in Australia ... winning by the biggest margins I'd ever done. I was a man on a mission, every training session I was racing that Danish guy ... every training session I dreamed about beating him ... I'd win by say five lengths on the Yarra and I'd sprint like I was dead level with him ... and the commentator every week would be saying 'last week Antonie finished at 45 strokes a minute' and I'd hear him and I'd have to do it again. It was great, I was gunning for Eltang.

For me this was like a good suspense movie where you wait, heart in mouth, anxious, sitting forward in your seat, hoping, awaiting the correct outcome.

LL: You beat him?

PA: No! I kept the pressure on in my training and I overtrained. I came ninth. I was shattered ... just totally shattered ... a year wasted.

LL: What year was that?

PA: That was 1985. I was so devastated ... but I thought back to the drawing board ... I came back home and dug in again ... and I realised nothing is ever really wasted ... I had a tremendous background of work that I was able to draw on later ... I won back home and got some really good form again.

I marvelled at Antonie's persistence, belief and strength of character. I thought how typical it was of the many great champions who had dreams, plans and disappointments, yet through sheer willpower and strength of character kept persisting through the tough times when all seemed lost.

'Keep going,' I said, like some starry-eyed child snug in bed, entranced by Dad's bedtime story of the white knight in shining armour riding in on his trusty steed, lance in hand, shield aloft, slaying dragons and monsters to rescue the princess.

PA: I finally got some good form back ... they just selected me ... they didn't want to, but they did ... and I went back overseas. We raced in the final, the Dane and me ... at the halfway mark I led because I'm a fast starter ... I didn't want to do it but I had two boat lengths on him at halfway ... he came at me ... and I could see him coming 'cos in rowing you can see your opposition — that's if you're in front. It ain't much fun if you can't see anyone, let me tell you ... anyhow, he kept inching up on me every stroke.

Just here I felt like jumping up and screaming, 'Go, Antonie! Go, son!' but I didn't think it quite appropriate there in his office ...

PA: I kept digging deep, concentrating, just saying to myself, 'world champion, world champion, fight, fight, guts, guts' with every stroke as he inched towards me.

Now I really wanted to jump up, wave my coat and cheer. I yelled, 'Get to the finish, man! Get to the finish!' Antonie went on, matter-of-factly.

PA: At the finish line I won by two 100ths. That was the hardest row of my life.

LL: Great! Just goes to show what a bit of good old-fashioned guts and persistence will do.

PA: Yeah! Later in the day Eltang came up to me and said, 'I got your message.'

LL: What message?

PA: Oh, two years earlier, I met a Danish guy in Melbourne who knew him and I said go home and tell your mate I'm coming to get him. Two years later, Eltang came up and said, 'I got your message.'

> *If a man has done his best, what else is there?*
>
> *George S. Patton*

Now we are great mates with the utmost respect for each other.

I was fascinated by this high achiever. As a coach I was eager to store as much knowledge from him as I could. One day it might be of value at talent identification camps for future athlete development, or I could see that simply by relating these stories to young people I just might put enough fire in their bellies to inspire them to chase their dreams and change their lives.

LL: Did you get much parental support when you started?

PA: My Mum and Dad are great ... you know ... they've always been supportive. They came and watched some of the events I was in when I was a kid and some of those when I was competing for Australia early on. They're getting on a bit now so they don't travel much. They certainly fostered my love for rowing, encouraging me to be the very best I could. My father was always very busy as a surgeon ... he came and watched me play rugby once and I got knocked unconscious ... he came over, looked in my eyes, saw that I wasn't dead and went home.

We both laughed ... great belly laughs.

LL: When was your first Olympics?

PA: 1988, Seoul, in a quadruple scull ... we finished fifth ... but I think ... that was ... that was creditable for our standard. I thought a bronze medal was perhaps achievable on a good row ... I thought really we could have got fourth, maybe, but a bronze on a good row ... but that was about the end of the day ... we got fifth on not as good a row as we could have. I had some great rows in those Olympics. The semi-final was one of the best races I've ever rowed in myself, even though we didn't win.

LL: How can that be if you didn't win? I thought winning was all important to you? Tell me about it!

PA: Winning is important to me but you can't always win. However,

> *The only limit to our realization of*
> *tomorrow will be our doubts of today.*
> *Franklin D. Roosevelt*

you can always do your best ... and ... we showed courage in that race. We rowed above ourselves ... we pulled together as a team. It was the best we could do at that particular moment in time and whether it be training or racing or working, you can't do better than your best.

'That's true,' I answered humbly, privileged to be the recipient of such wisdom from such a great man. I felt like some young child sitting at the feet of an ancient Chinese philosopher, listening, hanging on every word, soaking up knowledge.

LL: What happened in that particular race?

PA: It was very close to qualify for the final. We jockeyed for positions ... we controlled our technique under pain and pressure ... we showed good old-fashioned guts and determination ... the sort the old diggers would be proud of ... we just fought and scratched our way through to qualify in the top three of that race. So that was my first row at an Olympics, in 1988, and in my first year as a heavyweight rowing competitor — there were still no Olympic races for lightweights.

LL: When did you first believe you could be the Olympic champion?

PA: I had the opportunity to speak at a Rotary Club dinner ... I think it was probably March 1992. I was thinking about what I was going to say ... it was for kids in the area of Nunawading ... I think ... who, it was said to me, probably won't do much else in their lives ... but they've done a few things this year. The Rotary Club was going to give them some awards and they asked me to come along and talk. I sat down the night before and designed my speech and ... I thought ... that ... I'd just been playing the game of rowing in the heavyweight ranks and the Olympic Games ... to that date, I'd just been happy to compete, although I'd been a finalist at the World Championships for the last four years and won a bronze medal. I sat back and thought to myself that time I never really believed I could win, and I remember thinking at that moment ... that ... I hadn't really believed ... then I thought, well, why can't I win?

LL: You started to believe?

PA: Yes! You know, no one is going to say because you've got one leg or one arm because I've got two ... same as everybody else ... true I'm smaller ... I'm not six foot-six like some of the monsters ... I'm not 95 kilos. I'm 80 ... and I realised from that moment that it was possible that it could happen ... I didn't know how it was going to happen but by deciding and realising it could happen ... that there was no real reason why not ... I think that was a major milestone ... and I carried that belief with me right into the Olympic Village.

LL: Tell me a little about the Village and your thoughts there.

PA: We were pretty relaxed ... Steven's a quiet sort of bloke ... we were in the rowing village, a very peaceful setting ... we were busy with the rowing sessions ... we had the odd imagery and strategy session but by then our strategy was well worked out. Steven used to hit the hay about 8.30, put the ear plugs in and the eye shades on, and leave me to prowl around the place till about midnight 'cos I don't sleep a lot ...

LL: You had a lot of time to think?

PA: One night I'm wandering around and I realise I don't know 'Advance Australia Fair' ... it was 'God Save the Queen' when I was in kindergarten ... I thought ... this proves I'm not serious, so I'd better learn it, because we're going to have to sing the thing ... so in the dark, with Hawkins in the next cot with his eye shades on, I'm learning to recite the national anthem ... while cleaning the teeth, I'd think ... just drop the head so they can put the medal over the neck ... fantastic.

LL: Belief is an amazing thing.

PA: Yes, nothing happens unless you believe.

LL: Belief can be the catalyst for action.

PA: You're quite a philosopher.

LL: No, I just love to hear why people are successful, so back to you. When was the turning point in your career in terms of winning Olympic gold?

PA: That was ... no doubt ... and ... also the occasion of the final selection.

LL: Why?

PA: That '92 selection trial was the time Hawkins and I rowed together for the first time in a racing situation.

LL: It was good?

PA: Good? It went like a rocket.

LL: How?

PA: It was a natural thing. It was just brilliant.

LL: What happened?

PA: We were winning it easily. The race was going according to plan. We were comfortably in the lead, Steven was supposed to make the calls ... and in the last quarter of the race, as in 500 metres ... not a word ... the effort's there ... we're building the pressure ... we're building the tempo ... building a rating ... we're going faster ... there's no lagging, but the words are not there ... words like ... 'build' ... 'up' ...

LL: You actually call in the race to go faster?

PA: Oh yes, over the last 250 words like 'up' then every 10 strokes 'up' again as in ... up the intensity, up the effort, up the boat speed. There were no words. It was all happening. We were flying, but no words. At the end of the race it was posted as a brilliant time, six ten, which is extremely fast. We won comfortably. I felt like a million dollars ... pretty happy knowing we were selected for sure ... I turned around to say to Steven how good it was and there he was, flat on his back, completely breathless and exhausted, and I thought now I know why he couldn't get the words out.

LL: It takes a special type of person to be able to completely spend themselves in a race. These are the types of people who win when they are not supposed to.

> *It's not the size of the dog that counts*
> *but the size in the bite of the dog.*
> Australian women's hockey collection

PA: Yes, and this was exactly the type of person I needed to row with.

By now, Antonie's enormous pride and desire to be the best was obvious, but I was interested how the old man of rowing came to be partnered with this young kid.

LL: Well how did you happen to choose Hawkins as a partner?

PA: At the end of '91, when I came fourth in the single, I thought, righto, if I have a great row next year in Barcelona in the single I'll win the bronze ... now if I have a magic row, a beauty, a career best, I'll win the silver ... if everybody gets crook I'll win the gold ... I really believe that ... it was just going to be that tough.

LL: That's not like you to talk like that.

PA: That's being realistic ... I mean, I know it's possible ... but you also have to look ahead and be realistic ... so I thought I need someone to team up with and make a real good team, then I know we can win it.

LL: So, after careful analysis, realistically you believed you had a better chance in the double?

PA: Right ... remember, I know the opposition ... I see them every year ... a man's not stupid and I like to win ... so do what you have to do to win.

LL: You wanted to give yourself a better chance?

PA: I figured I needed a monster — a six foot six, 95-kilo champion monster ... goes all day ... lactate monster ... the works.

I couldn't help smiling to myself as he went on.

PA: We rowed the domestic season ... we have the trials ... we have fairly exhaustive trials ... four major races ... all the big blokes getting sick, falling by the wayside ... and someone said to Hawkins, 'Why don't you row heavyweight also and go for the Olympic Games?' We row the national titles and I'm in front, then my coach screams out from the side of the rowing course 'watch Hawkins'... there's about 700 metres to go on the 2000-metre journey ... he's sprinting to the line ... hammering ... as if it's 200 metres to go ... and ... he's rowed past me ... I had to respond immediately at that time and jump straight on it ... eventually I got through him, beat him by about a length ... we both rowed extremely fast times.

LL: That's where you got respect for him?

PA: Yes, and the selectors said how about you two row a double and in three weeks we test you again against the best of the others. We did that.

LL: What were your feelings?

PA: I thought, well, he's not the big guy ... he's not the six foot sixer ... he's not the 95-kilo monster I wanted ... he's 73 kilos max ... he's five foot eight in his socks ... the opposition will laugh at us for sure ... and they did ... but as soon as we had our first race for selection ... I knew it was a medal for sure ... and after our first race in Europe ... where we came second after a very, very conservative start which I'm not known for ... I rowed very conservatively in the start and we started our run too early at the line and ran out of legs just at the end ... I thought this thing has got gold all over it if we can do it right.

LL: Was Hawkins a good technician?

PA: Top shelf.

LL: Why?

PA: I think he grew up on this long rowing training at the two millemol lactate level introduced by the East Germans ... extremely high pressures but lower stroke rating ...

LL: Is that all?

PA: No, Tim McLaren, who coached him and who coached us for the Olympics, has a fine attention to technique. If it was 95 per cent right it was 100 per cent wrong. He just doesn't let anyone take any shortcuts, which so many coaches do.

This was music to my ears, because in my travels I see too many coaches standing around training venues not communicating with their athletes, just talking to interested parties around them, accepting mediocrity from their charges. If you accept mediocrity at training then you can only expect mediocrity when you race.

LL: Did this help your technique?

PA: Yes, even though I was so much older than him, I learned from him.

LL: How?

PA: I had to lift my game. I couldn't believe the mental concentration. It was every stroke the same, just churning it out, churning it out ... and ... I had to raise my standards of consistency to meet him.

LL: You let a young kid teach you?

PA: You're never too old to learn. There's no question I learned from him. If we were hit by a gust of wind or there was a ship going by or the water was a bit choppy I'd find my effort levels were varying but this kid was concentrated and composed ... bang ... bang ... bang ... perfect stroke all the time ... bang ... bang ... bang ... and I'm sure that was transposed into his racing. That mental concentration really shone through ... the coach had to take a lot of credit for this, so I thought, shut up, watch and listen to this bloke's coach 'cos he must know something.

LL: But he's 10 years your junior, isn't he?

PA: At least ... go back, '86 I won the gold in the single and the eight won the gold in the eight ... Tassie rowing club invited us down to Hobart for a night ... Steven must have been about 14 and I think I gave him a T-shirt, someone told me ... he got one of my old boats ... the boat builder sold it second hand to Steve's old man ... I reckon that gave him a bit of a buzz to go for it at that early age ... now, rowing with him, it's amazing ... the guy never stops ... his attention to detail and good application has taught me a lot ... it really has ...

I marvelled at Antonie's humility and his willingness to listen and learn, even though he was by far the most experienced sculler in the country. It was evident that he was prepared to listen and change if it was going to improve his boat speed.

LL: You spoke of Hawkins' mental toughness. I'm interested …

PA: He's the sort of person who can pull out something extraordinary. I was lucky to have him as a partner, yet …

LL: Yet to look at him you couldn't pick him as even a casual rower, let alone Olympic champion?

PA: True, but … he exerts himself so much to win that he'll suffer for months after … he'll just pull out a monster … and it'll put him down … like after last year when he wasn't properly recovered from training and racing in Mexico — he went to the World Championships and was leading this mad Scottish lightweight sculling world champion … Steve just faded and suffered over the last 100 metres and the Scottish bloke got through.

LL: Lots of people fade in the last 100 metres, Peter … everyone suffers if they're fair dinkum and having a dig.

PA: True, but one hour after the race he still had an elevated heart rate from the exertion, his heart was just thumping and wouldn't go down … he couldn't warm down … they had to get an ambulance … they have boats at regattas to rescue people because if you fall out when you're exhausted you can drown … he couldn't get his medal … they dragged him off the course … a lot of distress. That's the sort of bloke he is. He can dig real real deep, real deep, which is hard in the single 'cos the only momentum is generated by the sole person. Steven's the sort of person who can get that little extra out of himself. He has unbelievable mental strength. I tell you, there's only one Stephen Hawkins.

LL: There's only one Peter Antonie, too!

PA: You said that. I didn't. I don't want to push my case.

LL: So you found for your partner not a monster, but a tough little bloke with an extraordinary mental capacity … What else did you do to help to give you that elusive Olympic edge?

Peter with Stephen Hawkins after achieving gold in Barcelona.

PA: Once we were selected, I went down to Tassie for about two months. Plus we had a couple of long weekends. These were at Lake Barrington, in northern Tassie. They were great bonding sessions ... for us and the coach. We sat down with our coach and determined our goals and made plans as to how we would actualise these goals. Because I'd rowed in teams that had won medals internationally I knew that the gold was a distinct possibility as this thing, in my mind, was far and away better and had more potential than any of these other combinations.

LL: These long weekend camps were valuable?

PA: Yes. In other meetings there we designed our race strategy, the words we liked to hear ... the few words we say down the rowing course ... when we are going to put in the big effort down the course ... when we are going to build it up ... when we are going to look for the run of the boat ... when we're going to look for the togetherness ... the feeling ... the acceleration of the power through the drive of the stroke ... the smoothness ... the control ... all that sort of stuff ... we'd have key words, one word to bring out those factors ... we built that through those meetings.

LL: It must have been peaceful up there.

PA: We had relaxation sessions as well, all the way into the Olympics. We started those there in Tassie.

LL: How did you do that?

PA: The coach would go through a sequence. We'd chill out a bit, relax ... go through different portions of the race ... then, later, whenever we travelled, we continued these relaxation sessions in hotel rooms.

LL: What about in the Olympic year, anything special?'

PA: Throughout '92, as part of our Olympic preparation, there was a mental component ... relaxation and imagery ... planning ... discussing how we were going to race ... getting it all in order, rehearsing it ... I think it's important.

LL: Did you use a psychologist for this?

PA: No! This is the coach ...

LL: The coach?

PA: I reckon that's the way it's got to be. I really do, unless ...

At this point I couldn't help myself. Instead of listening, I butted in. I put my coaching hat on again and had to have my two cents' worth.

LL: As a coach ... I think a psychologist can be a crutch to cling to ... like a life buoy ... something the athlete should not need. I think, as a coach, it's your duty to make your athlete tough and independent ... and this, I believe comes from solid preparation ... doing tough things in training ... that's what builds confidence. I don't mind group sessions, using a psychologist to explain and to teach them mental rehearsal or imagery, but one on one — no way! When the gun goes they are on their own, and it is vital for a coach to develop independence in his charges.

PA: Yeah! You are probably going to go and see someone if you need help, but you shouldn't need help. It should be addressed. It's part of the organisation you need to have looked into. It's part of the total picture ... we went to the AIS in late '91 for a very preliminary selection for the Olympic team. These are the people in attendance with a chance of making the rowing team ...

LL: These are your opponents?

PA: Yeah! The selectors were looking at the likely people ... we had this meeting and this sports psychologist rolled in. I'm looking at the guy next to me, another rower, and I'm thinking I want to tear your throat out ... it's me or him or some other bloke who's going to make the team. The sports psych comes in and starts talking about teamwork. This is six months before the actual team's been selected and there are double the people there ... at that stage it's not teamwork, it's dog eat dog ... and so it should have been.

LL: How did you work on your imagery?

PA: I did it with the coach, but when I first started this I just couldn't do it. I couldn't concentrate ... but in the end I was right into it.

LL: How did you overcome this?

PA: Tim just kept persevering. He'd set the scene ... we'd have to close our eyes and imagine it.

LL: Such as what?

PA: Oh, it's a warm sunny day ... glassy water ... blue sky ... you're in lane three ... lane one is Canada ... lane two Poland ... four is Austria ... the favourites ... the Dutch are there, Olympic champions, lane five ... and Spain are lane six.

LL: Would he take you through the whole race?

PA: Sometimes ... but sometimes we'd just do a section of the race ... say it was the third 500 ... Tim would say, 'Go into it now.' And I'd know that about five strokes in Steven would say the word 'there' because we discussed and planned it at those weekend meetings at Lake Barrington in Tassie ... I'd know he'd say it halfway through the stroke and we'd both feel the acceleration through the stroke to the finish ... so that's how we'd be rowing ... he'd say 'there' about three times then I'd join in ... we'd both say it together ... so that we'd get the power together from the middle to the finish of the stroke ... this makes the boat really run fast and smoothly ... we'd keep our eyes closed, imagining the boat flying as we called 'there' in unison ... we'd dish that up for another 25 strokes and we'd be at about 750 to go ... at that stage we'd see some of the opposition fade out of the picture ... the good crews would be hanging on ... at 750 Steven would call 'squeeze' ... a little bit more, a little bit more, which was irrelevant because we were already totally extended ... but on 'squeeze' we would apply even more pressure to sustain the power to the finish ... but it was done in the context of smooth rowing, the technical perfection that Tim insisted on under the extreme pressures that are brought to bear in a race situation ... it was there that we just gapped the remaining crews completely as we'd take it through to the finish ... sometimes Tim would have us imagine another crew fighting us for the gold ... but we always won because of our better technical control under pressure ... and that's the way it turned out — even though during the race the Austrians were there, I just knew they could not sustain the pressure because I knew from our imagery sessions and our training what we were going to do down the home straight.

LL: We both agree that the mental side is of vital importance, probably the difference between winning and losing, but everyone is going to get beaten at some stage in their career unless you're Dawn Fraser or Herb Elliott. So what goes through your mind when you get beaten ... how do you keep going?

PA: As soon as it happens I'm working out what I'm going to do about it ... as soon as it happens. Probably ... I'll say good luck to the other guy ... he's better than you on the day and you can't deny that fact ... I don't go out and kick the dog or anything like that ... but I start to think after a little while ... why did this happen? And start getting ready, immediately, for the next one.

LL: Refocusing!

PA: Yes.

LL: Part of the Peter Antonie recipe for life?

PA: Yes, that's why, when I was world champion, Olympic champion ... to me they're the greatest things that have happened to me, but it lasts ... oh ... world champion? ... Ah ... 20 minutes ... Olympic champion? ... a couple of days ...

LL: Why?

PA: Because I know what's happening. There is someone there already training ... already ... to beat you ... the next campaign has already started. What you are is the Olympic champion for the four years past. It's time to start the next campaign.

I thought seriously about what he'd said. It was the Antonie philosophy on refocusing. It was a pretty basic philosophy. Once the crop has been harvested the wise farmer starts preparing the ground for the next crop. Refocusing is probably the one thing that appears to be lacking in many international stars, but for Antonie it was meat and potatoes, the very basic ingredient for future successes.

LL: You start straight away?

PA: Yep! The minute you start to bask in your own glory and fail to maintain solid preparation the opposition will latch on to your jugular.

LL: Once you're the champion everybody wants you?

Peter (left) and Stephen called their boat the 'John Coates', after the President of the Australian Olympic Committee. John Coates AO had been a section manager of the rowing team in Montreal in 1976, aged just 26, before moving through the rowing administration ranks all the way to the top of the AOC.

PA: Yes! I know because that's the way I feel.

LL: To change tack a bit, who's the greatest coach you know?

PA: Rowing? Unquestionably, Rusty Robinson!

LL: What's so special?

PA: Oh, when I trained with Rusty we would do some exceptional things. When you looked at it on paper at the end of the session you'd say that's not a lot of hard strokes, but it was more the way you did it.

LL: Why?

PA: Because of the nature of the guy, you would row every stroke as if it was the only stroke you would ever row in your life ... sometimes you'd be rowing and he'd say, 'We are going to do a bit of work up

Allsport

here.' And he'd just say the words, 'From now.' ... And you didn't know till when.

Peter let out a loud chuckle as he remembered Rusty. Then he continued.

PA: He could make you chase your dream. You'd tear your heart out for him. That was the nature of the guy. One of the two greatest people I know in the sport of rowing ever ... oh some of the sessions were just the hardest things I've ever done. You'd get to the stage where you'd almost cry ... you'd get into the boat for the next session and you'd be shaking still from the previous session ... still very, very tired.

LL: What success has he had as a coach?

PA: He was regarded as the most successful western coach when the Eastern bloc was big ... he coached the Olympic gold in the four for New Zealand in 1968 ... the Olympic gold for the eight, which is like the blue ribbon event, so they say, for New Zealand in '72 ... in '76 they got a bronze ... then he came to Australia. He coached the lightweight four which won gold in '80 and a lightweight four which won gold in '81 and the quad scull that got silver in '84 ... but they'd never give him the real premier boat in Australia ... politics behind it. He used to work himself to death ... hardest worker as a coach I ever knew. He led by example. You would walk over broken glass for him.

LL: Is he still coaching?

PA: No, he died carrying a motor boat up the hill in Sydney ... it was a tragedy ...

Peter's voice softened ...

PA: He was the greatest man I've ever known. I would do anything for him. He was a man that had so much experience of life, and he would share that experience. He had an aura about him as far as I was concerned ... He was just a brilliant man ...

His voice trailed off. It crossed my mind there must be thousands of unsung heroes out there in all sports that go quietly about their daily job of motivating and helping young people chase their dreams, never asking for or expecting anything. Just helping.

LL: As a young kid, did you have any sportsmen that you admired or looked up to?

PA: As far as rowing heroes ... Australia had a whole host of world professional rowing champions in the late 1800s. It's hard to know a lot about them. They were champions of their day. I love reading about them ... but the greatest sculler Australia's ever had, I reckon, is Bobby Pearce, '28 and '32 single scull gold medallist ... out of Australia ... brilliant I reckon ... Merv Wood is another. He rowed from '36 to '56 ... he went to four Olympics and they had the war in the middle, which deprived him of two Olympic representations. He won a gold in the single and a silver in the single and a bronze in the double ... but guys like Herb and Dawn Fraser, who I've known from drinking in her pub when I trained in Sydney.

LL: Did other Olympic heroes ever fuel your desire to go to the Games?

PA: The only year I've never been selected for Australia was 1980. That year I trained hard, ran a marathon, did a lot of weights, relaxed a bit, learned how to scull, which furthered my career.

LL: And?

PA: That year I used to watch the 'Olympic Minutes' on TV ... I can remember the music and the narrator ... 'You stand on the dais, you get the wreath on your head ... they give you the medal you are Olympic champion' ... and I wasn't going!

He thumped his hand as if he remembered not going. 'Weren't they great?' I enthused, focusing on the TV series.

PA: People like Zatopek, 5000 metres, 10,000 metres and the marathon ... the guy's had the greatest career of all time ... other champions like Lasse Viren, 5000 and 10,000 metres, 5000 and 10,000 metres ... in one of those wins he fell over, hit the ground, bounced up and gave chase ... not one moment in that race of any negative thought ... I reckon that's the greatest thing I've ever seen.

LL: It was amazing!

PA: I could go on and on ... Al Oerter, Abebe Bikila. Yes they all played their part. They gave me the dream.

LL: But you need more than just a dream?

PA: Sure! A dream without a plan and hard work is merely a fantasy.

Add to that the old Antonie persistence and refocus and you have a recipe for life.

He wanted to win, but not more than anything. Coach Wooden wanted to win very much but within the rules, within the guidelines he had set for the expression of his own and his players' competitive talent. Within those, he went all out. He understood the game totally. He eliminated the possibility of defeat.

Kareem Abdul-Jabbar on John Wooden

14 — Hockey Champs
Cutting no corners

I checked my camera bag, made sure I'd packed the long zoom and three extra rolls of Kodak Gold 400 ASA. Someone had told me that if you wanted action shots at the Olympic Games you needed 'fast film'. I glanced at my watch, dwelling momentarily on the Australian flag and Olympic rings on the face. The watch, a Seiko, was a spur-of-the-moment gift from Mike Bushel at an Olympic fundraising dinner, and since the function I'd scarcely had it off my wrist. I still had half an hour before the bus was to depart so I systematically started to cover my face and arms with 15+ sunscreen to get some protection from the searing Atlanta rays.

It was sweltering outside. The drink machines were continually being milked of water and Isosport by thirsty Australian athletes housed at Georgia Tech. They were following coaches' and medical advice to keep well hydrated.

It promised to be a long, hot morning at the Clark Atlanta University Stadium where the Australian women's hockey team was scheduled to practise. I was keen to check out the warm-up ground as well as the competition pitch. They were in two adjacent stadiums, just a few kilometres from the Olympic Village. Clark Atlanta University Stadium is a 5000-seat facility while the main arena, the Alonso Herndon Stadium, has capacity for 15,000 spectators in open concrete stands on either side of its synthetic turf competition pitch. Herndon Stadium is named after one of the most influential early black leaders of Atlanta, Alonso Herndon, who started out as a shoeshine boy and rose to a position of wealth and power in the community. So it was fitting that the ground in the heart of this African-American neighbourhood be named after an important black man from Atlanta's early history.

I'd been told it was a relatively easy walk over a fly bridge from one stadium to the other; I was looking forward to seeing the venues first hand. As I walked to the bus I thought back to the arrival of the Australian women's hockey team at Atlanta domestic terminal three days earlier ...

It was late at night and Michael Wenden was preparing to go to the Atlanta domestic terminal to meet the team. I was bushed. It had been a busy day servicing the needs of athletes already in the Village and preparing for those to come. I'd met some interesting people and I was looking forward to bed when he asked, 'Laurie, want to come with me to the airport to greet the women's hockey team? They're due to arrive in an hour.'

Here I am in the Atlanta Olympic Village with me'mate 'Baby Huey', the 210cm star of the Chinese women's basketball team.

'Sure, Michael,' I replied. After all, I wasn't here for a holiday. 'We got a car?'

'No way! We'll take the MARTA. It's quick and easy and it takes you inside the airport,' retorted Michael who, with Olympic swimming silver medallist, Lynne Bates, was responsible for coordinating the arrival and greeting of all Aussie teams into the Village for these Centennial Olympic Games.

'Have you travelled on the MARTA before?' I queried. (MARTA is an acronym for 'Metropolitan Atlanta Rapid Transit Authority'.)

'Yes.'

'Difficult?'

'No, easy!' That disc you've got attached to your accreditation gets you free transport on all public transport in Atlanta.'

'Good, show me how you do it.' I was slowly forgetting my tiredness.

We walked briskly out of the front gate towards the MARTA. I noticed the huge pin-trading tent that been erected just on the left of the village exit. There were not many pin traders active this late at night but it was early days yet and before the Olympics were over it would become a hive of activity, 24 hours a day, as athletes and fans came together trading, swarming like bees around a honey pot.

The train ride was uneventful. We arrived at the airport with plenty of time to spare. This gave Michael a chance to show me the airport surrounds and where the bus would pick up the girls to take them to the Olympic accreditation centre. Michael in his administration role was a stickler for details.

'Baggage collection down that lane,' he pointed, then added, 'McDonald's round that corner ... coffee to the left ... the bus that takes the athletes to accreditation is at the bottom of that escalator. We'll go down now so that I can show you.'

'How do you know all this?' I asked.

'I've been out here with Lynne to check it out ... I don't like surprises.'

'Were you this big a stickler for detail when you swam?' I enquired casually.

'You have to be. I like to be in control, and you feel more in control when you know where everything is,' he said.

'No wonder you won two golds and broke two world records,' I said.

'Hey! It takes a lot more than being in control. There was a lot of planning, hard work, and teamwork in those Olympic golds ... anyway, you can't live in the past. We've got a lot of work to do for this current crop of athletes to give them their chance to join the club,' he responded.

'What do you want me to do?' I queried.

'Remember this women's hockey party is going to be extremely tired ... they've travelled non-stop from Perth ... it's now almost midnight ... with flight connections, they've been on the road for almost two days ... all they want is a friendly, smiling Aussie face to welcome them and lead them quickly through this maze. If we can facilitate things and make things easier for all our athletes we are contributing in some small way to their success.'

'You want me to hurry them through accreditation?'

'Yep! The quicker the better.'

'We'd better hurry to get to gate 12,' I said after glancing at the arrivals monitor, 'the plane's just landed.' I pulled out my Olympic handbook to check names against faces in the women's hockey section. This little book had been invaluable to me so far. I'm a great believer, if it's possible, calling a team-mate by name even before you have been officially introduced. It makes them feel even more special. I looked at the pictures and repeated the names to myself: Michelle, Alyson, Louise, Renita, Juliet, Rechelle, Clover, Karen, Jennifer, Jacqueline, Nova, Katrina, Lisa, Danielle, Kate, Liane, Wendy ... I knew Wendy ... Ric ... I knew Ric ... Kathleen, Chris ... I knew Chris. We waited. The gates opened and weary red-eyed travellers poured slowly from the plane, Olympic team bags slung across their shoulders.

'G'day Ric. Welcome!' I enthused and squeezed the hand of Ric Charlesworth, team coach. 'How was the trip?'

'Tiring!' he replied, 'thanks for coming!'

> *We must all hang together, or assuredly*
> *we will all hang separately.*
>
> Benjamin Franklin

Well the last thing the girls expected after a 36-hour trip was a couple of mad fellow Aussies here to greet them in unfamiliar Atlanta, and their weary faces lit up with huge grins of relief at the pleasant surprise.

These girls were a happy bunch ... even though they'd arrived after midnight because of missed connections and long delays on the tedious flight from Perth, Western Australia. I recognised Wendy Pritchard, the women's team manager, immediately. Wendy had represented Australia for over 10 years as a player and was now one of Australia's most respected and efficient team managers.

'Wendy!' I called. She turned, saw me, eyes wrinkled behind her glasses and her mouth broke into a huge grin.

'Laurie, it's good to see a familiar face, even if it is way past your bedtime,' she quipped.

Wendy moved quickly and efficiently among her girls like a brooding mother hen around her chicks. Soon she had the entire Australian women's hockey team clustered around her. Her instructions were short, sharp and clear.

'Stay together, girls. Follow Michael and Laurie.'

'Who's Laurie?' interrupted Nova Peris with a mischievous twinkle in her eye.

Wendy continued patiently, 'Follow Laurie ... identify your luggage ... wait together ... I don't want anyone disappearing.'

'What about if you want to go to the toilet?' Nova called. The girls laughed.

Nova, from Darwin, had first made the Australian team in June 1993 for the Four Nations Tournament in Osaka, Japan. Her blinding speed made her a real asset to the team on the field, while her natural good humour made her equally valuable off the field in building team unity and team spirit — essential qualities in champion teams.

'Girls, listen! Once you have your bags the sooner we get to the bus which shuttles everyone to the accreditation tent the quicker we get through accreditation formalities. The quicker the accreditation the quicker we get into the Village. Understand?' I said.

'Yes!' they answered in unison.

'Good. Follow me!' I turned on my heel and set off at a brisk pace for the luggage carousel. The girls followed hot on my heels, conga-style, weaving deftly in and out of the huge airport crowd. It was hard to believe it was after midnight. The girls were now surprisingly awake, alert, and happy for a group that had left Perth over 30 hours earlier.

At the luggage carousel, Michael indicated that while I fast-tracked them through accreditation he would get back to the Village and have their rooms ready.

Once the luggage was identified, an Atlanta Games Organising Committee volunteer loaded it on large trolleys destined for security X-ray machines before delivering it to the Village.

I took off again with 20 female hockey players in hot pursuit, slicing through the crowd. I was rather enjoying this, as it was the first time in my 54 years that I had been pursued by 20 young women. The nearest approach before was when I was the 'lolly man' at my daughter's fourth birthday party. After sticking lollies all over an old raincoat with sticky tape, I ran around the large back yard and with 10 hungry little boys and girls in lolly pursuit ... what fun! This, however, was a little more serious. We must get to the escalator. I hustled them like the Pied Piper.

The German team had also arrived with a large contingent to be accredited and if we didn't get to the shuttle bus first we could be up to an hour longer becoming accredited. I knew where to go, and waved the girls on. Well drilled and disciplined, they responded magnificently. We bounded down the escalator two at a time. We were first on the shuttle bus. As the last hockey girl stepped onto the bus I called, 'That's it! Let's go, driver!'

As we pulled away, at Nova's instigation, the girls leaned out of the bus windows and waved a friendly goodbye to some of the German Olympic team ... we would be through accreditation quickly. I was hoping for a world record for accreditation.

The driver took us directly to a large marquee at the airport where all visiting Olympians could be accredited without fuss and at minimum inconvenience. I'd been through accreditation three or four times with other Aussie teams so I knew the ropes pretty well. I herded the girls through the photo identification and hand prints for Village security, organised cool drinks, sat them down to relax, changed TV channels, chatted with security guards ... as a result they were accredited in record time and ready for quick transport to the Village. I was feeling pretty pleased with myself.

'Okay, girls, we're done. Into the bus. We're off!'

They cheered, walked out in single file and piled onto the bus. I glanced at my Olympic watch. It was 12.45am. That was a record for getting an Australian group through. I puffed out my chest like a pouter pigeon.

'Let's go, driver, we're all here!' I called as the last girl sat down, then I turned round and said, 'Girls, we're home and hosed.'

I spoke too soon ... a rather large security guard strode to the bus,

Ric Charlesworth, one of the great Australian sporting coaches.

Sport: The Library

237

held up his hand, poked his head in the door and called, 'Hold for clearance, driver!' Then he turned and disappeared into the dark.

'Let's go, driver!' I called again.

'Can't, guy, we've got to wait.'

'What for, mate, we're all here?'

'Security clearance. Nothing moves here till the 'i's' are dotted and the 't's' are crossed.'

'Aw, c'mon, mate, it's nearly one o'clock in the morning and these girls have been travelling for almost two days.'

'Sorry, guy, I can't move till I get security clearance.'

Half an hour passed ... still no clearance. Some of the girls were starting to get a little restless, others were starting to nod off in their seats. Nova lay at full stretch on the bus floor with a carry bag propped under her head, eyes closed, trying to relax.

'Let's go, driver!' she kept calling, at five-minute intervals.

Another half an hour passed. The German team came out, climbed into their bus, smiled, waved and, having the last laugh, called, 'Auf Wiedersehen Australia!' as they drove off to the Village.

Now the girls who were still awake were really starting to get stroppy.

'Let's go driver! C'mon, what's the hold up?' they called.

'I can't go without security clearance!' the driver replied, but it was clear that he too was becoming a little frustrated.

Just then a giant, lone security guard appeared out of the dark, boots spit polished, shining by the light of the moon. He strode up to the bus, put his head in the door and called, 'Who owns the big silver steel trunks?'

Ric Charlesworth's eyes opened wide in surprise. 'I do,' he said.

'Well, guy, we need to open them to check some of the contents. The X-ray machine can't quite identify some of the objects. Can you come with me, please?'

'Ric's a terrorist!' joked a voice from the back of the bus.

'Don' ya mess round now, girl, or you'll be here all night,' the big man called back with a slight impatience in his voice.

'Mate, it's after midnight ... the girls are tired and we want to get to the Village as quick as possible,' I butted in.

'Sir, I appreciate your position but my responsibility is safety and security. I'm going to have to check the contents of those trunks before I can let the bus depart this airport.'

The girls moaned.

'Certainly, no worries,' said Ric politely, not wanting to antagonise such a huge man any further. Who was it that once postulated discretion is the better part of valour?

Wendy, ever the protective mother hen, jumped to her feet and insisted, 'I'll come with you. We shouldn't be too long. Don't get off the bus, girls.'

I'd only seen Wendy in action for two hours but already you could see why her managerial skills were so highly regarded by the Australian Hockey Federation.

'Don't worry about me, Wendy, I'll stretch out on the floor and have a bit of a rest. You take your time,' yelled Nova, as Ric and Wendy followed the huge man.

By this I was convinced that Nova was the team clown. I was right. The rest of the girls were surprisingly relaxed despite the fact that the clock had crept up to 1.30. They were all experienced travellers, having played international hockey all over the world, and were used to delays and adjusted quickly. They had learned from 'the Shrink' how to cope with all the little inconveniences that arise during international travel and not to let such things stress them out, sapping precious nervous energy that could affect their performance levels on the pitch.

'The Shrink' was the affectionate nickname given by the girls to Corinne Reid, the team clinical psychologist, who, by her own admission, was a sporting nerd. However, she had become an integral part of the team and their lives over the previous two and a half years. Ric Charlesworth recognised the importance of team harmony in team success. He was a master at covering all contingencies, so he brought in a psychologist to be part of his team, to help resolve team conflicts, to teach them to cope with any inconveniences that would threaten team performances, to build team unity and assist team morale. The girls had grown to like and trust the Shrink.

Ric, Wendy, and the huge man strode quickly towards an airport hangar situated about 150 metres away from the bus. It was here that the security X-ray equipment had been installed to screen all bags going into the Village. I followed three to five paces behind, occasionally breaking into a jog to keep up. As we walked into the hangar one of the security guards, who appeared to be in charge, motioned Ric over.

The Australian bags were piled on two large motorised trolleys. They had been checked and okayed, but Ric's two large silver trunks were still waiting clearance.

'Can you open these two big trunks, guy? We just can't work out what you've got in here,' called a guard standing by the machine.

'Sure,' ventured Ric and he opened the box to reveal the contents.

'What's all this?' the surprised security guard asked.

'It's my video equipment!'

'All this?'

'Yes!'

'What's this?'

'My editing equipment!'

'This?'

'Camera!'

'This?'

'Tripods!'

'This?'

'VHS pal NTSC converter!'

'Why do you need all this?'

'He's the Australian women's hockey coach!' I butted in, getting a

Allsport

Nova Peris-Kneebone in Atlanta, a key and very quick component of Charlesworth's gold medal-winning team.

little hot under the collar. I was anxious to get the team to the Village and into bed.

'You need this to coach hockey?' the security guard continued, ignoring me and directing his question to Ric.

Ric kept his cool, 'Yes, mate.'

'But all this?'

'Mate, I need this for daily video analysis of my team's training performance. I like to video all the girls' training sessions, the practice games, the opposition training sessions where possible ... so I carry all my own equipment everywhere I go. I carry recorders, playback machines, editing equipment, spare batteries, anything that makes us self-sufficient ... totally independent ...'

'Oh?' replied the interested security guard.

'Do you really need all that stuff? Surely it's more trouble than it's worth?' I quizzed while the guard checked the huge silver trunks.

'I find video a very useful coaching tool ... even if it improves one girl a little, enough to give us that elusive edge over our opponents, it's been worthwhile ... it's also very useful in analysing the strengths and weaknesses of our opposing teams,' continued Ric.

'Why didn't you hire some over here? It seems crazy to carry these big trunks all round the world,' asked the intrigued security guard. I must admit, I was a little intrigued myself.

'Maybe, but these little babies are like my assistant coaches. I know this equipment inside out and after each practice with all our own editing gear we can start editing training film on the spot. It is ready to show the girls before the next practice session. The video camera doesn't lie ... the girls get to know themselves, their strengths, their weaknesses ... in this way we can work to maintain their strengths and improve on their weaknesses. It's all part of this team's philosophy ... *To strive for continuous improvement.*'

'Do the girls mind being monitored?' I asked.

'Not really. They've come to understand its importance. If a mistake turns up often enough they know they have a problem. I can show them and encourage them with drills to overcome this weakness.'

'How?' I questioned.

'Oh, I set up especially for her repetitive skill drills that will turn that girl's weakness into a strength. So by using the video as a constructive coaching tool the girls can see their improvement — they welcome its use.'

'You mainly concentrate on strengthening weakness then?'

'I don't just practise weakness, but I believe that by strengthening

242

weaknesses you make that person a better all-round player ... I read somewhere once that the great Pelé's father saw that his son as a young boy was kicking only with his right foot. He encouraged the boy to use both feet. He made him kick and rebound the ball against a wall ... left foot right foot ... day after day, week after week, year after year ... until the young Pelé had unbelievable control and equal strength and power in both legs.'

The security guards were clustered around Ric at this stage, all ears, obviously impressed. I was, too, by his coaching excellence, knowledge and professionalism.

'Has the US got a field hockey team?' asked the inquisitive X-ray operator.

'Sure!' replied Ric.

'Any good?'

'Not bad. I've analysed your chances.'

'Beat you?'

''Fraid not, mate. We plan to win the competition,' Ric answered matter-of-factly.

'What about our team?' the X-ray operator was persistent.

'Well, the record of previous host nations would indicate that they have a good chance of getting a medal. Their strength will be their team spirit, discipline, fitness, corner battery, a couple of high-quality players and good goal defence. The addition of [Terry] Walsh, a former Australian assistant coach, will give them the best insight into what we are doing and may strengthen their belief in themselves to play what appears possible. They have beaten every team in the competition in recent times except Korea and ourselves. They will be very dangerous. The home crowd cheering for them will be a definite advantage,' replied Ric.

I was stunned and amazed at Ric's impromptu critical analysis of an opposition team in an aircraft hangar at 2am. It certainly enhanced my opinion of him as one of the finest coaches in the world.

I was struck by the hockey girls' dedication to the cause, their commitment to training and the savvy way they realised that if they wanted to win, then they had to pay the price.

'You sound like you are serious about the gold medal, man?' ventured the X-ray operator.

'We are!' I butted in again, keen to skite about this amazing team that Charlesworth had taken on and nurtured for more than 50 games for just one defeat — by Spain, the defending Olympic champions, in the pre-Games 'Atlanta Challenge'.

'Well, guys, good luck. If the United States can't win I hope you guys do.'

'Thanks,' I replied. 'Are we free to go? The girls are tired, it's 2am.'

'All clear, mates. Got any pins?'

'Sorry!' I answered quickly. There was no way I was going to waste precious Olympic pins on some dope who had kept us waiting for over an hour. Then I thought about Dale Carnegie and decided I may need this guy in the future, so amazingly I found three in my back pocket. I parted with three precious pins. It hurt, but it was an investment in the future.

Soon our ordeal was over and we were bussed into the Village. Michael Wenden, ever the organiser, had returned before us and was waiting up. He greeted us with a cheery, 'Hello, what kept you guys?' He had all the keys to the girls' rooms ready. They were on the first floor above Administration. Since there were no lifts, Ric had requested a lower-floor accommodation to save the girls' legs.

'Girls, we'll meet here at 10 in the morning dressed for a light run,' Ric ordered.

'You're so kind, Ric!' replied Nova. I was starting to enjoy her humorous little asides.

I helped the girls struggle with their gear up one flight of stairs to their rooms. Most of the girls were now excited, awake and hungry, so they headed to McDonald's, just 50 metres, away for an early-morning snack. It was way past my bedtime ... for me bed definitely had more appeal than a Big Mac.

Now, two days later, I was going to watch them practise. With my camera bag loaded and sunscreen applied, I headed for the bus stop.

The girls were already there. They were used to Ric's strict discipline. 'A team can't function without all members putting their shoulders to the wheel, girls ... and ... this starts with consideration for other team members ... be on time ... don't keep your team-mates waiting ...' he used to say. They dare not be late.

They were smiling, relaxed and had positioned themselves under a couple of shady trees to seek refuge from the searing heat which burned your throat and lungs as you breathed ... their first full training session was going to be tough. Most had a cool drink in their hand that they'd procured at a nearby drink machine with the free returnable token that came attached to their accreditation. Wendy was clucking around the girls as Ric approached with his assistant team coach, Chris Spice.

I looked at Charlesworth wandering along in earnest conversation with Chris. It was hard to imagine that this man, with a baggy canvas hat shading his face, his nose and ears protected by white zinc, was an Australian hockey icon, having attended four Olympics as a player. In addition, he had been afforded the honour of carrying the flag for his country at the Opening Ceremony in Seoul in 1988.

The bus arrived. We all piled in. I sat on the hard plastic seats next to Dr Tony Galvin, a four-time Olympian himself, who was the hockey team physician. I was anxious to find out more about Charlesworth, who had not been afraid to take on the challenge of coaching a well-credentialled women's team and proceeded to make them even better. Under his coaching they won the World Cup in Dublin in 1994 and since then had strung together 32 games without defeat, making them red-hot favourites for the gold medal.

'Tony, what makes Charlesworth such a good coach?' I asked.

'He's driven ... he's passionate and committed,' was Tony's simple reply.

'There must be more to the man than that?' I questioned.

'Oh yeah! He has enormous vision and reads the game well ... because

> *I do not know anyone who has got to the*
> *top without hard work. That is the recipe.*
>
> Margaret Thatcher

of his accomplishments as a player he has the players' respect ... and he does nothing but live up to that respect.'

'Is he hard?'

'He's hard all right ... remorseless but fair. He was such a high achiever himself ... politician for 13 years.'

'Wasn't he an opening bat for Western Australia in the Sheffield Shield?'

'Yes, but there's much more to Ric than that. Did you know he's a medical doctor?'

'I knew he was a 'pollie' but not a doctor. He's gone up in my estimation ... not that he cares.'

'No, it wouldn't worry Ric,' said Dr Tony Galvin.

'He studied medicine and succeeded while he was a player?' I queried.

'Yes, but he doesn't flaunt it. You know, even though he's a doctor he never questions my diagnosis of any girl's illness or injuries. I'm the doctor assigned to the team and he lets me do my job. He's content to draw qualified, committed people around him and give them responsibilities. Once you're part of Ric's team he has faith in you to carry out your assigned duties ... he works so dammed hard himself you dare not let him down.'

'He leads by example?'

'Don't all great leaders?'

'Yes ... but it appears to me, from talking to you, that his philosophy is to build a strong network of help around him.'

'He's very selective. He goes for the best ... and he never feels threatened in any way ... as is evidenced by the fact that he chose Brian Glencross as the man in charge of organising the International Tournaments and the day-to-day running of the team.'

'He values Brian's input into the team?'

'Oh yeah. Ric's the coach, but he listens to anyone. He will then sift out the chaff from the hay ... and use anything if he feels it is going to improve his team's performance.'

'It must be fantastic for Ric to have someone with Brian's experience to bounce ideas off.'

'By being open to Brian's ideas Ric can have the best of both worlds ... two former Australian captains sharing ideas.'

'I knew Brian coached the Seoul gold medal team but I didn't know he was an Australian captain. Where did he play?' I asked.

'He was a fullback ... a defensive player who captained the Australian team in Munich 1972.'

'And Ric?'

'A dashing, attacking forward with enormous flair and vision.'

'So the team is spiced with Ric's attacking flair and Brian Glencross' bulldog defence ...'

'That's about it ... Ric listens ... but he's in charge ... he makes the decisions and he's not afraid to delegate.'

'And delegating gives him the opportunity to do what he does best ... coach?'

'Yes!'

'But there must be other qualities or attributes that he has that have taken this team to be hot favourites for the gold?' I asked.

'Yes ... I guess,' and he paused, thinking carefully before he slowly and deliberately drew out a pen and started writing in a notebook.

'What's this ... a prescription?' I joked.

He remained silent and kept writing. When he'd finished he tore out the page and handed it to me.

'These are Charlesworth's strengths,' he said.

> **THE LIST**
> 1. *Plans well ahead*
> 2. *Well organised*
> 3. *Communicates*
> 4. *Gives responsibility*
> 5. *Shares responsibility*
> 6. *Expects excellence*
> 7. *Handles problems*
> 8. *Maintains pressure*
> 9. *Analyses opposition well*
> 10. *Builds team spirit*

I cast my eye over the list with interest and committed it to memory ... then I carefully folded the paper and put it in the bottom of my camera bag.

The list was burned into my memory bank, but I did not want to run the risk of losing it.

The bus pulled up. I had been so engrossed talking to Tony I hadn't even noticed the way we came. I'll have to pay more attention on the way home, I thought to myself. I alighted from the bus and followed the girls into the ground. They trooped into the open grandstand to watch the final 10 minutes of a practice match between Korea and USA. Our girls were extremely interested ... they sat and watched in silence. Ric had already analysed the Koreans as the team to beat for the gold medal. Our girls had beaten them in Australia the previous year but the Koreans had had three of their best players absent. He observed to the girls then that ...

'They remain the team most capable of scoring heavily against any opponent. Their method is sound without any obvious weakness. I believe we will play them for the gold medal in Atlanta.'

The Koreans were a well-disciplined unit — I could see why they were Ric's choice to play Australia in the final. Our girls sat engrossed, eyeing off their opposite numbers. The Koreans were fast. They would be worthy opponents ... a Korean makes a break down the right wing ... a US defender accelerates ... she slips on the slippery wet new astroturf and does the splits ... the Aussie girls groan, almost feeling the stretch ... the US defender regains her feet and gives chase.

'No way!' says Lisa Powell, whose sister Katrina was also on the team. 'If I did that I'd be on the physio table right now!'

'And stay for two weeks!' observed Nova.

The girls laughed in relief.

When the game was over the Korean girls, red-faced and dripping sweat, filed into the grandstand. They stopped three rows in front of our girls and commenced their post-match stretching and icing session in silence. It was almost a silent psych-out, as if they were saying to the Aussies ... we want you soon ... be ready. Our girls were unfazed and kept chatting.

However, they were soon stunned into silence when the Korean coach arrived. He started a tirade of abuse, yelling and gesticulating, that would have made any company sergeant major proud. The Korean girls stood in silence, bowing and nodding respectfully as the coach went troppo. He pointed and screamed at each one in turn.

'Oh put a sock in it, mate!' called everyone's favourite.

Nova had done it again.

Just then Randy Larson, the US Marshall in charge of field security, called from the bottom of the stairs, 'The field is now being readied for the Australian practice.'

Ric responded immediately and called to the girls, 'Down here girls ... pad up ... stretch ... get your ice vests ready.'

I watched fascinated as the girls filed to the two big eskies filled with ice cubes. Wendy Pritchard had them ready at Ric's request ... she was as efficient and as professional as Ric and his girls. The girls proceeded to cram the vests full of ice cubes. These were to be put on during breaks in play or strenuous training, or used by the bench players to help recover quickly from the extreme heat. Ric was leaving

nothing to chance. He figured that the sooner he could get the girls' body temperature down the more efficient and productive they would be back on the paddock.

While they were getting the vests ready, two uniformed volunteers took up two mounted fire hoses and started watering down the artificial turf pitch. Huge sprays of water cascaded into the air as the hoses were used like giant water pistols ... I really wanted to have a go — I reckoned I could make that group of gold-clad Aussie girls run for cover. While the girls prepared and I fantasised about playing with the big hose, Ric was busy setting up the field for practice. He scurried all over the field with coloured 'witches' hats'. He placed them carefully, some in a straight line, a blue one here, a red one there, some in triangular formations, others in zig-zag formation. Six portable hockey goal nets were positioned around the oval. Fifty or so white hockey balls were placed in the middle.

'Let's go, girls!' he ordered.

They moved as one. He jogged with them around the oval twice before detaching himself from the group and barking orders. On each command the girls responded quickly and efficiently ... left ... right ... high knees ... backwards ... forwards. Once they were totally warmed up they walked to the end of the field and on command turned and sprinted the length of the field. Nova Peris ran like the wind. She had speed to burn. It was obvious she was going to be a tremendous asset to the team if she had the hockey stick skills. They continued the aerobic fitness with a series of jog sprints over 50 metres. I marvelled at their discipline and fitness level. It was making me tired watching. Then they broke into pairs and started their drill work with stick and ball. Pass ... stop ... push ... extend the distance ... pass ... stop ... push ... extend the distance. All the time Ric barked instructions.

'Control the ball, girls! Watch the ball, girls! Trap! That's good! Keep your stick low! Step back, girls!'

As quickly as the activity started it stopped. Chris Spice gathered the girls around him to explain a new drill. Ric took one of the girls aside and spoke to her earnestly about her technique, taking the stick and demonstrating the stop, control and push. She listened and then worked on the skill while Chris kept the rest of the team working on a variety of skill drills.

While he scrutinised silently and nodded approvingly, I noted the way the coaches communicated. Chris worked on group dynamics with all the girls while Ric worked one on one, giving specialist attention to each of the girls in turn. Ric suddenly moved back to the centre of the group and called all the girls in. They responded quickly. I watched fascinated as the next drill was set ... a three-person dribble, a pass to the circle then shoot. One girl starts the drill and the rest follow like ants in military precision. The ball flies and spins. Water sprays from the damp surface and the ball thuds into the bottom wood in the back of the net ... straight, hard and accurate.

'Don't just pat it,' screams Ric. 'Hit it,' and he floats, skips, and encourages the team.

Dr Tony Galvin turns and remarks to me that the ball is already travelling at 120 miles per hour.

What can I say? The game's about to start and I want to hear you Aussies cheer!!!

I spun to observe the activity at the other end. A player dressed in helmet and face mask, chest protector, giant boots, oversized leggings and a giant mitt strides into goal. It is Karen Marsden, the Australian goalie — number 9. She is not recognisable. Kathleen Partridge, a former Australian team player, has been delegated the job of goalie coach. She is standing on the edge of the circle with a tennis racquet and a box of tennis balls. When Karen is ready Kathleen starts a barrage of tennis balls ... high, low, left, right. Karen's height is an advantage — at 176cm tall she is able to cover the goal easily, despite her cumbersome outfit. Her speed and anticipation are put to the test as she fends off one ball, kicks another, dives for another ... left, right, high, low.

The girls split up again. All girls are busy working on their own individual skills that are vital and needed for a personal best performance that will ultimately contribute to the overall team success. The defenders practise long passes, while the attacking players set up and practise moves for penalty corners. There is no time for inactivity; all are busy and professional.

Soon the practice is over and the girls jog off, red-faced from heat and exertion. They all put on their ice jackets before stopping at the drink station. Ric moves quietly among the girls, still communicating, trying to squeeze the last drop of juice out of an already successful training session. I watch enthralled from the sidelines. It is the first time I've watched an international hockey training session and I'm more than impressed with the girls' discipline, control, and urgency.

Now I understood why Ric is rated one of the world's best hockey brains and coaches. He took a group of good international hockey players, implemented a philosophy of attack accompanied by solid defence, then lifted their skill and fitness levels and developed them into an exceptional team that would go on to win the Olympic gold medal. His ability to bond the girls together is best described by Alyson Annan, who would score two goals in the gold medal game. Her comments on the team were recorded by Tracie Edmondson in *Aussie Sports Action* (vol.7 no.4):

We're great friends and we have a belief in each other. I don't think that there's ever been such a strong bond in any team in which I've played.

Ric's ability to get team members to sacrifice their personal ambitions is best described by Jackie Pereira who, for the first time in her 10-year international career, did not score a tournament goal in Atlanta. She is quoted in the same article in *Aussie Sports Action*:

Since Ric took over our style of play changed and so did my role, I was a bit disappointed at first but I had to put my personal goals behind me, I was part of a successful team ... When I went to the Olympics I thought no matter what happens I'm not going to be disappointed and I'd do whatever I could to help the team. I knew I was not the focal point. Sure it would have been good to score a goal, but to be in a winning team was far more satisfying.

With the practice over the girls piled into the bus dripping in sweat, still clad in their green-and-gold training uniforms. It was back to the Village for lunch. The girls were in high spirits. I sat quietly next to Ric, soaking up the team atmosphere, thinking how privileged I was to witness not only the professional practice session but also to experience the interaction of coaches with athletes and the incredible team camaraderie, a matrix that bound them together. Contrary to popular opinion circulating in the media, there appeared to be no obvious pressure on the girls as tournament favourites, rather; a quiet expectation of success. An expectation that can only come from the knowledge that you have planned well, worked hard and are totally prepared for the competition.

The driver put his blinkers on, pulled out slowly and headed back to the Village for lunch. This time I noticed the surrounds. They were depressing. It surprised me. The streets were narrow, the houses were unpainted wooden shacks, most windows had been broken, many were simply boarded over, and tiles hung broken, in disrepair, from the roofs. The yards were unkempt: long grass grew uncontrolled, trampled low in some parts by giggling ebony-skinned youngsters who played half naked in the grass or skipped along the narrow rubbish-strewn footpaths. An elderly man sat on the porch of one of these houses, puffing on a clay pipe and surveying the scene.

Australia's hockey champions have just won their country's ninth gold medal of the '96 Olympics, the most ever in a Games outside Australia.

As we approached the corner of Sunset and Magnolia Streets I could see a group of young African-Americans gathered outside an old corner store. Graffiti covered the shop walls. Two beautifully proportioned men were the centre of attention. One huge man with an afro hairdo and naked from the waist up clapped and moved rhythmically behind an upturned crate with a boom box balanced on top. The other man, a good six inches taller, with a mandatory back-to-front baseball cap, was also naked above the waist. He rapped, twisted, rolled, and spun in front to the squeals and encouragement of the crowd.

'Go brother! Move baby!' they squealed.

'Have a look at this!' yelled Juliet Haslam, who was first to spot the excitement.

Some of the girls, keen to get a clearer view, stuck their heads out the window. Ever vigilant, Wendy reacted immediately to protect the girls.

'Sit down, girls. All heads inside the bus please.'

No sooner were the girls seated than the bus lurched to a stop at the corner. The driver, anxious to get out of this undesirable area, pulled the wheel a little hard, accelerated and scraped against a stop sign in the narrow street. The driver then seemed to go into panic mode. He reversed, accelerated, reversed, accelerated ... soon the stop sign was flat underneath the bus. While this was going on the two huge men cut the music and ran across the road. It happened so quickly ... pandemonium! The bus jerked to a stop. One huge guy was standing, legs astride, arms raised in front of the bus while the other started belting the driver's side wall with closed fist. He let out a string of profanities, which would have made any old time Aussie bullocky proud. The ashen-faced driver was screaming for help into his two-way radio.

I put my head down, frightened. I could see why the 11,000 volunteer police contingent from all round the world, housed at Morehouse College, affectionately known as 'the Hood', were advised not to leave the college at night, and under no circumstances, were they to leave the premises alone, day or night. Two Australian volunteer police officers had fired my fear of the area earlier in the week when they related tales of four shootings, and shots being fired into their accommodation block each night after midnight. All security officers were transported by bus in and out of the college accommodation block for their Olympic duties, escorted by the US army and armed police ... of the 180 Aussie volunteers 90 per cent wanted 'out' after two days.

The boys kept screaming abuse and belting the bus ... the bubbly girls fell silent ... you could feel the tension in the air. It was then that Nova Peris, the Aboriginal girl from Darwin, leapt to her feet and roared ...

'Hey driver! I think our friend is dirty because you've knocked his stop sign over!'

The tension eased immediately. The girls in the bus roared with laughter ... and so did all the men. Buoyed by the effect she had on the team, Nova, ever the joker, turned to all in the bus and shouted: 'Guys, at moments like these it's everyone for themselves!'

With that she put her head out the window, waved and called out ...

'Hello, Brother!'

The girls roared with laughter again. Within a couple of minutes four patrol cars arrived and escorted us back to the Village. I'd had a great day. When we got off the bus at the Village Wendy rummaged in her bag, pulled out a pile of papers and asked, 'Laurie, I wonder if you could organise to have these typed and photocopied so that I can give them to the girls?'

'No problem. What are they?'

'They're a collection of motivational sayings the girls have collected themselves over the last three and a half years and Ric wants to hand them out as a little reminder this week as we lead into the competition.'

An hour later I had them finished and copied. I went in search of Ric, and found him in his room, bowed over a TV set examining some of the plays and drills from the morning's training session. He was leaving no stone unturned in his drive for the elusive Olympic gold.

'Ric, here are the motivational gems your girls have collected.'

'Thanks, Laurie,' he said without raising his head.

'Ric, would you mind if I went around and put one saying on every door in our accommodation block ... I just feel the girls' collection should be shared with the entire Australian Olympic team.'

'No problem.'

I went straight to the athlete liaison office and photocopied enough to stick on every door in our four-storey accommodation block ... an hour later the job was complete. I kept a complete copy for myself, and believe they are worth sharing — consequently, many of them are featured through this book. I have reproduced them exactly as I received them. Where possible, the author or source is recognised.

It's a funny thing about life —
if you refuse to accept anything but
the very best you will often get it.

W. Somerset Maugham

 **James Hardie**

15 — A Penny for Your Thoughts
The power of self-belief

As I sat in the quiet of my cramped Olympic accommodation, preparing to interview South Africa's Olympic swimming heroine, I couldn't help but remember back to Rome 1994. I was there for the World Swimming Championships with my daughter, Jane, a real water polo head.

We'd been flitting between the swimming and the water polo. I had accreditation, she had none, but we were just having a ball together, father and daughter bonding, catching public transport, avoiding the gypsies, exploring the Colosseum, sitting on the grassy embankment at the Circus Maximus sipping water, eating pizza and discussing what the excitement must have been like over 1000 years ago as the chariots thundered by, whips cracking, hooves flashing, dust flying. Late at night, after the swimming, we would sit by the Trevi Fountain, watching it dance and cascade as the night lights played tricks on its movements.

One day, prior to the commencement of the swimming, as we sat in the foyer of our two-star centrally-appointed hotel, a stocky South African strode quickly up the steps towards the receptionist. He was quite agitated — his brow was furrowed, and beady drops of perspiration filled the furrows then rolled out and down his cheeks. His hair was dishevelled, his jawbone tense, his shirt hung half out of his jeans. His wife, too, a strong-looking woman, was flustered and red-faced. She followed just two steps behind.

He marched to the desk and demanded, 'I've just had my wallet stolen, call the police!'

'They do nothing ... but I ring,' was the concierge's reply as he shrugged his shoulders and threw both hands in the air in a manner that could only be described as 'Italian'.

As they sat in the foyer with us, waiting for the police, he retold the whole sorry tale ... a crowded bus, a jolt, a tug, an accomplice, a missing wallet. They were resigned to the fact that the money was gone and they would have to move in with some friends if they were to see their daughter race. When they mentioned their daughter racing my ears pricked.

'Is she swimming at these championships?' I enquired.

'Yes, she's the South African champion for breaststroke,' he replied.

'Great! I'm a swimming coach from Australia. One of my swimmers is competing in the World Championship marathon.'

'Really? Where's that being held?' his question was more of courtesy, as he had more pressing things on his mind.

'On the coast, south of here, at Terracina ... but tell me more about your daughter.'

'Well, she's now training in the United States ... she's having a few problems adjusting but she loves it,' said the proud father.

'What's her name?'

'Penny Heyns.'

'Oh, she races Sam Riley and Becky Brown.'

'That's right.'

'Look, I've written a book of short stories about some of the many champions I've come in contact with over the years. Let me give you a copy for her. It might help her.'

'Thank you. That would be nice.'

I went upstairs got a copy from my room and gave it to them.

'Don't get it stolen!' I joked, but that went over like a lead balloon.

They left that afternoon and I haven't seen them since.

How ironic it was to be sitting at my little desk in Atlanta, fiddling with my mini-disc recorder two years later, preparing to interview their daughter, now world record holder and Olympic champion, conqueror of our own world record holder, Sam Riley.

Penny Heyns sat down at the study of the little room I shared with Herb Elliott. I pressed a variety of buttons and tried to look as if I knew exactly what I was doing with my new mini-disc recorder before finally turning on the microphone and shoving it close Penny's mouth. A rattle of a key in the door before I even started my interview wasn't very promising. In walked my room-mate, the great Herb Elliott.

'Sorry to interrupt!' he blurted.

'No worries. Since I can't get you down on tape I thought I'd take the opportunity to hear what another world record holder and Olympic champion has to say about preparation.'

I'd been trying unsuccessfully to pin Herb down to actually record some of those magic late-night bedtime discussions we'd had on Percy Cerutty and his training philosophies.

'Penny, meet Herb Elliott. Herb, Penny.'

'Pleased to meet you, Mr Elliott. My Dad has told me all about you. He was a track and field enthusiast.'

'Thanks, young lady ... and congratulations to you as well. It was a fabulous performance — I was at the swimming for both your gold medals.'

There was genuine admiration in both their voices. I thought how lucky I was to be in the company of two Olympic champions. Herb rummaged around in the top drawer of the dresser.

'Oh, you've still got my top drawer I see,' he joked.

'Yes, don't touch the top drawer,' I replied.

Penny smiled at our good-natured banter. Her easy smile disguised the relentless, ruthless, single-minded determination that had propelled her to Olympic gold.

'Penny, don't worry about him. Tell me how you got involved in swimming?' I asked.

She smiled again and replied, 'I guess living on the coast in Durban, South Africa ... I was always in the water ... when I was around seven I started swimming with my school ...'

'What about club swimming?' I butted in.

'I joined a swim club when I was 12.'

'But when did you start showing potential?' I interrupted.

'Oh, at 14, I made my first Senior Nationals and won a bronze medal ... then I just tried to keep improving each year ... two silvers the following year and ... three gold at our National Championships in 1991.'

'The year before the Olympics?'

'Yes ... I went to Barcelona ... but I'd say my swimming only took off when I came to the States in January 1993, to the University of Nebraska.'

'How old were you when you went to the University of Nebraska?'

'I'd just turned 18.'

'How was it?'

'Oh! It was a real adjustment period for me ... I came in December for the first semester and swam NCAA for them.'

'You go okay?'

'No, I only came something like 18th ... I was bitterly disappointed ... I went on home and realised that at that stage I needed to change my stroke ... adapt quite a bit and figure out the weight thing.'

'The weight thing?'

'Yeah ... because of my age I was starting to put on weight.'

'You needed discipline in your diet?'

'Yes.'

'What did you do ... did you make dramatic changes to your diet?'

'Well, I needed to learn ... when I was at home my mother was always cooking for me ... always healthy, well-balanced meals ... But when I came to the States suddenly I was in dorms and there was as much food as you wanted ... the first semester I put on a lot of weight.'

'How much?'

> *Once we contemplate success it is already in the making. For that reason, I sank my resolve so deeply in my mind that I had virtually no choice but to succeed.*
>
> Hans Linderman, who once crossed the Atlantic in a canvas raft, alone, in 72 days

'A lot of weight.'

'A lot of weight?'

'When I went home after that disastrous NCAA I realised I gotta start figuring out a few things if I'm going to be serious about swimming ... I need to know how I'm going to eat because I'll be living on my own and cooking for myself.'

I looked at that hard, lean, muscular body and wondered how she could ever have a weight problem and how she conquered it ... discipline, I thought. Discipline to treat your body like a fine racing machine. I thought then of the legendary Mick Doohan, and wondered what his reaction would have been if someone had put low-octane fuel into his 500cc racing machine. Great athletes are no different — they have to treat their bodies like finely tuned racing machines and must be fuelled only with the very best foods for maximum performance. She went on ...

'I've learned a lot over the last few years and now I know how to balance my meals for the best nutrition.'

'Percy was a great advocate of eating natural foods,' chipped in Herb.

'Go back to your packing, Herb, I'm talking to Penny, and I want to find out how she got herself disciplined,' I joked.

'I just realised that if I wanted to be successful in swimming I was going to have to make some drastic changes to what I was doing,' Penny continued. 'I needed to get my mind in order. I returned to the University of Nebraska and became associated with Jan Bidrman. He became my coach in August 1993.'

> *We will land a manned spacecraft on the moon ...*
> *before this decade is out. We choose to do this thing*
> *not because it is easy but because it is hard.*
>
> JF Kennedy, May 1961

'Everyone needs a mentor,' chipped in Herb. 'Perc was just great for me. So passionate.'

'Funny, Jan is exactly the same,' Penny replied. 'He's from the Czech Republic ... when he was 19 he defected to Sweden ... swam for them ... then came to the University of Nebraska in 1990 and swam for them for a year ... competed at the Olympics in Barcelona ... retired after that and started as an assistant coach at Nebraska.'

'So you were 19 when Jan started coaching you?' I asked.

'Almost 19.'

'How old are you now?'

'Twenty-one.'

'Your progress in two-and-a-bit years has been remarkable.'

'Yes, I think by coming to the States I had the opportunity to compete against people who were a lot better than me.'

As she spoke I wondered why it was that tough competition and higher expectations made people strive for and achieve higher standards. Why it was that seemingly impossible tasks, once achieved, became almost a daily occurrence. She went on ...

'Jan knew what was required for success, but until now I was only a dreamer, not a doer. I started to get my mind in order and I became receptive to his ideas as I watched athletes around me achieve.'

'What athletes?'

'I remember my first NCAAs. I was just as overwhelmed there as I had been in Barcelona ... and ... it detracted from my swimming ... but the mind-set in the States is that the athletes don't limit themselves ... they just expect to get better and better all the time ... I never experienced that in South Africa ... we didn't have that mind-set ... Jan then gave me the expectation of going a 1:09, from a 1:12, and getting down to a 2:34. ... I set those goals and that was a big thing,' she said, 'but it's more than that, it's belief and the courage to follow those goals to conclusion.'

'I guess belief is a big thing in any athlete being successful ... once you believe you can do it ... it enables you to. As Herb says, keep persisting until you're successful,' I mused.

'No, Laurie it's more than that. It's the remorseless march towards the inevitable. Nothing will stop that, if you believe, and your mind-set is right,' corrected Herb as he threw the last of his underwear into a carry bag.

My mind flashed back 20 years to the great Steve Holland, the doyen of 1500 metres swimmers, and I silently cursed as I thought of how Steve journeyed to America to train with Mark Schubert after I went into temporary coaching retirement. In America, Steve swam in the squad with a young guy named Brian Goodell ... Goodell watched the world record holder and saw Steve's tremendous work ethic as well as the extraordinary quality he expounded in workouts, session after session. Goodell learned that to beat Steve he would have to change his training habits, and he did. A belief was born that it was possible to beat Holland if he was prepared to change and chase. The result was a gold medal in Montreal for Brian Goodell, defeating Steve Holland, in one of the most exciting races in Olympic history.

I was pulled back to the present as Penny spoke.

'Jan made me realise that there was so much more we could do ... I didn't do a lot of mileage when I was back in South Africa ... I trained maybe five times a week, Monday to Friday, for an hour a day, maybe 2000 to 3500 metres ... that was it. I didn't even know how to do breaststroke drill when I went to my first Olympics in Barcelona.'

'So this time your preparation there had to be dramatically better?' I added, but you didn't have to be Einstein to work that one out.

'Yes, this and Jan's encouragement gave me a confidence that I'd never had before. I just knew I would reach the time goals Jan and I had set

'... to me, no matter what happened, I was going to reach those goals ... those times of 1:09 and 2:34 seemed quite achievable ... even though I was a long way off, I just knew I would reach those times and nothing was going to stop me.'

I marvelled at the steely determination in this young woman's voice. Sitting on the edge of my bed listening, I could feel the desperation and hunger for success dripping from every word. The quest for her goals had consumed her. Herb's words flashed before me as I contemplated her 'remorseless march towards the inevitable'.

'Perc used to say there's always room for improvement. Even the most perfect world record, on reflection, has the possibility for improvement, be it in the preparation or the execution,' Herb chipped in again.

'What did Jan build you up to?' I asked.

'Right from the start it's been doubles three times a week and singles the other days ... nine workouts a week. Initially we were only swimming four and a half to five kilometres a session for the first season, just because I wasn't used to it, but we were doing plyometrics and gym.'

'What? In addition to the swimming?'

'Yes, I'd never done that before. It was a big jump for me, but it strengthened my confidence in my ability to reach my goals ... I just knew 1:09 and 2:34 were only a matter of time. My goals were clear.'

'Tell me more about your training,' I quizzed, hungry for more information.

'The following year we increased the yardage again ... there were times when we did 8000 yards a session, but that was only about six weeks of training cycle, and then we'd be going down to 6000 or 6500, which seems to be about right for me.'

I was fascinated, but interested in my coaching beliefs that to be good in a particular stroke or event you had to be very stroke specific and training specific to that event. I asked in the form of a statement.

'You do a lot of breaststroke!'

Penny in Atlanta establishing a new world record in the 100 metres breaststroke ... in the heats!

Allsport

'Just about every session we do breaststroke, and there are times in the 6000 yard workout when I would do 5000 yards breaststroke ... whether it be broken up in pull or kick or swim ... but more than that ... looking back on my programs, we work on a threshold system, so when Jan says T+1 that would mean an 80 per cent effort ... we do a lot of that stuff.'

'Ah! I said, inspired. 'So a lot of quality in your workouts. Every day?'

'Every day!'

'So you think quality is the key to your success?'

'Not only quality. When I look at myself and other swimmers, we generally do the same kind of work. The only thing I've noticed is ... people get in the water and they are thinking about other things ... I figure if I'm going to be in the water for two hours I may as well be there mentally as well.'

Her simple beliefs were really starting to hit a chord with me. It was becoming more and more apparent from the conversations I'd had over the years with many great champions that to be the very best in the world you really must have the mental capacity to focus on the job at hand, to discipline yourself and not let your mind wander. Concentration appears to be that magic key that opens the door to achievements. Mental concentration in the various stages of training will allow the mind to go almost onto autopilot during the major competitions. It takes a very special individual to be able to apply the mind incessantly to the task at hand, not wavering day in day out without wearing of it. Gautama Buddha, quoted by Wynn Davis, sums it up perfectly ...

As the fletcher whittles and makes straight his arrows so the master directs his stray thoughts.

She continued. 'As for physical commitment, that's always been a plus for me and every single workout I work hard ... I just don't see the point of working out and not putting in 100 per cent.'

'You just give it to yourself every single session?' I interrupted.

'A lot of times I get broken down very quickly during the season and I will need to step back and take a couple of days easy ... and the reason I think I get broken down very quickly is that when Jan gives us our recovery days I tend to go hard as well which, I think, is one of the reasons why I probably do so well. I think this harks back to my training in South Africa. The workouts were so short that everything I did was hard ... about 100 per cent effort. I'm used to working out like that so I find it very difficult to pace myself during a workout.'

Here the great Herb Elliott commented on his own training regime and how often an easy run became a punishing training session, as his fertile imagination took control of his body and he could sense opponents on his shoulder, almost feel their heavy breath there like a blowtorch, challenging him. On these occasions, psychologically, he would be compelled to punish himself mercilessly — whether he be on forest trails, on long, lonely dirt tracks, around the backstreets of Melbourne on cold winter nights, or sweating up the unforgiving sand hills at Portsea, conquering one opponent after another. Herb was building, in training, a mental toughness that would take him to the top of the world in business and sport.

My mind flashed back to the great Tracey Wickham. I recalled the intensity with which she trained and how on occasions her lean muscular back would become blood red from the effort expended in training. Later she would slump on the blocks, cheeks flushed, exhausted but happy, having demolished all her training partners.

Often she would still be feeling the effects a couple of days later; unable to accomplish time goals set for her in training she would let the body recover by swimming aerobically lap after lonely lap. But I couldn't allow myself to be sidetracked. I was here to learn.

'You did nine water workouts. How much dry land and what was it?'

'I'd say the most intense dry-land exercise would be in preparation for these Olympics. It was very structured — Monday, Tuesday, Thursday, Friday, weight programs. They were planned to be around 45 minutes long but they did work out to be longer than that. Monday and Thursday were power days where we did hand cleans and more free weights ... you know ... body stabilising exercises and stuff like that ... a lot of power work ... then on Tuesdays and Fridays we'd do circuit work.'

'Plyometrics here?' I interrupted, trying to sound knowledgeable.

'No, the last time I did plyometrics was the 1994 season. I haven't done it since then — I've done more free weights, but then our free-weight program incorporates a lot of plyometric-type exercises.'

'But what was the big turnaround for you from the World Championships just two years ago in Rome and your incredible confidence and tremendous form here in Atlanta?'

'I think lots of things ... I went to the Commonwealth Games in Victoria, Canada, ranked fourth in the world. That was the first time I'd ever been world ranked and South Africa thought I was a medal hope ... but it was just so inspiring for me to watch swimmers like Samantha do so well ... I started looking at their stroke and I thought there's no reason why I can't be that quick ... I guess my belief systems started to work there.'

'Belief is powerful,' added Herb.

'You went from there to the Worlds in Rome?' I pressed.

'Yes, I really expected to do better there. I was seeded second going into the final.'

'What happened?' I questioned.

'I didn't swim my own race. I got caught up in the whole enormity of the event. I didn't concentrate on myself. I worried too much about the opposition and I got sixth. It was a big disappointment for me.'

I wondered how many times huge disappointments had contributed to the motivation of people, driving them to persist when all seemed lost. Disappointment and adversity, coupled with belief in one's ability and one's destiny, seem to travel hand in hand, making determined individuals tougher and more resilient.

Once we understand that failure is a natural consequence of trying, then the strong-minded can continue their 'remorseless march towards the inevitable'.

'Why didn't you give it away?' I quipped to Penny, tongue in cheek.

'I thought about it,' she continued 'I thought, well, you can give up — you've reached sixth in the world, that's pretty good — or you can persevere and make use of the disappointment.'

'Perc used to say disappointments are stepping stones of future successes,' observed Herb.

'Yes, I had to make a choice, but now I really believed ... so the choice was easy. I knew I must become technically perfect and totally efficient under pressure, with the ability to concentrate on myself and not be distracted by others around me. I watched a lot of videos and just realised I could do it. I remember saying, "I can break the world record" after Samantha broke it.'

'You actually believed you could break the world record?'

'Yes! I honestly believe that truly was the turning point for me. That was a big goal, but having set that goal, there was no turning back.'

'The remorseless march towards the inevitable,' interrupted Herb again.

'I believed I could do it,' Penny continued, 'but, realistically, I knew it would take time. Jan had reminded me many times of how the constant dripping of water would gradually wear away even the hardest rock. I didn't expect to do it in a year but I totally envisaged that I could do it within two years. I set incremental goals. It was my goal that the following season I would go in the low one minute eight second range ... I did that at the nationals and I knew the following season if I improved at the same rate I could and I would break the world record. I went to the Pan Pacs in Atlanta a year before the Olympics.'

> *Failure is so often the*
> *fertiliser of success.*

'How did you feel when Samantha Riley was disqualified there?'

'Really disappointed. I wanted to race her ... winning without your main rival, someone you really want to beat out, made the victory a little hollow, even though I swam a low one minute eight seconds.'

'What did you do then?'

'From there I went to the World Student Games ... and I think if I had actually aimed at the world record there I may have got it, because I went 1:07.84 in the preliminaries.'

'Close to the world record. Were you disappointed?'

'No, it didn't faze me because I'd always said I was going to break the world record in March 1996.'

'You knew you were well on track to break the record.'

'Yes, but strangely, training did not go that well in the beginning of that season. It was only in December–January that I got my act together.'

'What, were you slack? Did you miss training?'

'No! I didn't miss a single training session ... but there was a lot of stuff going on and I was very distracted ... I was going there doing the work but mentally I just wasn't putting in as much effort as usual ... normally it's total concentration for me. I go home and I think about swimming all day long. I just love it. I analyse my stroke, ask questions of myself. Where's the best place to pull? Where's the best place to kick? Where do I put my head? How do I maintain the wave? I wasn't doing this, I was just swimming through the meets.'

'What got the urgency back into your training?' I pressed.

'Jan was a big help; he was always totally honest with me. Sometimes you need your coach to be brutally honest with you. He was. It got me focused back on my goals to break the world record.'

It was refreshing to hear a swimmer acknowledge the important part her coach had played in her success.

'You started concentrating on technique again?' I asked.

'Not only technique … times, effort, as well, because without quality training you are deluding yourself.'

'Did you videotape yourself?'

'Some of the college meets we taped but mainly I studied my swim from the World Student Games, which to date had been my fastest. I spent hours watching that video because I really believe breaststroke is so highly technical. Of course you need strength and power, but looking at the rest of the girls I'm racing I think one of the things that really helped me was my technique, and I spend a lot of time thinking about that.'

'Why are you technically superior?'

'Well, first of all, the theory behind the way I swim, even though it may not look like it, and I'm sure it's the same for Samantha, is Barrowman's wave technique.'

'He certainly revolutionised breaststroke.'

'Yes, you have to cut down all resistance. The idea I have is to come up and over the water … a lot of breaststrokers are coming up but they are pushing the wave in front of them, I want to time my kick and drop my head so that I can get in front of the wave and the wave is actually pushing me … well that's the basic idea, anyway.'

'Anything else?'

'There are a couple of other things. I always look at the guys' strokes and wonder why they are so much faster than the girls'. I've watched the boys and noticed their kick is so much stronger than the girls. Not only was it stronger but technically they tend to kick directly back while the girls for some reason tend to kick down … maybe it's something to do with our hips. Somehow I've managed to kick back and as a result I think my kick is so much better and stronger than anyone else in the water.'

'You consciously developed this?' I asked, intrigued at what a student of swimming this young woman was.

> *I never could have done what I have done without the habits of punctuality, order, diligence, without the ability to concentrate myself on one subject at a time.*
>
> Charles Dickens

'Yes, when I do kick sets I'll be thinking about my kick all the time ... I don't just do kick sets — I concentrate on my kick technique 100 per cent, because you can't make changes without conscious effort.'

She was making a lot of sense, so I asked, 'Does it hurt in kick sets or do you just concentrate on stroke?'

'It hurts all right! I would probably build up more lactate than the other girls in the squad or even the boys for that matter. I keep up with the boys and can beat most of them.'

I looked at Herb. I could see the look of admiration in his eyes. It was obvious we were talking to a very special athlete, and I wanted to get as much of her philosophy on tape as possible.

'Penny, what makes you different? What gives you that winning edge?'

'I think most of the girls who swam in the final are all physically fit ... some may have had problems along the way but physically we are all in shape. But the thing that stood out for me is that I believed in myself ... I committed to total preparation.

Here was the self-belief factor that comes from good preparation shining through strongly in the conversation again. Many of the world's great thinkers over the years have documented its importance. It is vital for people striving for goals and dreams to have that power of self-belief.

'It must have been gratifying to break the world record in the prelims?' I interrupted.

'I wasn't happy with that swim 'cos I made mistakes in that race ... that's why it's not hard for me to know I'm going to break the world record when I swim again shaved and tapered ... it makes sense to me ... everything is so logical ... if I can correct those mistakes ... and I

The only realization of tomorrow
will be our doubts of today.
Franklin D. Roosevelt

train a little harder or do a couple of things a little bit better, then obviously I must be better and swim faster next time ... every time I race, every time I get out of the pool, the minute I touch the wall, I can look back and see where I've made mistakes in my swim,' she replied matter of factly.

I was captivated by her belief and self-assurance but I wanted to find out more of her thoughts leading into the Olympics.

'When Amanda Beard beat you in May, just six weeks out from the Olympics, what were your thoughts?' I enquired.

'I didn't expect Amanda to go that well. Up until that point I was totally convinced Samantha was the girl I was going to have to beat. Amanda would be there, but I didn't think she'd be a problem ... and it was a bit of a surprise ... in fact the timeboard malfunctioned and showed 1:05.25. The ':05' should have been ':09'. I thought, no way, that's the time I'm shooting for in the future ... that was a bit of a shock ... then I realised it was a mistake ...'

'Did this worry you ... the defeat, I mean?'

'Some people made a big fuss about it ... especially back home. They were worried, but I knew how tired I was from my work and weights and, looking at Amanda's body build, I knew that even if she was working as hard as me she couldn't be as tired because she didn't have as much muscle as me.'

'You weren't fazed?'

'No, I know that when I shave and taper I drop a lot of time ... I just have to focus on myself ... I can't control her.'

'Talking about tapering! How long did you taper for and what yardage did you drop down to?'

'Oh! I swam a meet on June 30, three weeks before my major competition, and went 1:09.40. It was an all-out race. I did a time trial a week before we came here at Auburn and I went 1:09.24 and then a week and a half later here I swam the world record 1:07.02.'

I was happy. 'Thanks, Penny, that will do me. I appreciate your time.'

At this point Herb Elliott, who like me had been fascinated with Penny's thoughts, said, 'Laurie, what do I get out of this ...'

'Ask her a question, Herb,' I said holding the microphone up to his face.

'No! I don't want to ask a question! Turn that thing off!'

I made a movement to turn the recorder off but, no way, I wanted to capture the entire conversation.

'There, it's off!' I lied. Herb went on ...

'What I get out of this is the absolute inevitability of her going to win. Penny continually thought she was going to win. Her technique was changed for the express purpose of winning. Weights were added. Everything she did in training was aimed at winning. It was there, confronting her all the time. The intensity of training was there, even on easy days. The two key points for me were the focus on winning and the intensity of training which makes it possible.'

'Were they things you did?' I asked, but he saw that I still had the tape rolling.

'No you can't do my interview now! You can't get me that easily.'

Just then Penny came to my rescue. 'Were you a hard trainer, Mr Elliott?' she asked respectfully.

'Yes! I was intense. Always in my mind when I was training I had my competitor on my shoulder and when I was running up a hill and got tired and wanted to slow down that was the signal to accelerate and get away from him. You practised your race millions of times and you always won in your own mind by never giving in. The intensity of training was there ... you finished like a mad dog, almost frothing at the mouth ... it was just crazy training intensity, so it just automatically followed into racing intensity.'

'So, logically, you're saying the habits you build in training are the habits you take into a race?' I interrupted.

South Africa won three gold medals in Atlanta. One came in the men's marathon, to Josia Thugwane. The other two were won by Penny Heyns.

Allsport

'Gee you're perceptive, Laurie!' Herb quipped. Penny laughed. I cringed. Then I went on unperturbed.

'I admit I'm a slow learner, but once having grasped the information I retain it.'

'I keep trying to tell you, Percy believed your mind creates the winning habit in training so that winning becomes inevitable,' said Herb.

'Yes, but Penny's saying she would often go hard in easy sessions depending on how she felt. How about you?' I asked.

'Yes! Same! I'd go out for an easy jog and next thing I'd be going for it. I couldn't stop myself.'

'Same for me!' Penny responded. 'There's time when it's planned to be an easy session but I feel great ... so I figure why not just go for it, this way I know I give my very best every workout. Sometimes I think I'm going to get overtrained but Jan gives me the opportunity to discuss my training with him and let him know how I feel because I'm really getting to know my body very well, and hence I have a certain say in my training.'

'Doesn't that pose problems in that you may look for an easy way?' I asked.

'I don't try to shirk anything ... but I think Jan is trying to develop an independence in his athletes, having them become more self-sufficient ... so there is less need for him.'

'Yes,' Herb commented. He was starting to revel in the three-way exchange of ideas. 'But the coach is your eyes, isn't he?'

'Of course, he has the experience!' I butted in, fearing I might be left out of the conversation.

'Well, Jan in particular, because he's been an athlete himself, knows the feelings you must be experiencing but, being a European, I think he would be quite intense,' added Herb.

'He is! But, more importantly, always he's honest. He praises, but he tells you the way it is,' she added.

'Percy was like that ... he'd stand up to you ... totally honest ... sometimes he'd tell you things you didn't want to hear.'

'But he made you think,' she observed.

'I was always honest as a coach,' I said, trying to become involved in the conversation. 'And, since we're talking honesty, would it worry you if your coach wasn't at the meet? Some swimmers would freak out.'

'In all the time Jan has been coaching me, the Pan Pacs in Atlanta and the Olympics are the only two international meets he has attended,' she said. 'Obviously I respect Jan but I know I am the one who has to race. He can't be there holding my hand.'

'So you learned to stand on your own two feet,' I observed.

'Necessity is the mother of invention,' added Herb.

'Yes, if I come in to warm up and Jan is not there it wouldn't bother me, because I've done it so many times before ... World Championships, Commonwealth Games ... I know what I have to do, whereas a lot of other swimmers would panic if their coach wasn't there.'

'He's taught you independence — that's good coaching,' I solemnized.

'Which gets back to what I was saying ... total preparation, belief and intensity in training makes winning inevitable,' said Herb.

'Yes! Do you know, before the Pan Pacific Championships one year before the Olympics, Jan had never seen me race long course?'

'I can relate to that. If you're independent you can relax more,' said Herb, 'although I used to still get butterflies in the tummy before I raced.'

'Do you get butterflies, Penny?' I asked.

'Yes! Although I must admit I've never been as relaxed around a meet before as I was at these Olympics. I really enjoyed the pre-meet atmosphere ... I wasn't nervous at all. Maybe it was the fact that Jan was around if I needed him but, like he said, we were prepared, so enjoy it.'

'What worried you about the final?' I asked.

'I was a little bit anxious for the final of the 100 metres ... not because I was frightened of the other girls but because I knew I could go faster!'

'But you broke the world record in the heats?'

'Yes, but I made mistakes ... I knew I could go faster.'

'You eventually swam slower in the final.'

'That's because in knowing I could go faster I really wanted to break the world record. I think that's where I went wrong ... I shortened my stroke and was trying to rush it just to swim faster, instead of taking my time and swimming relaxed like I did in the morning.'

This was priceless information for all competitive athletes, particularly swimmers, and as a coach I couldn't help but wish some of the young Australians with dreams of making Sydney Olympics could be privy to this conservation. This tape would become a valuable teaching aid in future.

Herb was totally immersed in the conversation now and observed, 'Laurie and I were discussing track and field and the desirability of training by yourself or training with a group. I found that in running I needed 80 per cent of the time to train solo.'

'I still disagree, Herb!'

'No, by yourself you are so focused on all of your feelings and constantly challenging yourself ... whereas, if you run with others, you're joking, you kid around for a while, you start racing each other but your mind is on the other person instead of on yourself,' said Herb.

'Funny you say that,' said Penny. 'We did six to seven weeks working out in Lincoln ... it was all short-course yards ... in fact we even worked out in the diving well because there were problems with the water for a week or so. All during this time I was training with Julia Russell, another South African, in college meets and training. We are very close and often have to race each other.'

'Yes!' said Herb. He'd finished packing his gear and he sat down on the bed to join in the conversation.

'After that we went to Puerto Rico. We were supposed to train there for two weeks long course. I felt it was too big an adjustment for me to work out long course. It wasn't going very well,' Penny said.

'Well it's a big enough adjustment having to go long course without thinking about some other girl you have to race,' added Herb.

'Exactly! I was so focused on beating Julia in training and being beside her in workouts that I was not concentrating on myself, and I really didn't know what I was doing,' she said, looking at Herb. I was right out of this conservation now.

'It takes an enormous amount of concentration to control technique under pressure, let alone have your mind distracted by competing with someone beside you in training,' Herb answered.

'Right! Funny, I had a gut feeling that I needed to go back to Lincoln on my own, work out and concentrate on myself for a week,' she said.

'That's rubbish!' I said. 'I would have been cranky if I had been the coach.' It was good to get back into the conversation.

'That's just your coaching ego,' cracked Herb.

'I know it didn't make sense. Jan and I had the biggest argument about it ... but I had a feeling I had to concentrate on my own swimming ... I really believed in my own heart that this is what I had to do. Even if it didn't make sense, whatever I believed in was going to work best for me ...'

'It makes sense to me,' applauded Herb.

'I went home ... swam hard, concentrated ... Jan came home a week and a half later and I swam the best workouts I'd done to date.'

'Long course or short course?' I asked.

'Short course! I did all my workouts apart from two weeks short course.'

'You're kidding!' I replied.

'Look, you guys are going to have to excuse me ... I'll miss the plane ... great to meet you, Penny ... great to listen to you, too,' waved Herb and he was gone.

Penny politely followed. This young woman seemed to break many of the conventional rules of swimming success, yet I knew in my heart that a powerful belief in her own ability, coupled with consistent hard work and persistence in the tough times, had propelled her to be an Olympic champion.

On Monday, July 19, 1999, after watching Pat Rafter's gutsy five-set victory over Todd Martin that gave Australian victory over the USA in a Davis Cup rubber in Boston, I settled on a plane and, as usual, turned first to the sports pages. The headline said it all.

'BROWN'S RECORD TO HEYNS'

At the Janet Evans Invitation meet in Los Angeles Penny had astounded everyone, including herself, by breaking Rebecca Brown's world 200 metres breaststroke world record twice in one day. She was supposed to be merely preparing for the August Pan Pacific titles, to be held in Sydney.

Penny had had an ordinary competition year, by her standards, after the Atlanta Olympics, and had needed to do something drastic to get back on track. In the glitz and glamour that inevitably came with being South Africa's first gold medallist (a double gold medallist at that!) since her nation's expulsion from the Games in 1960 because of its apartheid policies, Penny had lost her way. Her coach and mentor, Jan Bidrman, had left the University of Nebraska, where she trained, to take up a coaching position at the University of Calgary, in Canada. Penny swam on without him, but could not win a medal at the 1998 World Championships in Perth. It was crisis time.

Penny had to refocus or wither on the vine.

In an all-out effort to defend her Olympic titles in Sydney, Penny made what she considered to be the best decision for her to achieve this goal — she decided to return to her old mentor. The no-nonsense, strictly disciplined Bidrman had played a key role in making Penny fiercely independent. In all the years of coaching her, he had only attended one major meet with her, yet there seems to be a special bond between them, born of mutual respect. Together, they developed a new plan. More importantly, they worked hard on that plan. Without implementation, a good plan is only a pipe dream.

In five weeks through July and August 1999, Penny set an astonishing eight world records and won two Pan Pacific titles. In doing so, she once again demonstrated the importance of good teamwork and the importance of being able to refocus goals. With her Christian beliefs to strengthen her and the mental toughness and resilience that is necessary for success, Penny Heyns has climbed the mountain once again. In doing so, she has shown many future champions the way.

Where to now, Penny? Sydney and beyond. The quest for perfection is endless.

The most memorable event is always the last one. That's why I did it, but then the next one I do will be the most important one to me ... I always try to look forward ... When I'm finished in 10 years I can look back over the total thing and see where the greatest amount of pleasure occurred, but at the moment, it's always the one I just finished or the one I have to do tomorrow.

Daley Thompson

16 — Sam
Never beaten

It was January 1994. It was one of those typical balmy, sticky Queensland summer nights at the Queensland swimming championships, just a month before the Commonwealth and World Championship swimming trials. A fresh-faced smiling teenager bounced into the pool, warmed up and later exploded from block four, breaking the Australian record and missing the 200 metres world record by just 100th of a second.

A new queen was born. Rebecca Brown had arrived.

The former queen, Samantha Riley, smiled bravely, leaned over the rope and congratulated the new champion. Long live the Queen, the old Queen is dead!

Sam then slipped quietly into the women's change room at Chandler Aquatic Centre. She sat quietly in the corner away from the prying eyes of media and public, hung her head in her hands, threw her towel over her head and sobbed quietly and bitterly, trying to expunge the frustration and disappointments that accompany defeat from her mind.

'Why am I always destined to be the bridesmaid?' she whispered out loud.

Then she thought how Lara Hooiveld was an Australian representative when she was a young developing swimmer in the Lawrence squad. She remembered the Commonwealth Games, 1990. In 1991, Linley Frame arrived to thwart Sam's dreams to become the world champion and Australian darling in Perth. The pain eased a little, and momentarily she smiled to herself, as she thought of her Olympic bronze in 1992 and the national championships gold medal in 1993 but then it was back to the present, 1994, and she whispered to herself again.

'Why now? It's just not fair. Why would any just, higher being send another challenger now? Why Commonwealth Games year?'

Her thoughts were interrupted by the announcer calling for medallists in the 200 metres breaststroke to attend the victory ceremony. She wiped her tears, put on a brave face and hurried over. She smiled and congratulated Rebecca Brown even though she was hurting inside.

Just one month later I was poolside, race calling and announcing for the Queensland Swimming Association at the Commonwealth Games and World Championship trials when Rebecca Brown smashed the world record. Sam Riley was bridesmaid again.

I thought back 12 years when, as a skinny asthmatic kid, Sam was dragged by her mother through the big, wide, clear glass doors of this very pool and entrusted to my care with the words, 'I don't want any champion, Laurie, but she needs to swim to control her asthma. The doctor told us this is the only thing that can help her health.'

I looked at Sam. She was shy, nervous, skinny, weak, sickly-looking and, I hate to admit it, I thought momentarily, 'Gee, I'm a bit too busy to bother with another shy, skinny, sick kid, especially when I need to spend more time with the elite athletes training for national championships.'

Then I admonished myself, thinking of the universal law of nature, of how a handful of seeds cast to the wind can make a majestic forest. We must sow seeds before we can reap the harvest, and the more seeds we sow that fall on fertile ground, the more we have the opportunity to reap. Often, by giving a little more of our precious time to nurture the planted seed, we can reap rewards we never thought possible. Reluctantly, I turned to this skinny kid with the big brown eyes, and grinned:

'Young lady, you can train, on the proviso that whenever you come training you must complete all the workouts, no excuses. I hate people who are talkers not doers. Talkers often never reach their full potential ... to me ... actions speak louder than words.'

She looked me in the eye and said a simple 'Thank you', and then her face lit up with the most dazzling smile I'd ever seen.

'Well, young lady, if you can swim as good as you can smile you'll be a champion,' I said. With that, I turned on my heels to focus on the other swimmers ploughing up and down the pool, striving for future Australian honours.

Well, I must admit, for the first 12 months, with her asthma she was not a regular at training, but when she was there she kept up her end of the bargain. The regular committed athletes were training six days a week, 5am to 8am, and in the afternoons four o'clock till seven o'clock, as well as attending school or holding down casual jobs.

During Sam's early days her asthma was so bad and her training so spasmodic that I would often joke with her as she came through the door by asking her to sign the visitor's book. In spite of her poor health that necessitated 20 visits to hospital between the ages of seven and 15, she possessed this bulldog determination, a quality much prized in athletic circles. She exhibited this both in the pool and in the gym. She impressed me so much that at just 15 years of age I decided to take her to the Olympic trials for Seoul, before she had even swum

Sam Riley shows her trademark, one of the most recognisable smiles in Australian sport.

in a Queensland championships. There, this inexperienced kid made the final, vindicating my faith in her guts, ability, and potential.

For Sam a dream was born. She realised that if she could make the finals of an Australian championship on that much work, at her very first attempt, she would surely give the next Olympic team a real shake, if she could control her asthma and attend training regularly. She dreamed, but more importantly, she believed and started to work.

Over the next few months, Sam worked in the pool and gym beside world record holders Tracey Wickham, Jon Sieben, Duncan Armstrong and a host of Australian age and open champions. She was learning by association. She could see that these great superstars were just normal people whose success depended on doing abnormal things. She was learning that ...

Winners are different. They have a clear vision and are prepared to pay the price.

Many a time I gathered my squad in that dingy back room that doubled as a gym and demanded total dedication to their preparation so that when the race was complete there could be no anguish pangs of 'what if'. They'd crowd in close, bonded together for life by the musky smell of perspiration, their scent of success. There I'd relate stories of people who were different. Winners all. American swimmers such as Dave Berkoff and Mike Barrowman or Olympic legends such as Karoly Takacs. Everyone needs heroes. They make dreams tangible goals. They help people believe.

These stories would always come as welcome relief from hard training when, as coach, I felt they were in need of an easy recovery training session because their bodies were so torn down by the quality and quantity of work they'd been doing.

The Karoly Takacs story was a particular favourite of mine. They'd heard it a dozen times. Takacs, a sergeant in the Hungarian army in 1938, was one of the finest rapid-fire pistol shooters in the world and was expected to dominate the 1940 Olympics set down for Tokyo. These Games would ultimately be cancelled because of the conflict of war. One day, on military manoeuvres, a defective pin caused a grenade

he was holding in his right hand to explode. It blew off his shooting hand. Most people in this situation would wallow in self-pity, feeling sorry for themselves, but not Takacs. As soon as he was out of hospital he started practising with his left hand. He would stand for hours holding the pistol still with his left hand, aiming carefully, practising dry shooting in the privacy of his own home. Only when this was mastered did he venture to the practice range. He then set himself a regime of daily dry shooting practices at home coupled with frequent visits to the rifle range. Poor shots on the range only strengthened his

Karoly Takacs, Olympic legend.

resolve to get better. He saw temporary failure as part of his bigger plan in his inevitable march to competition success. Slowly but surely he gained proficiency.

When he turned up for the national pistol shooting championships, other competitors thought he was there to watch. He competed and won. This only fired his determination to improve. He practised even longer and with more determination.

At the London Olympics, now an army captain, 10 years after his hand had been blown off, he competed, broke Argentinian Carlos Valiente's world record, and won Olympic gold. He defended his title in 1952 at Helsinki. I take delight in quoting Takacs from Bud Greenspan's book *100 Greatest Moments in Olympic History* ...

Everybody was giving me things except for the thing I wanted most. So I gave myself a present. No I gave myself three presents. I had three right hands made, especially for skiing, swimming, and boxing.

Sam learned her lessons well. She knew that failure was an inevitable companion on the road to success. She had read Theodore Roosevelt's quotation that hung on the wall every time she ventured into the gym at Chandler.

The credit belongs to the man who is actually in the arena; whose face is marred by dust and sweat and blood; who strives valiantly; who errs and comes short again and again; who knows the great enthusiasms, the great devotions, and spends himself in a worthy cause; who at the best knows in the end the triumph of high achievement; and who knows at the worst, if he fails, at least he fails while daring greatly.

An Olympic bronze in 1992 was nice, but not the colour she yearned for. Now, just as Sam was ready to become Australia's No. 1 breaststroker, Rebecca Brown was here to spoil her Commonwealth Games party ... another disappointment loomed. However, this disappointment at the Commonwealth Games trials was just the catalyst she needed for success. Now she had a challenge.

How often are setbacks and disappointments the fertilisers of success? They are sent at times to help people refocus on their goals, and make them more determined not only to chase these dreams with all the fibre in their being but also to value the spoils of victory. Rebecca's win and world record now became a driving factor in Sam's quest for Commonwealth Games glory. She was highly motivated and prepared to accept this challenge. She went to her coach and together they formulated a plan for success — for without a good plan all good intentions are doomed to further failure. Intelligent planning is the beginning on the journey to success.

Scott Volkers proved to be a coach with an inquiring mind. The Australian Institute of Sport scientists, led by Bruce Mason, studied in detail, recorded, and supplied a stroke analysis of the first three placegetters in all strokes at the Commonwealth Games trials in Brisbane. The world record holder, Rebecca Brown, travelled one and a half metres with every stroke. Sam travelled two metres, much further. Sam was more efficient, but unfortunately her long graceful stroke fell apart under race pressure. Scott, with the help of Queensland

> *Anyone can wish for something — and most people do. But only a few know that a definite plan, combined with a burning desire, is the only way to get there.*
>
> Australian women's hockey team collection

Academy of Sport scientist Dr Maw, analysed the underwater stroke rate and plotted it against Sam's swimming speed. They noticed something very interesting. Every time Sam tried harder and increased her stroke rate she actually swam slower. The harder she tried the slower she went. They showed her this.

Sam was amazed. The three realised they had to modify her training schedule and devise ways to overcome this deficiency. Experiments and analysis proved Riley was most efficient when she swam 22 strokes every 50 metres. Scott designed a whole series of innovative power breaststroke drills for Sam to use so she could control her stroke more efficiently. Many of these involved the use of specially designed swim paddles and fins.

With this plan in place she attacked these drills with a new purpose and zeal. She worked on the drills daily. Slowly but surely she learned to control her stroke and keep it long under pressure. Now, when her body screamed in pain, she would maintain a steady rhythm, keeping her stroke long and smooth, resisting the temptation to muscle her stroke and speed up the tempo. She concentrated and constantly strived for 22 strokes per 50 metres. Failure was now forgotten and it became the catalyst for improvement, as she chose to focus on future successes. Scott would march along the pool deck, with a stopwatch in each hand, eyes glued to his pupil, counting strokes per lap, shouting instructions, checking heart rate, stroke rates and times. After each effort he would lean over the end of the pool to communicate stroke rate, stroke count, streamlining, technique, rhythm, and times to the breathless Riley.

Besides the gruelling swim training sessions, she was required to go into the gym three times a week to improve her strength. This strength

Sam at the 1994 World Championships, single-handedly resisting the Chinese invasion of women's swimming.

improvement, too, was monitored, to give her positive feedback. This positive feedback is so important in keeping the motivation levels high — with positive feedback the athlete can see the improvement and the fire is stoked internally to improve even more. No one could have predicted the amazing results from this plan-work-communicate ethic that the Volkers–Riley team had put into place.

At the 1994 Commonwealth Games in Victoria, Canada, Sam harvested two gold medals as she lowered the colours of Rebecca Brown. She swam an amazing 1:08.02 for the 100 metres.

Ten days later in Rome, at the World Swimming Championships, the amazing Chinese juggernaut arrived. Powered by special Chinese 'herbal medicines', they dominated women's swimming in the way the East German women governed in the late '70s and early '80s. The first night of the Championships, the Chinese won every event, breaking world records in the process. Shock waves permeated the world swimming community. Coaches from several countries publicly accused the Chinese of cheating, of being on performance-enhancing drugs, questioning how their swimmers could beat drug cheats.

> *The anticipation of failure
> is a recipe for defeat.*

Newspapers screamed 'Chinese on Steroids'.

These types of accusations and coaching attitudes serve only to sap the confidence of swimmers and should not be broached at championship time because to win, whether it be in international competition or local competition, there has to be a blend of physical readiness and psychological confidence, a belief in one's ability to win. Without a marriage of both the physical fine-tuning and psychological control, success cannot be attained. Some coaches in Rome unwittingly defeated their athletes before they even competed against the Chinese by intimating publicly that the Chinese were on 'the juice' and it was not possible to beat them — by anticipating success for their opponents and failure for their charges they doomed their athletes to defeat. It was into this negative cauldron that Samantha was thrust immediately after her successful Commonwealth Games campaign.

As a young impressionable kid, Sam had been exposed to Sieben's and Armstrong's unexpected Olympic victories over world record holders, so she believed victory was always possible. She also appreciated the significance of concentrating on controlling the controllables. She knew she could not slow the Chinese swimmers down. She had to concentrate on making her performance perfect.

Sam and Scott had planned her preparation carefully, right down to the last tiny detail. She had executed it to perfection. She had been true to herself by doing everything to the best of her ability. She knew that for maximum performance she must concentrate on making her own performance better. Worrying about things over which she had no control would only be detrimental to her own performance; after all, competition is about striving to win. She must relax, go out and celebrate her talent.

So physical preparation, belief, and psychological toughness saw Sam bounce onto the world scene in Rome. She became the only female swimmer in the world to halt the Chinese domination of the World Swimming Championships, winning both the 100 and 200 breaststroke. As a bonus, she broke the world record in the 100 metres breaststroke, swimming 1:07.75 including, amazingly, 22 strokes in the second 50 metres, the exact target she had worked so hard and so long for in training.

The hard work and planning had paid off. Her swims there earned her Australian Sportswoman of the Year and World Female Swimmer of the Year. The Atlanta Olympics beckoned; back in Australia endorsements and accolades followed. Sam was on top of the world.

Nineteen ninety-five was a year of triumph and disaster. She met them 'face to face' again, proving her resilience, commitment and toughness. Illness, a stressed rib fracture and disqualification in her best event by an over-officious American referee at the Pan Pacific Games in August in Atlanta failed to halt the Riley avalanche as she marched towards her major goal, Olympic gold. Two days after the disqualification she went within 0:05 of Rebecca Brown's world record. Sam, in all situations, remained totally positive and regularly studied the gold ring sporting the Olympic symbol on her right hand, a public reminder of her commitment to the Olympic dream.

In December 1995, at the World Short Course Championships in Brazil, she had the time of her life. She broke two world records within 24 hours as she demolished the world's best. Her smile dazzled the world. Eight thousand Brazilians in the stands of the open air pool on Rio de Janeiro's famous Copacabana Beach danced the samba and celebrated her 1:05.70 second world record when she finished more than two seconds ahead of second placegetter, Ukrainian Svetlana Bondarenko. So dominant was she that former Great Britain coach, now resident AIS coach, Barry Prime, raved over her 2:20.85 200 metres world record and claimed Riley was ahead of her time. She was still on track for Olympic gold ...

Life is funny, and sometimes when we least expect it something happens to crush our dreams. It takes a very special character to stand firm and keep fighting despite adversity.

At the Queensland swimming championships in 1996, the start of

Nicole Stevenson, Sam, Sarah Ryan and Susie O'Neill after taking silver in the medley relay in Atlanta.

the Olympic year, her year, the year she'd dreamed of since she was a skinny asthmatic kid, Sam Riley's world crashed. Sam was laughing and talking with her good friend Susie O'Neill, who shared the same Olympic dream, when Scott Volkers, his face ashen, called her over. The news was catastrophic. She couldn't believe it. The blood drained from her face, her knees went weak, she had to sit down on one of the red plastic chairs beside the pool. The news? She had tested positive a month earlier at the Championships in Rio. He'd just got the news. She couldn't believe it. How? When? Where? Why? Her head spun, her mind raced. It was just not possible. She would be branded a drug cheat. She hated drugs and was a vigorous campaigner against them. Why? How?

It's amazing what a month can do. On December 4, she was dancing the samba in Brazil, the dual world short course champion and double world record holder; now, in January, she was racking her brain on how she could possibly test positive.

'Maybe somebody spiked my drink?' she thought.

Question after question flashed through her mind.

'How would she cope? What would her mother say? How could she face her team-mates? What would her sponsors say? Surely they would desert her in droves?'

Her world was on the verge of collapse. No one wanted a drug cheat. Tears welled up in her eyes and rolled down her cheeks like huge drops of rain. She wanted to disappear somewhere and cry out loud. Later, in private, she put her head on Mum's shoulder the way she had when she was a little girl and sobbed bitterly.

Scott Volkers was driving along on his way home from training when it hit him like a bolt of lightning. He pulled off to the side of the road, slumped over the steering wheel and hit his head three or four times with the open palm of both hands as he thought about it. How could he have been so stupid? He remembered the mongrelled-up blister pack in the bottom of his swimming bag, smelling of rubbing liniment, one tablet sealed and intact. He was supposed to be a professional swim coach meticulously covering every last little detail. He was responsible for formulating and executing the world champion's program. Now his whole world was collapsing. His star pupil had tested positive. It had to be his wife's headache tablet. There was no other explanation. Why did he leave them there? What possessed him to be so stupid as to give Sam his wife's headache tablet that had been in the bottom of his bag for three years? He just didn't think. Why didn't he send her to the doctor? He was a swimming coach, not a doctor or a pharmacist. Why? He just didn't think. He broke the No. 1 rule of successful coaching 'pay meticulous attention to detail'. A simple mistake now not only threatened his career but the career of his prize pupil. Should he remain silent and let her ride it out?

'No!' he screamed out loud and banged his hand on the steering wheel. First he'd have to ring a chemist to confirm his worst fears. Then he would have to tell Sam. If he had inadvertently spiked one of Australia's best gold medal chances for Atlanta he was going to have to tell her. It was going to be the hardest thing he had ever done in his life.

That afternoon he sat down and broke the news to Sam. She was devastated. He was repentant, but the damage had been done.

Tuesday, February 13, the story broke in all the national newspapers. Headlines blared across the nation:

'RILEY TESTS POSITIVE FOR DRUG!'

The nation was in shock. Riley, the country's best chance for Olympic gold and a long-time campaigner for a no mercy hard line on drug cheats, had tested positive to a banned substance dextropropoxyphene contained in the headache tablet Di-Gesic. That day, at a specially called press conference, they whole story came out. Sam was seated in front of an Australian flag and flanked by a drawn, chastened Volkers and her lawyer, Peter Bastion, who had been lobbying the FINA executive in Berlin. Scott explained his stupidity.

'We came to the conclusion I was a moron,' said Scott.

The press didn't disagree.

'Do you blame Scott for all this?' a journalist asked from floor of the packed conference.

She looked at him kindly. 'At times I feel so angry with him. I feel like grabbing him by the throat and shaking him but I know he'd never ever deliberately hurt me. I owe him so much. He's going through hell at the moment ... probably more than me because he feels the guilt.'

At the media conference, crushed but not defeated, Sam faced a barrage of questions. She answered with quiet dignity that highlighted her fighting qualities.

'I'm still training ...

'I hope to defend my World Championships and win gold for Australia in Atlanta ...

'I support FINA 100 per cent ...

'I'm not a cheat ...

'I've never cheated ...

'I'm trying to stay as positive as I can ...

Sam's fellow breaststroker, Helen Denman (centre), with Hayley Lewis and Michael Klim in Atlanta.

'I still want to do all I can to fight steroids ...

'Two years is not fair for a headache tablet ...

'Obviously I am devastated ...

'The thought of missing the Olympics is crushing me at the moment ...

'I hope I get a fair trial ...

'I hope they see that it was an innocent mistake ...'

The grilling continued. She answered bravely, but the stress showed on her face.

The next day the nation was convinced that Riley's only crime was ignorance and Volkers was a fool.

The following four days were absolute torture for Sam as she waited to hear FINA's decision. She jumped every time the phone rang. Finally, on February 18, the nation rejoiced as headlines blared:

'SAM CLEAR!'

So ended the most stressful six weeks of her young life. Still, a dark pall hung over her. No judgement had been passed on Scott. He may not be with her in Atlanta. What would she do? The stress continued.

She struggled to find the old Riley zing and sharpness at training. The Olympic trials approached.

On Monday, April 21, 1996 at Homebush Aquatic Centre, another bomb fell on the already shellshocked Riley. Western Australian breaststroker Helen Denman stunned both Riley and the Australian public as she relegated Sam to second place in Sam's best event at the Olympic trials.

Riley finally succumbed to the pressures that had enveloped her for the past four months. Chinks were appearing in her armour. It was her first defeat in two years. In the 200 metres breaststroke another bomb. This time diminutive Nadine Neumann, hungry for an Olympic spot, claimed Riley's scalp.

History showed the stress was too much for Sam in Atlanta. Her Olympic dream was shattered. The only real joy in Atlanta came as the fab four — Susie O'Neill, Nicole Stevenson, Sarah Ryan and Sam — combined to win a silver medal in the 4 x 100 medley relay.

When she arrived back in Australia she had some serious decisions to make. Sam was at the crossroads in her career. Should she retire, or continue on to Sydney 2000? She knew there would be a host of new pressures, new challengers with five rings in their eyes chasing the honour of representing Australia at their home Olympics. There would be triumphs and heartaches. She expected that ...

She'd be the 'granny' of the team ... She knew that. She stared at the Olympic ring on her finger and closed her eyes. Her destiny seemed to be controlled by a battered old sign that hung on a gym wall.

The credit belongs to the man who is actually in the arena; whose face is marred by dust and sweat and blood; who strives valiantly; who errs and comes up short again and again; who knows the great enthusiasms, the great devotions, and spends himself in a worthy cause; who at the best knows in the end the triumph of high achievements; and who at the worst, if he fails, at least he fails while daring greatly.

Sam, Sydney awaits!

Certainly in the Olympic field, the one who wants to win the most will win. The margin of physical ability isn't that great. Generally the eight people in the final have similar physical ability; it is what the person thinks and feels that is critical.

Lynn Davies

17 — It Ain't Over ...
Till the fat man lifts!

I stuck my head inside the door of the Athlete Services Office in the Atlanta Olympic Village, surveyed the hive of activity and called loudly to the beefy, greying, middle-aged man hunched over a computer on the far side of the room:

'John, I'm just going down to the pool to watch the swimmers train this afternoon.'

'Fine,' John Devitt, 1960 Olympic gold medallist, now assistant Chef de Mission of the Australian Olympic team to Atlanta, replied without lifting his head. He was engrossed in the computer.

'If you need me, catch me on the mobile,' I said and waved the little Nokia from side to side in front of my face.

I couldn't believe it. A few years earlier I had labelled the mobile phone a 'yuppie' toy. How time brings changes. The yuppie toy had become an integral part of my daily communications, saving time, energy and enabling me to be in constant touch with office and family.

'Fine!' John responded.

I was quite excited at the prospect of getting back to the Olympic pool. Yesterday I'd watched Kieren Perkins punch out some fantastic 50 metre sprints in the training pool. He'd positioned himself in a lane beside his young challenger Daniel Kowalski. It was obvious Kieren was fast approaching his best form and had been keen to let his young opponent know that he was not going to abdicate the crown easily. If Daniel wanted the Olympic wreath he would have to earn it, and part of the deal was that he would have to face the psychological pressures that Kieren would dish out in the two weeks leading into the 1500 metres race at the Games.

> *The mind is the master ... and the bridge. All the instructions come through the mind and everything you do physically comes through the mind. Fear is mentally under control. The mind controls the fear ... it controls the adrenalin glands. Too much and you're scared stiff ... if the mental pre-competition was getting on top of me, I'd go to bed, read Edgar Wallace and smoke my pipe.*
>
> Bob Tisdall, 400m hurdles, 1932 Olympic gold, LA

In all the lead-up competitions Daniel had dominated the swimming pool, beating Kieren at Olympic trials and continuing his dominance in the Telstra Grand Prix Shortcourse Series. Daniel had grown in confidence with each victory and now believed he could beat Perkins, the world record holder, in his favourite event.

It's a funny thing about belief — if you believe something is possible then you become a very dangerous opponent. Kowalski believed, but more importantly, so did his coach Bill Nelson, who 12 months earlier had nursed Daniel through a serious shoulder injury and a period of self-doubt. The burly ex-coalminer's determination and faith in his young charge never wavered, and he carefully planned each training session with Olympic gold in mind. One person believing they can win gold is powerful, but when two people combine to chase the golden dream they become formidable opponents.

Kieren, who hitherto had been undisputed 'king' of distance swimming, with world records from 400 to 1500 metres, now had a real battle on his hands to retain his Olympic title. Franklin D. Roosevelt put it beautifully when he said:

The only limit to our realization of tomorrow will be our doubts of today.

Kieren's coach, the cagey old John Carew, was aware of the challenge and had a few ideas up his sleeve on how to help keep Kieren focused as well as keeping some psychological pressure on young Daniel ... maybe even shake Daniel's growing confidence a little.

John knew that when the time came to race the gruelling 1500 Kieren had to be totally prepared. Because of this, after Kieren's defeat at the Olympic trials, the canny coach had reappraised all training and started a new, tougher work regime designed for Olympic success. John knew that the greatest pre-race talk or the best cheer squad in the world couldn't help any athlete who had cheated on his preparation. On the other hand, he believed that if you prepare well you earn the right to be confident and this confidence will enable you to compete ferociously at the highest level.

With this thought occupying my mind, I hitched my Australian team bag over my shoulder and set out happily for the pool. It was going to be a top afternoon's training, and my heart beat a little faster in anticipation of watching the psychological warfare between these two great mates, Perkins v Kowalski, continue. What would Kieren do today to let Daniel know he was still around and was not going to abdicate the crown easily? How could he shake Daniel's growing belief in himself? I thought of the little poem I'd read and memorised when I found it in Howard Ferguson's great book *The Edge*:

If you think you are beaten you are;
If you think that you dare not, you don't;
If you'd like to win but you think you can't,
It's almost certain you won't.

If you think you'll lose, you've lost;
For out in the world you'll find
Success begins with a fellow's will.
It's all in the state of mind.

If you think you are outclassed, you are;
You've got to think high to rise;
You've got to be sure of yourself before
You can ever win a prize.

Life's battles don't always go
To the stronger or faster man;
But sooner or later the man who wins
Is the man who thinks he can.

I was so engrossed in my thoughts that I almost collided with Steven Kettner, the big 108-plus kilogram Australian super-heavyweight weightlifter, at the top of the stairs.

'Are you coming to watch us train?' grunted the big man.

'Well, I ...'

'Are you coming to watch us train?' grunted Kettner again, but this time it had more the feel of an order than a question as he interrupted my stammer.

'Well, ...' I hesitated once more and looked nervously around. I really wanted to go to the swimming but I dare not tell him that.

'Are you coming to watch us train or was that all just talk at the team briefing at Athens University in Georgia?' the big man persisted even more firmly.

My mind flashed back to the team briefing in Athens, where the lifters sauntered into the briefing room late. Slowly and deliberately they spread themselves around the room, as if to say, 'Well, we're here. What's this all about?'

They sprawled over the chairs as one and sat with deadpan faces, waiting. I'd seen bikie gangs intimidate people in the movies merely by their silent presence but I never thought it would happen to me. My best friendly efforts at Village information sprinkled with my attempts at humour were met with stony silence. The big man sat like a statue, with folded arms, a cold stare and a blank expression.

Michael Wenden had made me even more wary of the lifters when he remarked to me casually, 'Oh, you don't mess with that big fellow.'

I remembered spelling out very clearly to the lifting team that it was my responsibility to look after them in the Village — anything they needed, just call. And, of course, I'd be coming to watch them compete and train.

Now with the giant of a man blocking the stairwell exit of our sleeping quarters at Georgia Tech and asking the question,

'Are you coming to watch us train?'

I made a quick decision in the interests of self-preservation. Daniel and Kieren's psychological tête-à-tête would have to wait until tomorrow; I was not prepared to risk serious injury by refusing Mr Kettner's request.

'I'm with you, big fella,' I called.

I raced back up the stairs two at a time, old grey camera bag bouncing on my hip, to let the office staff know of my sudden change of plan. Then I hurried after my new-found friends ...

Unfortunately, they were nowhere to be seen ... weightlifters wait for no man. They were already down the stairs with the insides of their thighs rubbing rhythmically, glutes bulging, as they slowly sauntered across the road to the tramstop. The tramstop consisted of four aluminium poles, which formed the frame for a white canvas shade cover that offered no respite from the oppressive Atlanta heat.

As they leaned against the poles waiting for the tram I couldn't help noticing that the tramstop was crammed between two tall imported Australian gum trees. Some bright spark had nailed two tiny toy koalas two metres up the tree ... the gymnasts blamed the basketballers.

The happiest I ever saw Big Steve Kettner in Atlanta was at the Closing Ceremony.

The basketballers insisted the gymnasts stood on each other's shoulders.

I could hear the distinctive whine and rattle of the battery-powered tram, the internal transport system of the Village, so I quickened my pace to join the boys. The tram was crowded, but this made no difference to the weightlifters — they muscled, pushed and grunted their way on board. As big Steve put his weight on the step the tram visibly tilted and groaned. I followed. I was happy with my new friends ... people were actually moving aside for me.

'Sit here next to me,' ordered big Steve ... of course I obliged. The five-minute trip was squashed and silent. I wondered why he insisted I sit next to him. Maybe he didn't want me to escape.

We got off at the stop that would allow us out of the Village and onto the shuttle service between practice venues. This would be my first time out of the Village since being accredited, so I was on a learning curve myself. When in doubt stay back, watch, learn, then go for it. I'd heard stories about the weightlifters before, but I was about to experience one first hand. Led by Steven Kettner, 'the boys' marched up past the entrance and proceeded to exit. The security guards sprang to their feet. At last they had something to do. The lifters bulldozed on, following big Steve. He reminded me of a runaway Mack truck followed by a convoy of little trucks ... nothing was going to stop them ... not even Village security.

'Sorry, guys, this is the entrance,' announced a United States village security guard.

'We just want to go there,' grunted Steve and he pointed his stubby finger at the bus and kept pushing on, following his massive stomach ... the mini convoy followed.

'Hey guy, this is the entrance!' insisted the security guard.

Big Steve, without saying a word, turned right, right again, back through the electronic surveillance gates, then hard left to the other end of the entrance to exit ... the mini convoy followed in silence, conga-style, enjoying the dance but showing no emotion. I brought up the rear, totally confused, as were the hapless guards.

'Oh! Let them out this time, Chuck,' called the frustrated guard. Steve marched out, his face deadpan, followed by his loyal followers and little old me bringing up the rear.

'I only want to go over there,' Steve grunted again.

'Hey buddy, next time can you go out the correct door?' called the stunned security guard.

'You no worry, mate, I fix it good next time,' said Yurik Sarkisian, the little Australian–Armenian who won a silver medal for USSR at the

Yurik Sarkisian, all 59kg of him, giving it all and more for his country.

Allsport

Moscow Olympics. Since then he had brought his wife and twins to Australia for the peace, stability and security of the Australian lifestyle.

I had been sure the bus ride to the weightlifting stadium was going to be boring. I'd been told a few stories about the lifters, tales of how dumb they were, so unfortunately I had a strong preconceived idea of what these guys were like. How wrong can you be?

I sat next to Damian Brown, our representative in the 76kg division, and started to chat. He was a physical education teacher, highly intelligent and an engaging, entertaining conversationalist. We chatted about the current Australian team members, their personalities, their training quirks, past Australian weightlifting personalities, the training venue, international competitors.

Kilogram for kilogram, this bloke could be the greatest lifter of them all ... Naim Suleymanoglu wins gold in Atlanta!

Allsport

'We've had some characters in this sport in Australia,' enthused Damian.

'Big Steve scares me!' I said, nodding to the huge man who had taken up the entire front seat of the bus.

'Nah! He's as gentle a guy as you can imagine, just quiet ... doesn't say much ... wouldn't hurt a fly.'

'I guess it's because he's so big ... and he never seems to speak ... he just stares right through you.'

'Once he gets to know you you'll be right. He'll chew your ear.'

'I don't want my ear chewed by any heavyweight lifter!' I replied.

No one laughed so I asked, 'Is it right the heavyweights eat copious amounts of food?'

'Oh! These big blokes love their food all right, they get real hungry,' butted in Harvey Goodman, a 91kg-division lifter whose hobby is home renovating and who was sitting in front listening to our conversation.

'Tell Laurie about Nick Cimino!'

'Oh yeah!' started Damian and he smiled as he recalled the incident.

'We were overseas on a competition trip once in Bulgaria when Nick, one of the supers, accidentally locked himself out of his room ... well he had a case of Coke and some snacks locked in his room. The big fella, six foot four and 165 kilos, got a bit peckish. The supers get a bit peckish at times. When he couldn't get into his room he started to get a bit anxious ... food withdrawal symptoms ... so he got over the balcony in my room and inched his way to the balcony on his room ... talk about the human fly, we were two storeys off the ground.'

'Can you imagine big Steve doing that? What a sight,' I said.

'Those big guys'll do anything when they're hungry,' said Harvey, before quickly changing the subject by asking, 'Ever been to the lifting, Laurie?'

'I saw Suleymanoglu lift in Seoul. He broke six world records in one night. I'll never forget it. That was big. I doubt if I'll ever witness anything as exciting as that again,' I added, trying to contribute a little to the conversation.

'Legend!' they chorused.

All the time we were talking Yurik was continually moving. First he had sat on the bus feeling his quadriceps tenderly with his right hand. Then he'd stand, hold onto the bus seat and squat one leg at time, first the right leg then the left leg, always checking and feeling the upper thigh with his right hand. In between squats on his left leg he'd put his hand over his knee and bend the leg three or four times, muttering to himself before repeating the procedure. His team uniform, in contrast to many of his team-mates, fitted him perfectly. Apparently, he had been to the uniform store in Athens many times, searching for the perfect fit until each item of team issue looked tailor-made for him. At the mention of Suleymanoglu he thrust himself into the conversation.

'Little man very strong,' he said in broken English.

'Suleymanoglu's five feet tall standing on tip-toes in high heels,' said Damian.

'He looks a bit like a midget,' I observed.

'Good levers for lifting. If he wins here the crowd will go berserk. It will be his third consecutive Olympic gold·medal. There are a group of Turkish countrymen who follow him all round the world to watch him lift,' added Harvey.

'Yeah! You wait! They'll pack one section of the stands, wave their red-and-white, moon-and-a-star flags and dance and sing as their pocket Hercules mounts the stage to lift ... dead silence as he attempts the lift ... then they'll go bananas as he makes each lift. He is Turkey's most celebrated athlete.'

'Turkey give one million dollar Bulgaria become citizen for Seoul Olympics,' said Yurik.

'What?' I said trying to work out what he meant.

Damian interpreted, 'Suleymanoglu was born in the mountains on the Turkish–Bulgarian border. The Bulgarians coached him in their special lifting program. He became world junior champion, but he defected when he came to Melbourne for an international lifting competition. Turkey adopted him. The borders are so close. There is some friction. The Bulgarians would only release him to lift for Turkey if they paid a million dollars. He's a big star in weightlifting. He's a superstar!'

The bus arrived at the venue much too soon. We strolled into the big gymnasium, which was set up especially for weightlifting.

'Watch Yurik!' said Damian, 'He'll take up that mat right in front of the entrance where everybody can see him. Oh, he's a little show pony! You watch!'

Sure enough, Yurik selected the mat right in front of the entrance on which to do his workout.

'Watch Harvey, he'll take the mat at the back. We're a superstitious lot, we like to train in certain areas of the gym. See you after, I have to grab my mat.'

I was enthralled. I sat there, close by Yurik, watching everyone intently. Yurik wandered over to where I was sitting to explain he would not be lifting anything too heavy this afternoon.

'Knee too sore. No lift heavy.'

While Yurik took it easy the other members of the team went through their various warm-up routines, moving slowly and methodically from mat to mat, shifting weights, buckling and unbuckling support belts, grunting, lifting, sitting. Before and after each lift they'd ice niggling injuries. I'd never seen a weightlifting training session before so for me it was captivating stuff.

Half an hour flew. A Channel 7 camera crew appeared at the door. Damian wandered over to me and whispered,

'Watch Yurik, he'll lift a monster now that the TV cameras have arrived.'

The little man's demeanour changed immediately. He became alive. He started skipping, bounding, preening like a too-proud turkey. As the cameraman came near he stood by his weight stack, bowed and did a two-footed kangaroo-like leap over the bar. Yurik certainly had everyone's attention!

'Soon I lift a record!' he said. The little man with the sore knee who was going to have an easy afternoon had suddenly come to life.

The cameras whirred. Sure enough, he lifted a Commonwealth record, bowed, rubbed, iced his knee, looked towards the cameras and shrugged.

'I lift more, but knee sore.'

The crew left happy. I had a fascinating afternoon, made a bunch of new friends, and as we returned to the Village I promised them I would come to watch them compete.

Days later, I was about to head out to the Georgia World Congress Centre, on my own by Village bus (invariably a slow, laborious process), to watch Yurik Sarkisian and Stefan Botev lift when I chanced to meet John Coates, Chef de Mission of the Australian team.

'Where are you off to today, young Laurie?' he questioned, even though I know I was born many years before him.

'The weightlifting, Mr Coates.' I used 'Mr Coates' as a mark of respect. My Dad, an old shearer's cook, had instructed me to always keep sweet with the boss.

'I've promised the boys I'd go see them lift,' I added.

'That's where we're going! I have an official car at my disposal and this young man's my driver. You're most welcome to come with us!' he said invitingly.

I didn't need any second invitation. I jumped at the chance. 'Stumpy' would be smiling in his grave if he knew his son was off to the weightlifting with the Chef.

'Thanks, Mr Coates!' I replied respectfully.

'John's the name! Let's not get too formal,' he said easily.

We walked towards his little golf buggy that all the Chefs had as a private means of transport within the Village. I could tell it was going to be a top day.

> *I would like to be remembered as an
> athlete who took chances and never let
> anyone tell him that what he thought
> he could do was not possible.*
>
> Carl Lewis

'We'll just pick up Pauline. She's waiting at the front gate ... then we're out of here with the help of this young man,' he said nodding to the young driver, a university student on holidays, who had volunteered his services for the Olympics.

'Do you get to go into the various events?' I asked the driver.

'Sure do! I go everywhere Mr Coates goes,' he replied, with the biggest smile.

'What a scam! How good a job is this!' I jibed.

He smiled even more as he contemplated his good fortune. 'It sure is a great way to spend a university vacation,' he added.

Pauline, John's wife, was waiting patiently for us by the main gate. She smiled and waved we approached.

John introduced me. Some people have the gift of being able to make people feel completely at ease immediately. Pauline was that sort of person. It felt the most natural thing in the world to be sharing a VIP car with the boss of the AOC heading down Peachtree Street to the weightlifting.

As we approached the arena security guards checked our IDs and waved us through. Soon we were parked.

'I want to go through the athletes' warm-up area to see the boys,' said John.

'You go ahead then! I'll take our young friend to the official seats,' replied Pauline.

'What about you, Laurie, do you want to see the boys?'

'Can I?'

Mr John Coates, a good fella to know around Olympics time.

'Well that accreditation won't get you in but if you want to chance it you'll need to stick close by me.'

'I'm with you, Mr Coates. Lead the way.'

I'd used all sorts of ingenious ways to scam my way into Olympic and World Championship venues in the past ... but on the shirt tail of the boss?

Never!

It was easy. All I did was follow. In no time we were among the action. It was a hive of activity as athletes from all nations went through their pre-competition lifting attempts. I had never seen the coaches so active. They were not only concerned with their own athletes' form, but were also continually moving, watching, assessing competitors' practice lifts with eagle eyes. An informed decision on the weight chosen to lift in the competition arena could mean the difference between success and failure.

John could see how busy they were so he turned to me and said, 'We'll just wish them our best and get out of the road.' Which we did.

Soon we were seated in the VIP area, right in front of the lifting apron with Chefs and IOC delegates. I wished my Dad was alive so I could spin him an Olympic yarn when I got home of how I hobnobbed it there at the weightlifting with the IOC delegates the way he used to spin me yarns of his exploits in the shearing sheds.

Soon Yurik, the little man who went into camp to train with the Russian team after his selection for Australia, came out to lift. He snatched 125kg on his first attempt — a good start. This looked promising, but he failed to secure the bar overhead at his second and third attempts at 130kg. In the clean and jerk, 155kg posed no problems but, unfortunately, his weak knee couldn't cope with 160kg, which trapped him in the full squat position. You could see the disappointment in his face as he failed at his third attempt and hobbled off stage clutching his knee.

Later, John and I went to the athletes' area to commiserate, congratulate, and thank Yurik for the fine job he did representing Australia.

'Sorry, boss, next time I do better. Knee sore. Seven no good. No good.'

'Seventh is very good, Yurik. Don't you worry, we are all very proud of you,' said John. I simply took Yurik's hand, looked him in the eyes and squeezed his hand firmly. No words were spoken. There was no need. I knew what he was feeling and he knew what I was thinking.

Luke Borreggine, one of the weightlifting coaches, appeared with some ice for Yurik's knee. When he saw us he said, 'Don't miss the super heavyweights, it's going to be a weightlifting war. Stefan will be lifting against Chemerkin of Russia and Weller from Germany.'

With that he began packing Yurik's knee with ice.

'We'll get out of your way! Well done, Yurik! See you back at the Village,' enthused John Coates.

Back inside the arena the atmosphere was building. There was a real electricity in the air as the fans waited for the heavyweights to strut their stuff.

Once the heavyweight contest got underway I moved to sit in the VIP area, spellbound by the high drama unfolding before us. The German hero, Ronny Weller, affectionately known as 'the slab', was desperate for gold. Two years earlier, at the World Championships, he had been denied gold by the Russian man mountain Andrey Chemerkin. As the contest unfolded the Australian, Stefan Botev, took the bronze. The battle for gold, though, would be fought out between Weller and Chemerkin.

Weller, dressed in his black, red and gold lifting tights, had to lift before Chermerkin. He was under tremendous pressure — to win he needed to lift a weight that will make it impossible for the giant Russian to match. He sat alone in the corner chalking his hands, listening to Brahms, visualising the weight being hoisted above his head. The German coach, knowing it will take something huge ... something special to beat the giant Russian, called for the attendants to ready the bar at 562 pounds. The audience was stunned. Weller was going for the world record. It's all or nothing.

This was the moment Weller has worked for all his life ...

Now is the time to celebrate his talent, to show the world he is worthy of the Olympic gold medal. The coach, although he has faith in his charge, is nervous, and the strain shows on his face. Is his protégé ready for a world record? Weller oozes confidence and shows no sign of nerves. He knows he has prepared well. He walks slowly to the brightly lit, four metres by four metres, solid wood lifting platform and positions himself behind the huge weight. He stares at the bar loaded with a world record. Slowly and deliberately he grasps the bar, licks his lips and manouevres his feet for better purchase. Now he is ready for the challenge.

As he takes the strain he emits a scream like some ancient warrior chief leading his men to battle. This is war. The scream echoes round the hushed stadium as his huge quadriceps strain under the world record weight. The crowd murmurs aloud in disbelief and anticipation as he stands upright and steadies the bar, ready for the final jerk above his head.

Pat Welsh, commentating for Australian television, calls, 'Weller at the moment has gold within his grasp. This will ensure it, I think, unless Chemerkin can pull out some amazing performance.'

Three seconds later, the world record is broken when Weller hoists the huge weight above his head. The crowd erupts into sustained cheering. Welsh screams, 'He's got it! He's GOT it! A world record. He deserves the gold.'

It's pandemonium in the stadium as the crowd celebrates a demonstration of strength never seen before.

Weller cannot contain his emotions. He throws his arms, fists clenched, above his head in victory before falling onto his back in pure joy. He can smell the gold medal. Three seconds later he springs to his feet, rips off his lifting sneakers and throws them to the adoring fans in a victory dance. The German coach and team manager, too, embrace each other in a victory celebration.

However, there's an old saying in the sporting world ...

It ain't over till the fat man sings.

The challenge has been set for Chemerkin, the giant Russian world champion with the huge stomach.

And Chermerkin responds to the challenge. His coach signals to load the bar with 260 kilos. Five hundred and seventy three pounds. The crowd is silent in disbelief. This is eleven pounds heavier than the world record that Ronny Weller had just set. Were they about to witness something special? Something they could tell their grandchildren about in years to come?

Chemerkin, sweat dripping from his brow, stands seemingly unperturbed behind the massive weight.

Pat Welsh announces, 'This bar will groan.'

Belly shaking, lips curled, Chemerkin lifts. Successfully! Welsh screams, 'Oh yes sir! Six and a half kilos more! Andre Chemerkin! He has lifted a weight we may never see lifted again. He throws his coach around like a rag doll. Two hundred and sixty kilos!! That is amazing stuff!!!'

It's over now!! Andrey Chemerkin has just won a thrilling weightlifting mega-battle.

I was taken up in the emotion of the evening. While I rejoiced for Chemerkin, I bled for Weller.

The German sat motionless, stunned, sweat running down his face, dripping in great blobs onto his team uniform. A plain white Adidas T-shirt was clearly visible as the straps on his lifting uniform were pulled down to his waist. He had broken the world record and thrown his sneakers into the stands in a victory salute yet was denied gold by his great rival's mighty lift. The look on Ronny Weller's face after he saw the gold medal slip from his grasp will live with me forever. While Chemerkin celebrated, Weller walked slowly away, with his coach's arm on his shoulder, both pondering what might have been.

Later, as I discussed the evening's events with Australian coaches Luke Borreggine and Martin Leach, we came to the same conclusion — as coaches we have a duty to install into our charges not only a real love of their chosen sport but also the importance of personal best achievements. If athletes have an intense passionate love for their sport, the long hard hours necessary for success will be palatable as they chase new personal horizons.

The cycle of continuous improvement in sport and life is love, hard work and satisfaction with personal successes as they occur. These personal-best successes are crucial in maintaining enthusiasm when you're losing, because disappointment is a constant companion in the quest for victory.

Ronny Weller has to be satisfied with a personal best. In this way he will live to fight another day. In life, and in sport, we must all keep punching, because the quest is never ending ...

It ain't over till the fat man lifts.

Become a winner

with Laurie Lawrence

Laurie Lawrence is in strong demand as an inspiring and entertaining corporate speaker. His messages of success from the sporting world translate brilliantly to the world of business, and his infectious good humour, ability to inspire and the passion he brings to his presentations make him the ideal keynote speaker to open and close your conference.

For bookings, contact Jennifer on 07 3341 7260 (phone/fax), email Laurie at lauriel@winshop.com.au, or write to Laurie Lawrence, PO Box 392, Currumbin Qld 4223.

From the Laurie Lawrence Collection ...
Lawrence of Australia — a book of motivational stories: $20.00 plus $2.00 postage.

'Gold Medal Collection' — four audio tapes: $30.00 each plus $2.00 postage per tape ...
1. *Los Angeles and Seoul Recollections*
2. *Barcelona Recollections*
3. *Atlanta Recollections*
4. *12 Midnight*

Poetry CD: $20.00 plus $2.00 postage.

Video — *Babies can Swim*: $30.00 plus $2.00 postage.

To order any item from the Laurie Lawrence Collection, please contact Jennifer on 07 3341 7260 (phone/fax), email Laurie at lauriel@winshop.com.au, or write to Laurie Lawrence, PO Box 392, Currumbin Qld 4223.

kids alive

DO THE FIVE

1. Fence the pool
2. Shut the gate
3. Learn to swim
4. Supervise
5. Learn to resuscitate